THE PATRIARCHS

ENCOUNTERING THE GOD OF ABRAHAM, ISAAC, AND JACOB

BETH MOORE

LifeWay Press®
Nashville, Tennessee

Dedicated to Lee Sizemore,

Lead Video/Audio Producer—

When we came together years ago for the very first taping, who would ever have believed God would give us 10? I remember our first conversation so well. As you shared what LifeWay envisioned, I asked if the anointing of the Holy Spirit and the warmth so critical to women's Bible study could ever be experienced through video. I fight back the tears as I reflect how God Himself answered the question.

Lee, I'm not sure God has ever put together more handicapped hearts than ours to perform a heavenly task. He wanted to make sure that no one but Him could take an ounce of credit. God alone, my friend. God alone has accomplished this work. May He gain all the more glory and continue to spread a holy passion for His Word.

Keith joins me in this inadequate attempt to express gratitude. You've faithfully kept your promise to him, and he doesn't take it lightly. You stand tall to my Texas man. Thank you, thank you, my dear friend and partner in sharing the gospel. You are dearly loved.

Beth

Published by LifeWay Press®
© 2005 • Beth Moore
Second printing October 2005

ISBN 0-6330-9906-6

This book is the text for course CG-1053 in the subject
area Bible Studies in the Christian Growth Study Plan.

Dewey Decimal Classification Number: 222.11

Subject Headings: PATRIARCHS (BIBLE)\ GOD\ BIBLE O.T. GENESIS 12–50

Atlas map © 1998 Broadman and Holman Publishers, all rights reserved.

Photography: Michael W. Rutherford. The photographs were taken on location in Egypt and Israel
during the taping of *The Patriarchs.*

Illustrations: Dan Brawner

Unless otherwise indicated, Scripture quotations are from the Holy Bible, New International Version,
    copyright © 1973, 1978, 1984 by International Bible Society.
Scripture quotations identified KJV are from the King James Version.
Scripture quotations identified AMP are from The Amplified New Testament
    © The Lockman Foundation 1954, 1958, 1987. Used by permission.
Scripture quotations identified NASB are from the New American Standard Bible
    © Copyright The Lockman Foundation, 1960, 1962, 1963, 1968, 1971, 1972, 1973, 1975, 1977,
    1995. Used by permission.
Scripture quotations identified CEV are from the Contemporary English Version, Copyright © 1991,
    1992, 1995 American Bible Society. Used by permission.
Scripture Quotations identified HCSB are from the Holman Christian Standard Bible®, copyright ©
    1999, 2000, 2001, 2002, 2003 by Holman Bible Publishers.
    Used by permission.
To order additional copies of this resource, WRITE to LifeWay Church Resources Customer Service;
    One LifeWay Plaza; Nashville, TN 37234-0013; FAX (615) 251-5933; PHONE (800) 458-2772;
    ORDER ONLINE at *www.lifeway.com*; or VISIT the LifeWay Christian Store serving you.

Printed in the United States of America

Leadership and Adult Publishing; LifeWay Church Resources
One LifeWay Plaza; Nashville, TN 37234-0175

Contents

About the Author 6

Introduction to *The Patriarchs* 7

Weeks of Study

1. Leave Your Country 10
   Day One The Call of Abram 11
   Day Two Down to Egypt. 15
   Day Three Parting Company 19
   Day Four Man of God Against Kings 23
   Day Five God Most High. 28

2. The Approaching and Approachable God ... 34
   Day One The God Who Sees Me 35
   Day Two The Covenant of Circumcision 40
   Day Three No Longer Sarai 44
   Day Four Anything Too Hard 47
   Day Five Smoke Rising 52

3. Triumphs and Tests 58
   Day One Not That Again 59
   Day Two Laughing Out Loud 63
   Day Three God Heard 67
   Day Four The Eternal God 72
   Day Five To Mourn for Sarah 76

4. Eyes on Isaac 82
   Day One A Jar on Her Shoulder 83
   Day Two This Is from the Lord 87
   Day Three He Loved Her 91
   Day Four Longing for A Better Country....... 95
   Day Five Ishmael and Isaac 99

5. The Heel Grabber 104
   Day One The Babies Jostled 105
   Day Two An Appetite for the Intermediate 109
   Day Three The Generational Impact 113
   Day Four Stolen Blessings............. 117
   Day Five Destructive Consolations........ 122

6. For the Love of Jacob.................. 128
   Day One When Jacob Saw Rachel........ 129
   Day Two An Unexpected Bride 133
   Day Three Winning Love 137
   Day Four Speckled Blessings 141
   Day Five Fleeing from Uncle 144

7. God of the House..................... 150
   Day One The Embrace of Brothers........ 151
   Day Two Nightmare in Shechem 154
   Day Three El Bethel 158
   Day Four But His Father 162
   Day Five Public Dreams 166

8. Dreams and Disappointments........... 172
   Day One Tamar's Trap............... 173
   Day Two The Lord Was with Him........ 178
   Day Three Forgotten................. 182
   Day Four A Jog in a Cupbearer's Memory ... 186
   Day Five Public Dreams 191

9. A Fragile Band of Brothers 196
   Day One Can't Quite Forget........... 197
   Day Two Unrecognizable Recognition 200
   Day Three And Benjamin Also 204
   Day Four Fears to Feasting........... 208
   Day Five A Set Up and a Stand Up 212

10. Epic Endings to the Beginning 218
    Day One With All That Was His 219
    Day Two The Years of Pilgrimage 223
    Day Three Crossing His Arms 227
    Day Four Prophetic Blessings........... 231
    Day Five The Grandest Finale 234

Christian Growth Study Plan 240

About the Author

Beth Moore was born on an Army base in Green Bay, Wisconsin, during what her father describes as the worst thunderstorm the city had seen in five years. He affectionately says, "The Lord brought her into the world with a drum roll."

The fourth child of a retired Army major and a homemaker, Beth was raised in Arkadelphia, Arkansas. Her father managed the local cinema where each of her four siblings had a role to play. Beth's job was to hand out samples of popcorn and soda. Growing up in the theater had its perks. Sometimes Beth would be allowed to slip into a movie with a bag full of popcorn and a cup of Coke®.

There in a theater chair, wide-eyed and filled to the brim with Coca-Cola®, Beth began a lifelong love for stories. She loved to tell them, write them, and hear them. The story that captured her heart and consumed her life, however, was not told in a movie theater; She heard it in Sunday School. It was the story of Jesus Christ, a Savior who loved children and who thought she was special. A seed was planted in her young heart that would grow to mark her life with a passionate love for Christ.

At the age of 18, Beth sensed God calling her to work for Him. Although she couldn't imagine what that would mean, she made it her goal to say yes to whatever He asked. Beth graduated from Southwest Texas State University with a degree in political science. She later received an honorary doctorate in humanities from Howard Payne University. In 1978 she married Keith, and soon after, the Lord added Amanda and Melissa to the family. As a young wife and mother, Beth served the Lord by speaking at luncheons and retreats, working with Mother's Day Out, and teaching Christian aerobics.

When Beth took a Bible doctrine class at her church, a love for God's Word took root in her life. Her teacher Buddy Walters, a former college football player, taught the Scriptures with tears streaming down his cheeks. Beth fervently prayed for such a passion for God's Word. It was Buddy who first taught Beth, along with Keith, how to study the Bible.

Beth founded Living Proof Ministries in 1994 with the goal of teaching women how to love and live on God's Word. She has written numerous books and Bible studies, including *Breaking Free*, *Believing God*, and *When Godly People Do Ungodly Things*. These resources have been read by women of all ages, races, and denominations. American missionaries and expatriates have even taken the Bible studies overseas, resulting in Beth Moore Bible study groups popping up all over the world. Beth's Living Proof Live conferences have taken her to 39 states since 1994 and have been attended by more than 421,000 women. God has graciously given her the opportunity to speak to the body of Christ in many different countries, including Ireland, England, Singapore, the Philippines, Puerto Rico, and India. With great joy, she began a radio ministry in 2004 called "Living Proof with Beth Moore."

Ever the storyteller, Beth is known to pepper her teaching with stories and poems written from the perspective of pertinent characters. She communicates with great energy, passion, humor, warmth, and grace.

Beth remains very dedicated to her home fellowship, Houston's First Baptist Church, where she teaches a 700-member Sunday School class. There she hosts an interdenominational Tuesday-night Bible study for women in her city. Because of her burden for unity in the body of Christ, Beth counts serving women of all denominations as one of her greatest privileges.

Keith and Beth have been married over 26 years. They enjoy traveling, sipping coffee on the back porch, eating Mexican food together, and making each other laugh. The Moores live in Houston, Texas, with their two dogs, Beanie and Sunny.

Introduction to the Patriarchs

Dearest One, As I invite you to join me on this—the 10th—Bible Study, I am more amazed and humbled than ever. I put the last period on week 10, day 5 only last night, came out of my chair, and went face down to the floor before God. I just don't understand a God like ours. Isn't it enough that He pulls a life out of a pit? Why would He also go to the long-term trouble to teach that messed up child to walk a healthier path–even when it was two steps forward and one step back? And why would He care enough to rebuild a broken mind, one patient piece at a time?

Beloved, one thing I can tell you at this point in my walk is this: God is committed to His children. Perhaps that's the message of the patriarchs in a nutshell.

God is committed even when we're not. God keeps covenant even when we don't. Somehow His plan gets accomplished, and anyone who has been privileged to be part of it is left without a shadow of a doubt that it happened through God alone. That's exactly what I said to Him this morning. My heart spills over with such love and gratitude that I'm not sure I can express myself to you.

The simplest words may be all I can articulate: God loves you so much! I am deeply humbled that He would allow me the joy of washing your feet, spiritually speaking, with the water of the Word. I am both blessed and frightened at the prospect of walking by your side as we journey through God's Word, daring to comment on it and coax you to apply it. God is the only One who can be taken entirely at His Word. With fear and trepidation I place this offering before you and tell you that where I've mis-stepped or inadequately applied, I ask your forgiveness, patience, and prayer. Some of the material in this study is as difficult and as exciting as any I've tried to tackle, but my heart is pure of motive. My soul's desire is to encourage you to love your God more through the study of His inspired Word. I encourage you again, Dear One, to protect yourself by staying under many teachers. At the same time, I am humbled and blessed beyond words that you'd allow me to be one of those. I do not take such responsiblity lightly.

So, welcome! Welcome to *The Patriarchs: Encountering the God of Abraham, Isaac, and Jacob.* Unless you've studied Genesis 12–50 in-depth before from a similar angle, I can assure you that you've never taken a trip quite like this Bible study journey. At least I hadn't. It is wild! You'd never believe the situations in which we'll find ourselves with the historical figures of Genesis. In fact, I'll warn you that even if you've taken some of my other studies, you might be surprised by the topics I'm forced to address in this one. I finally had to come to this conclusion with the more sensitive issues that come up in Genesis: if God talks about it, He means for us to talk about it, too. So, brace yourself.

The awkward and uncomfortable moments are few, and we'll survive them ... and learn volumes from them. One thing is certain: you don't have to wonder whether God can handle pertinent issues and address cultural crises. You will be shocked by the patriarchal narrative's relevance to our present lives. Rest assured, God knows the ways of mankind. The most shocking part is that God raises people like Abraham, Isaac, Jacob, you, and me out of the mire of this troubled world and brings Himself glory.

Even though God has caused each of the 10 studies to be unique, He has given us a pattern and approach that has worked well for us. Like most of the others, this Bible study is video driven. In other words, your member book is a very important part of the journey but not the only part. You're also invited and urged to join me for the weekly video messages that complement the written part of the study. If you and your group are holding to the optional 11-week schedule, we'll have time together on video followed by your own personal time with God in between through your five increments or "days" of homework. If you happen to be in a situation where you cannot view the video segments, I will direct you to read the pertinent passages of Scripture, but you will miss our face-to-face time.

Don't let the word "homework" scare you! You are going to have a blast with God! He will speak intimately to you, transform you, direct you, answer you, and bring you immeasurable healing in all sorts of ways as you meet with Him. God's Word never returns void! In fact, you can confidently thank Him in advance for all He's going to do.

Here are a few suggestions for making your journey through the pages of Genesis more meaningful: On the inside of the back cover you'll see a map of the lands involved in the patriarch stories. When I tell you we've got some miles to travel with Abraham, Isaac, Jacob, and his sons, I'm not kidding! You'll quickly learn why they were called "sojourners."

To keep the travels and the travelers straight, I urge you to get three highlighters of different colors and assign one to Abraham, another to Isaac, and another to Jacob. Every time Scripture records one of them in transport, mark the route on your map in the color you assigned to that patriarch. You can even customize the legend on the map by filling in the box beside each patriarch with the color you choose for him. You might also mark the phrase in your Bible in the same color. Personalize the experience! Let God make the journey rich and real for you as you fully participate. Underline phrases in your Bible, circle important words, and jot notes in the margins if you like. God wrote His Word to you, Dear One! Write back!

To enhance your learning and application of Scripture, *The Patriarchs* is written in an interactive format. I encourage you to complete all of the written work in your workbook. The Holy Spirit uses your efforts as you seek to answer the questions and respond to the activities in your own words.

You'll find five Principal Questions listed at the beginning of each week. Each comes from one of the five lessons during the week and deals with facts from the lesson. They will be identified in the week with a symbol like this: 🐪. Your small group will likely discuss the Principal Questions when you meet each week.

In addition to the Principal Questions, you will find Personal Discussion segments identified with a symbol like this: 🐫.

These learning activities help you personally apply the material by relating the events to your own life. Your small group will allow time for you to share about your Personal Discussion responses, but you will not be required to share unless you so desire.

I can never thank you enough for coming along. Oh, for words to express the love God has given me for you! Knowing and serving you is one of the greatest joys of my earthly life. When I write, I picture faces like yours and speak as directly to you as I would from across your breakfast table. I hope that's how you'll see it as well: two believers studying God's Word together. Malachi 3:16 says that every time people who revere God speak to one another (presumably about Him), He listens and hears and a scroll of remembrance is written in His very presence to record it. Let's keep the angels of heaven busy writing records of our conversations and boastings in the Lord our God this next 10 weeks!

I bless you, my dear fellow sojourner, in the name of the God of Abraham, Isaac, and Jacob. May He meet you on every page.

With deep affection,

I love you,
Beth

Introductory Session

God issued this promise to Abram in Genesis 12:2: "I will make you into a great _____."

Read Genesis 11:1-9.

1. God responded to man's "_____, _____ _____" with His own. The order of the consonants in the Hebrew word for "let Us confuse" is _____. The order of the consonants in the Hebrew word for "bricks" is the reverse: _____. "Will He _____ what they _____?"

2. The rebellion in Shinar was first and foremost an attempt by the people to make a _____ for themselves. (See Gen. 12:1-2.) From the resulting table of nations, God birthed a nation to _____ His Name and _____ the world with His blessing. Interestingly, since *YHWH* (the Tetragrammaton, "LORD") was considered the _____ name, one of the most common titles that God has been called in Jewish tradition is *Ha-Shem*, literally meaning "The _____" (2 Sam. 6:1-2).

3. We commonly identify this chosen nation as "the _____," but they were not called by this name for centuries.

Names or Identities:

- Abraham and his descendants were first called _____.
- After God renamed Jacob *Israel* and established the 12 tribes from 10 sons and 2 grandsons, Abraham's descendants also became known as the _____ of _____ or _____.
- The tribe of _____ and the small tribe of Benjamin, however, remained as the Southern Kingdom known as _____. After Judea fell to the Babylonians and the people were taken into exile, they became known as the _____ and the religion they practiced _____. Eventually all Abraham's descendants became generally known by the name of the largest remaining tribe (Judah) and the name was shortened to _____.

4. In keeping with His character, God told the _____ of a nation through _____.

WEEK ONE
Leave Your Country

Day One'
The Call of Abram
Day Two'
Down to Egypt
Day Three'
Parting Company
Day Four'
Man of God Against Kings
Day Five'
God Most High

Why are we about to invest precious time studying lives from early antiquity when time has never been at a higher premium? Isaiah 51:1-2 suggests a motivation. "Listen to me, you who pursue righteousness and who seek the LORD: Look to the rock from which you were cut and to the quarry from which you were hewn; look to Abraham, your father, and to Sarah, who gave you birth. When I called him he was but one, and I blessed him and made him many." While the people of Israel were blood descendants of Abraham and Sarah, Scripture shows that you and I are spiritual descendants. We make up the "many" God referenced. We will look to the rock from which we were cut and to the quarry from which we were hewn. Rest assured, we will learn. As you approach each day, ask God to give you eyes to see and ears to hear. Treasures await you in this archaeological dig, Beloved. During your first week, watch particularly for the principal questions that you will review in your small group:

This Week's Principal Questions

Day 1: According to Hebrews 11:8, where did Abram think he was going?
Day 2: What did the Lord do on behalf of "Abram's wife Sarai" (Gen. 12:17)?
Day 3: What kind of division developed between Abram and Lot (Gen. 13:5-7)?
Day 4: What was Abram called in Genesis 14:13?
Day 5: Who was Melchizedek and what made him unique?

When I first began researching the patriarchs of Genesis, I decided to mark every place name (such as Shechem, Bethel, and the Negev in day 1) with the same color highlighter in my Bible. Every time I see yellow highlighter in Genesis, I automatically know a location is recorded. Consider doing likewise. You'll also trace the journeys of the patriarchs on the map on the inside back cover. Use a different color for each patriarch.

Day One'
The Call of Abram

Home. That's what he once called Ur. Back then Abram didn't know to look for "a better country." Like many of us, he knew too little of the more to be dissatisfied with the less. When you don't have God, any god will do. At his age the ache in his soul could have been rheumatism for all he knew. Of course, at 75 Abram was only in the throws of middle age. The sun's light would climb up and down the tiers of Ur's famous ziggurat every day for another century before setting for the last time on the back of Abram far, far away.

Life throbbed in the soles of at least two hundred thousand pair of feet tramping the streets of ancient Ur. Like intravenous needles, two harbors drew lifeblood from the rich, silted waters of the Euphrates. Ur was a wealthy metropolis in Mesopotamia whose excavated history boasts elaborate systems of writing, impressive educational facilities, mathematical genius, extravagant business records, and highly-practiced religious life.

All in all, Abram was a city boy. He had a city life and a city wife. They were true Ur-banites, you might say. Well-taught students of patriarchal history will quickly cease equating antiquity with inactivity. Archeology has proved many ancient cultures astonishingly developed. Let's give these famous Urbanites a little pulse and picture them in sync with a high-energy environment. While we're at it, also picture them crawling in family.

Today's Treasure

The LORD had said to Abram, "Leave your country, your people and your father's household and go to the land I will show you."
Genesis 12:1

Now these are [the records of] the generations of Terah. Terah became the father of Abram, Nahor and Haran; and Haran became the father of Lot. Haran died in the presence of his father Terah in the land of his birth, in Ur of the Chaldeans.
Genesis 11:27-28, NAS

Abram lived under the nose of his father, Terah, whose tribe probably shared more spontaneous meals in a week than we share family reunions in a decade. An active extended family interjects an entirely different dynamic into any household. Life can be rich, but boundaries can be blurry. Sometimes people we invite into our home life tend to make themselves at home in every room. Still, closeness is worth it as long as we can appreciate the challenges. For instance, imagine how many times Abram and Sarai were asked when they were going to have children, what might be wrong, and how they could still be happy. No telling what Sarai might have given for an explainable diagnosis like endometriosis. And Abram? Picture being 75 and still wondering whether your father thinks you're a real man.

Complicate family matters with the death of Abram's brother, Haran. We can assume Haran died prior to Terah's family's departure from Ur (see Gen. 11:27-28, NAS).

Keith and I can testify how much death can affect family dynamics. He lost two siblings, one a small child and the other a very young adult. My heart grows tender as I muse that both also died, like Haran, in the loving presence of their earthly father. We are marked both positively and negatively as a family by those losses. Many households are torn apart by grief, finding the fellowship of pain intolerable. If anything, the fabric of Terah's family seems to have tightened. Add a little depth perception to the family dynamics with a dominant religious life. At the zenith of Ur's pyramid-type ziggurat stood a three-story terrace structure comprising the inhabitants' central worship center. People worshiped many gods in Ur, but Nanna, the moon god, was the city patron. Although the name sounds like someone's grandmother, it wasn't. Like all idolatrous gods, Nanna stole the security and dignity of his worshippers and throttled them with his insatiable appetite. To obtain his favor, worshippers served him with endless offerings, sacrifices, and demeaning rituals.

We might like to think Abram's family knew better than to worship false gods, but what does Joshua 24:2 say about the old family practices?
❑ Abram was a monotheist   ❑ Abram's family worshipped other gods

Bits of Hebrew tradition teach that Abram refused to participate in his family's religious practices, implying that God called him because he was set apart from the others from the start. The Bible remains completely silent about Abram's character prior to his call, however, so I am far more comfortable attributing God's choice of Abram to the mysteries of His sovereignty. I have less trouble imagining God's elect neck-deep in idolatry than positioned as the perfect choice when he was called. Isaiah 51:1-2 implies that God dug Abraham, and therefore all his spiritual descendants, out of the pit.

How deeply enmeshed were Terah and his family in the worship of the moon god? Several resources suggest that Terah, Sarai, Laban, and Harah were each named after the moon, the moon god, or his associates.[1] The family tree grew out of idol roots. We have no biblical reason to believe Abram and Sarai were looking for another god, but God was undoubtedly looking for them. To me, that beautiful fact provides the perfect place for our study to begin.

Read Genesis 12:1-9. What two verbal commands did God issue to Abram (v. 1)?
❑ Leave ... and cleave   ❑ Leave ... and take   ❑ Leave ... and go

How does Acts 7:2 recap the encounter?

Imagine! The "God of glory appeared" to Abram. What appearance do you think God took? Scripture doesn't tell us anything else about the divine encounter, but out of this holy confrontation monotheism was reborn in a heinously idolatrous world culture. This encounter was thus one of the most pivotal moments in human history.

Why didn't Abram simply add the "new" God to his old ones? We'll see hints that some of his family members bowed to multiple gods. What made Abram different? He was the only one among his people at that time who actually saw the glory of this God. Anyone who closely encounters the one true God of glory knows instinctively and immediately that none is like Him. To make a monotheist out of a polytheist only requires a hair-raising encounter with His Highness, the One and Only. Abram may have had other questions after that moment, but whether any other god was worth worshipping was not among them. There was One, and Abraham had met Him personally.

Our study hinges on Genesis 12:2-3. I'd like you to familiarize yourself so thoroughly with God's promises to Abram that you could recall the details at any time.

Why should we be interested in God's promises to Abraham (Gal. 3:6-9)?

_____

_____

So let's go ahead and get familiar with the specific promises. Please circle in the margin Scripture every time God makes an "I will" promise.

Underline God's concluding promise—the result of His "I will" actions (v. 3).

We've already stumbled onto one of the most vital points and paramount applications we can draw from God's promises to Abram. God's purpose in blessing one is to bless many: "I will bless you" (v. 2) "and all peoples on earth will be blessed through you" (v. 3). If God blesses us, we don't have to ponder whether that blessing has further purpose. We're blessed to bless. Blessed with spiritual gifts? Bless with them! Blessed with intelligence and skills? Bless with them! Blessed with finances? Bless with them!

Think of a few more examples and write them in the margin.

You and I have been blessed. Nothing mystifies me more than why God has chosen to bless a former pit dweller like me. Others tell me they feel the same. Imagine being Abram, however. One blessed man among all peoples on earth. Why Abram? Bruce Feiler reflects the mammoth significance of God's covenant promises to Abram in Genesis 12:2-3.

> "With these words, God asserts his decision to create the world anew. As before, with Creation, he uses only words to call the world into existence, to conjure firm ground out of the chaos. Only this time, Abraham is the navel of the world, the sacred starting point. The Rock."[2]

Abram never set out to be a navel. I can't picture him as a little tyke boasting, "I want to be a navel when I grow up." So, I ask you again, why Abram? Genesis 12:4 suggests a marvelous initial answer: "So Abram left." Perhaps one answer is simply, "Because he'd go."

monotheism
the doctrine or belief that there is but one God

polytheism
belief in or worship of more than one god

I will make you into a great
  nation
and I will bless you;
I will make your name great,
and you will be a blessing.
I will bless those who
  bless you,
and whoever curses you
  I will curse;
and all peoples on earth
will be blessed through you.
Genesis 12:2-3

Family/Friends
Freedom of Religion
Creativity
Sharing mistakes/lessons

🐪 Hebrews 11:8 impresses me even more. Where did Abram think he was going?

_____

We'll find that Abram was deeply flawed just as we are, but we'll also find that faith and obedience went a long way. Literally. Sound scholars are divided on the actual location of Abram's ancient Ur. Some place it in upper Mesopotamia, but "most scholars still maintain the identification of Ur with the Lower Mesopotamian site."[3] The lower site, 220 miles from modern Baghdad in southern Iraq, has ample biblical support, so we'll adopt the same view. How far can a little faith and obedience take us? Abram may well have traveled a thousand miles on his walk with God.

Genesis 11:31 and 12:5 could lead us to believe Abram's call came in Haran, but Acts 7:2-4 clarifies the matter. What was the sequence of travels?

_____

Note from Genesis 12:4-9 every move of Abram and mark it on your map. You can be virtually certain he took a route by a river for fresh water. The "land where you are now living" in Acts 7:4 refers to Israel.

When you read Acts 7:4, you no doubt noticed that Abram and his family settled in Haran for a while. Not knowing why allows us to imagine. Why do you think they may have settled short of their destination, not departing until Terah died?

_____

Consider all the things "Terah" could represent as you read the following quote by F. B. Meyer, and write some of those things in the margin. "It becomes us to be very careful as to whom we take with us in our pilgrimage. We may make a fair start from our Ur; but if we take Terah with us, we shall not go far … Let us all beware of that fatal spirit of compromise which tempts us to tarry where beloved ones bid us to stay. 'Do not go to extremes,' they cry; 'we are willing to accompany you on your pilgrimage, if you will only go as far as Haran … ' Ah! This is hard to bear, harder far than outward opposition."[4]

Where were Abram, Sarai, and Lot when they arrived in the land God announced He'd give to Abram's offspring (Gen. 12:6-7)?

_____

What did Abram do after God said He would give the land to Abram's offspring?
❑ Fell on his face as if dead ❑ Built an altar to the Lord ❑ Wept aloud

"Leave ... and go" (Gen. 12:1). God is never aimless. When He tells us to leave our lives of sin, He wants us to proceed to lives of victory. When He tells us to leave one place as He told Abram, He has another place for us to go. God may not reveal the destination for a while, but we can rest assured we're never called out without being called to.

All God told Abram about his ultimate destination was that He would show it to him. In other words, "The only way you're going to find it is to walk with Me. When we get close, I'll show it to you." And He did. "So [Abram] built an altar there to the LORD" (Gen. 12:7).

Join me on a journey leading us far away from our "Urs." What is Ur to us? Let's adopt the name of Abram's former home as an acronym for "Usual Routine." God calls us to leave our familiar spiritual countryside—our ruts, our comfort zones, and every hint of mediocrity—and "go" to a place He will show us. Let's not settle for Haran. Let's go the distance.

Tell God you want more; Challenge yourself

Day Two

Down to Egypt

I keep thinking about Abram's city wife. The God of glory did not appear to her. Sarai had nothing but Abram's word on which to base the most radical move of her life. Can any wife relate? Any daughter? Long before one of my favorite childhood sitcoms, "Green Acres," Sarai's heels dug a path all the way from city-Ur to country-Canaan. A rare woman wants to be a wanderer. We prefer purses to back packs and porcelain cups to Styrofoam™. We don't have to have a fancy home, but a wise husband knows to find us a place we can call our own. By gender, we are nesters and not adventurers.

"But, Abram, did God actually say, 'Take Sarai your wife'?"

"He didn't have to say it, Dear. We go together."

"What if I stay until we sell the house? The market should improve, let's say, in the next year or two."

"Get your purse, Sarai."

"The beaded one?"

How many of those miles do you imagine Abram traveled next to a cold shoulder? Scripture suggests we'd be mistaken to picture Sarai minus an outspoken opinion. How do we explain our callings to those affected? Especially those who have never met the Caller personally? Until she fully internalized this new monotheism, imagine how Sarai may have thought Nanna the moon god mocked her every time she tossed and turned under a night sky without a roof to call home.

To top it off, soon after Abram's clan reached Canaan, a famine hit (Gen. 12:10). If Keith is going to take me somewhere I don't want to go, he will either entice me with good shopping or good food. Shopping is out of the question at the deer lease, so good food ordinarily becomes our *pièce de résistance*. Imagine Abram and Sarai being met by famine in their destination of promise. "To your offspring I will give this land," God promised (Gen. 12:7). Historically, famine was an indictment against the land and the elements, in Sarai's eyes, Canaan clearly didn't put its best foot forward.

"Happy wife, happy life," I heard one husband say. If that's the case, Abram could have used a little pity. But before we become overly sympathetic, we'd better read today's text.

Today's Treasure

Now there was a famine in the land, and Abram went down to Egypt to live there for a while because the famine was severe.

Genesis 12:10

Write a one-sentence summary capturing Genesis 12:10-20:

_____

Glance at Genesis 12:9. According to this verse, Abram was headed toward …
❑ the Negev   ❑ Egypt   ❑ Canaan

We sometimes experience emotionally what Abram and his fellow sojourners experienced logistically. Negev included desert regions in southern Canaan. The word *Negev* means "dry." Realizing that God has spoken a word over you and perhaps has made you a promise is a spiritual high—and rightly so. Nothing is like a fresh realization that the God of the universe knows we're alive and that the voice that spoke the planets into orbit has spoken to us. However, the honeymoon period we spend swimming in the spring of a direct word from God is sometimes followed by a trip to the desert.

Take a look at Matthew 4:1. Where was Jesus led and why?

_____

What had Jesus just experienced at the conclusion of Matthew 3?

_____

We can be sure the people of God to whom promises come will be tested. For God to strengthen our faith, He must allow us to find cause to doubt. Only Jesus always passed the doubt test. The theme of tested promises will make us squirm, but perhaps we can learn to be more prepared for it.

🐫 **Have you ever felt that you followed God in obedience to a promise only to find yourself in a desert soon after your arrival?** ❑ yes ❑ no **If so, explain.**

_____

The weaknesses of God's children do not strain the strength of God.

Egypt was the land of dynasties, pyramids, and Sphinx, reputed for overflowing granaries blessed by the fertile Nile. We should not be surprised that Abram turned south. However, I am astonished once again at God's apparent security in not minding that we know His chosen servant and carrier of the blessing was so frail of character that he lied at the risk of his wife's honor. God has not opposed our knowing, and He fully intended us to know. His forthright inspiration of Scripture bids us to learn from past examples, both poor and good. The weaknesses of God's children do not strain the strength of God.

Let's face it. We are prone to lie when threatened. Furthermore, we can go from prone to lying to premeditated lying at the first hint of trouble. Surely you did not miss how well Abram planned his deceit. He had a ready rationalization. After all, Sarai was a relative. Genesis 20:12 even indicates she could have been his half sister. And isn't a half-truth still half true? Somehow, I don't think God sees it that way.

When my grandmother became too feeble to help around the house, she amused herself by listening on the other phone to what my brothers, sisters, and I assumed were private conversations. Sometimes the only way we'd know she had eavesdropped would be a familiar chide. Head shaking and lips as tight as a squeezed accordion, she'd say, "What a tangled web we weave when at first we do deceive." She was right, of course, but I always found her blind spot to her own deception as intriguing as her misquote of Sir Walter Scott.

Abram's blind spots can remind us of our own. One commentary reads, "Scholars debate the proper understanding of Abram's plan."[5] Let a bleached-blonde with a simple mind help them: Abram was scrambling to save his own skin. I know because I've done the same thing. Surely, somewhere along the way, you have, too. Perhaps we haven't recently scrambled in such a way because we finally learned that lying tends to backfire. The heat radiating from those backfires can be enough to burn us and teach us some very important lessons. We will have reason to doubt how well Abram learned from the consequences of this mistake in weeks to come.

We are left to wonder how Sarai initially responded to Abram's plan. Think about his thoughtful wording, "I know what a beautiful woman you are."

Mark on the scale where Sarai's initial response to these words may have fallen.

∞———————————————————————————————∞

fright   flattery

Beauty is often in the eyes of the beholder, but Sarai was obviously beautiful no matter who was beholding. Remember, she was only middle-aged at that time. Having blushed and powdered my own late-40s face in the mirror this morning, I'm still impressed she was admired for her physical beauty.

Consider the predicament in which Abram placed his wife just to save himself. After presenting the plan to Sarai, Abram reached Egypt only to have his fears realized. Take a good look at the words, "When Pharaoh's officials saw her, they praised her to Pharaoh" (Gen. 12:15). I believe many of us recall being "praised" like that, as if anything honorable or complimentary was intended. I'm not a male-basher, and, thankfully, I have a long list of fine men who keep me from the temptation. At the same time, I can recall humiliating encounters of passing a group of profane, godless men who liked to "praise" women. The difference is that these Egyptian hagglers had a friend in high places.

The next thing we know, Sarai was taken into Pharaoh's palace. What happened while she was in residence? We don't know, and we may not want to know. What did Pharaoh mean when he demanded of Abram, "Why did you say, 'She is my sister, so that I took her to be my wife'" (Gen. 12:19)? I want to be very careful with your minds, so I ask you give intelligent consideration to Scripture without proceeding to mental images. My purpose is that you try to fathom the magnitude of consequences Abram's plan could have invited. Pharaoh's words could mean the worst. Let's hope they didn't.

Have you discovered that decisions made in panic or self-protection mode can have undesirable consequences? ❑ yes ❑ no If so, how?

_____

_____

Glance back at Genesis 12:16-17. Scripture is clear that God came to Sarai's rescue even if Abram was busy counting sheep … and cattle, male and female donkeys, menservants, maidservants, and camels. Good grief.

What did the LORD do in behalf of "Abram's wife Sarai" (v. 17)?
(The terminology may suggest that God responded in this way because of Sarai.)

_____

Ah, Sarai obviously had a Friend in a much higher place than the hagglers'. This won't be the last time a Pharaoh has a serious encounter with God over His people. Beloved, God goes to our defense, doesn't He? No one trifles with us without treading dangerously on divine turf.

One of my favorite passages in the Psalms speaks to finding ourselves in the distress of battle. How might Psalm 55:16-19 speak to Sarai's scenario?

_____

As I consider the Pharaoh's question of Abram, I am grieved that a pagan ruler acted with more integrity than a child of God. Pharaoh basically asked, "Why didn't you just tell me the truth?" My stomach turns as I recall a time when I acted more sinful than the less "spiritual" people I knew. I cringe when I hear stories of Christians acting less ethically than those who make no claim of faith. We must be careful to allow God to build bone-deep character in us. The reputation of the whole family of God is at stake. We will undoubtedly make lots of mistakes, but let's admit them and testify when our actions are inconsistent with God's teachings.

Since we've placed Abram on the hot seat today (and not for the last time), let's check to see whether we could have come up with a better plan than his passing off Sarai as his sister. Remember, Abram wasn't wrong in his prediction; he was wrong in his plan.

What might Abram have done differently?

_____

_____

I want to conclude by offering you F. B. Meyer's proposal of an alternative plan because it instructed me deeply. Absorb it. Apply it.

> "How much better would it have been for Abraham to have thrown the responsibility back on God, and to have said, 'Thou hast brought me here; and Thou must now bear the whole weight of providing for me and mine: here I will stay till I clearly know what Thou wilt have me to do.' If any should read these lines who have come into positions of extreme difficulty, through following the simple path of obedience, let them not look at God through difficulties, as we see the sun shorn of splendour through a fog; but let them look at difficulties through God. Let them put God between themselves and the disasters which threaten them. Let them cast the whole responsibility upon Him. Has He not thus brought you into difficulties, that He may have an opportunity of strengthening your faith, by giving some unexampled proof of His power? Wait only on the Lord, trust also in Him ... He will provide."[6]

Day Three'
Parting Company

Our text today unfolds with the words, "So Abram went up from Egypt to the Negev, with his wife and everything he had, and Lot went with him. Abram had become very wealthy in livestock and in silver and gold" (Gen. 13:1-2).

The curtain lowered on our previous lesson with Abram and Sarai urged by Pharaoh to leave with haste, door prizes and all. "Take her and go!" (12:19). I can almost picture the ruler digging frantically in the drawer of his royal bureau for a return policy on Sarai. Of course, God doesn't have to ask permission or acquire cooperation to have something returned that belongs to Him.

I wonder what the trip back to Canaan was like. Can you imagine the conversation between Abram and Sarai? Was it heated? Tearful? Nonexistent? In today's culture the damage caused by comparable events would be considered virtually irreparable. Don't think for a moment that God's silence over certain events renders them without consequences. Likely the events were handled privately or left open-ended to exercise our imaginations.

If you were Sarai, what would the ride back to Canaan have been like?

_____

We'll consider our text in two segments today. Begin by reading Genesis 13:1-13.

List significant similarities between Genesis 12:8-9 and Genesis 13:3-4.

_____   _____

_____   _____

Among the more obvious and sacred similarities, I see Abram backtracking: Bethel–Negev–Egypt followed by Egypt–Negev–Bethel. He got off track, turned around, and retraced his steps back to the place of worship and fellowship with God. You might be blessed to know that the word *restores* in the familiar, well-loved Psalm 23 ("He restores my soul") means "to turn back, turn around, return. . . . Essentially denotes movement back to the point of departure."[7] When we've moved far from God, often we'll say, "I don't know how to get back." Beloved, sometimes we need to go back just the way we came—to the last place where we met God. We've already seen Abram build two altars, and we'll see others before our study ends. As New Testament believers in Christ, we might wonder how we can apply the concept of altar building to our lives.

Read Romans 12:1.

We are urged to offer our "bodies as _____ _____, holy and pleasing to God" because this is our "spiritual act of worship."

Today's Treasure
So Abram said to Lot, "Let's not have any quarreling between you and me, or between your herdsmen and mine, for we are brothers. Is not the whole land before you? Let's part company. If you go to the left, I'll go to the right; if you go to the right, I'll go to the left." Genesis 13:8-9

Dear One, every time we bow down and offer ourselves afresh as living sacrifices to God, we build a holy and pleasing altar as surely as Abram did. Notice that next the focus switches from Abram and Sarai to Abram and Lot.

 What kind of division developed between Abram and Lot (Gen. 13:5-7)?

_____

 Overcrowding increases conflict, but that may not have been the only issue. What does Proverbs 13:10 consider a breeding ground for many quarrels?

_____

In an ideal world, we'd protest that pride, jealousy, and rivalry have no place among family members. However, in the real world, we sadly find ourselves at odds with family more often than with friends ... or even foes. The competition can be fierce—especially when only certain gifts or interests such as music or sports invite the family blessing. We see the wiser side of Abram as he takes his place and insists such quarreling should not exist among "brothers."

What was Abram and Lot's actual relationship (Gen. 11:31)? _____

Abram's wording in Genesis 13:8 either meant family or brothers under the same God. Abram knew that peace in this situation would only come through amiable separation.

How did Abram soften the blow of suggested separation (v. 9)?

_____

How did Lot choose his portion (vv. 10-11)?

_____

In which direction did Lot go?   ❑ North   ❑ South   ❑ East   ❑ West

apostasy
renunciation of a religious faith; abandonment of a previous loyalty

God's Word is full of symbolism and rich repetitive themes. I was intrigued when a dear friend from Israel told me that Jewish people consider "going east" a phrase for apostasy. Many scholars point out parallels of eastward moves in Scripture that resulted in greater distance from God's fellowship. The first eastward move is recorded in Genesis 3:23-24.

What were the circumstances and central geographical location in this Scripture?

_____

After the exodus, the children of Israel wandered east of the Jordan in unbelief; they had to move west to dwell in the fulfillment of God's promises. The Holy of Holies was located in the western extremity of the tabernacle; but, praise God, the tribe of Judah was planted right by the eastern gate. Jesus, the Lion of the Tribe of Judah, is our holy transport from our wandering and unbelief to the promises of God. Before you take the concept of moving east or west literally, remember that on this round planet we all live east of someone. The idea is to keep moving toward deeper intimacy with God.

Whether or not they were directionally challenged, Adam, Eve, Lot, and the unbelieving generation of wandering Israelites each distanced themselves from God on the basis of what looked good. Abram gave Lot the choice of the land, and Lot chose what appeared to be the best property. Those who earnestly desire to please God (and therefore place others first) may sometimes think humility turns out badly. We can even convince ourselves that being godly means being beaten down—the more pitiful we are, the more piety we have. Untrue! God wants to bless us! That's why He insists on our obedience. God wants to teach us to seek His will because what He gives us will always prove better. When we're motivated by selfishness, what appears to be a good move may find us unintentionally pitching our tent near Sodom.

Read Genesis 13:14-18. What happened after Lot parted from Abram (v. 14)?

_____

I'm not sure we can overemphasize separation's role in Abraham's story. The first statement of promise followed Abram's separation from his country, people, and father's household (Gen. 12:1). The second statement of promise immediately followed his separation from Lot. Later we'll discover the third statement tucked in the context of Abram's willingness to separate himself from the dearest treasure of his life (Gen. 22).

Make no mistake. God tests our willingness to follow Him in obedience even if no one will or can go with us. We won't embrace with both hands what God has for us if we hold our old lives in a death grip. Like any Bible concept that seems radical, we are wise to view separation against the backdrop of the whole counsel of God's Word.

Compare 2 Corinthians 6:17 and Matthew 28:19-20. How do you reconcile these two seemingly opposite commands?

_____

_____

Sadly, some people who lean toward instability and extremism look for anything in Scripture to claim God's support of their bizarre behavior—no matter how they have to twist it, turn it, or isolate it. We are not meant to pack up our belongings, barricade ourselves in the mountains, defy the government, and become separatists. Christ called us to be in the world but not of the world (John 17:14-16). Our great challenge is to take our place in loving ministry to a lost world without getting lost in worldly loves.

Compare God's second statement of promise to Abram in Genesis 13:14-18 to His first statement of promise in Genesis 12:2-3. Record any additions or noteworthy ways God expounded on the first.

_____ _____

_____ _____

One of my commentaries pointed out a tiny word expressed in the Hebrew that I found fascinating. It is not represented in the NIV, but it is translated "now" in the *King James Version* of Genesis 13:14: "Lift up *now* thine eyes, and look" (emphasis mine). Consider the following:

> "Many translators ignore the small Hebrew particle *nā'* in the divine speech, but it is reflected in our translation as please, which is its normal English equivalent. It occurs many times in the OT, some sixty times in Genesis alone. But only four times in the entire OT does God use the word in addressing a human being: here, 15:5; 22:2; Exod. 11:2. In each of these four passages God asks somebody to do something that transcends human comprehension."[8]

If we translated the Hebrew particle according to these scholars, we might consider the verse, "Lift up please thine eyes, and look." Before we are horrified over the mere suggestion that God might lower Himself enough to say "please" to mortals, consider the word as an urgent and strong affirmation rather than a plea. That's why we see the word "now" in the major versions that translated *na* in those four verses. Why am I bothering to emphasize such a small word? Because I am deeply moved that God is urging His child to believe He is believable. In other words, "Abram, please believe Me when I tell you to lift up your eyes and look around you. I will give this land to you and your offspring forever."

God's willingness to urge us to believe Him is profound. As the psalmist mused, who is man that God is mindful of us? That He would bother with us? (See Ps. 8:4.) After all, if we don't believe and don't receive, isn't the loss ours alone? Beloved, try to absorb this: God lacks absolutely nothing. He is the I AM. The self-existent One. He created us out of the overflow of love and fellowship with His Son. Before time began, God had nothing to lose. When He created us, He placed His heart at the great and certain risk of loss.

When we choose not to believe God and follow Him, we all lose. Might we consider that God has allowed Himself to experience some element of loss? Neither His plan nor any measure of His glorious essence and authority is lost. However, our part in the plan that He cherished, His great pleasure in our participation and our fellowship with Him, is lost—if only momentarily. Hebrews 4:15 says of Christ, "we have not a high priest which cannot be touched with the feeling of our infirmities" (KJV). Oh, that God allows Himself to be touched by our infirmities! He willingly feels the loss of our losses!

In view of all that we've learned today and all the places God wants to take you during this study, imagine God saying to you, "Will you please, will you now, believe Me, Child? Would you really miss your part in My plan for the world?"

Do you sense that God might be asking you to believe and trust Him in some area? If so, write your response to Him below.

_____

_____

_____

_____

Day Four

Man of God Against Kings

As I prepare for today's scene, my eyes fall once more on Genesis 13. After God issued the second statement of promise, He instructed Abram to "Go, walk through the length and breadth of the land, for I am giving it to you" (v. 17).

How differently do you think the ground felt on the soles of Abram's calloused feet after God told him the land was his?

_____

Can you think of an experience in your own life when something felt different because you were told it was yours? If so, explain.

_____

_____

Today's Treasure

When Abram heard that his relative had been taken captive, he called out the 318 trained men born in his household and went in pursuit as far as Dan.
Genesis 14:14

Through our journey we will see several prominent themes rise like the pages of a pop-up book. The concepts of covenant and blessing will undoubtedly be among them. However, we cannot overlook how both those concepts involve another prominent theme: land. Never mind the fact that Abram's world never viewed him as a landowner. He wouldn't have viewed himself as such, but he certainly knew Whose the land was to give. So did the psalmist.

According to Psalm 24:1, how did the psalmist view property rights?

_____

Though I have always loved and longed for open spaces and outdoors, I have not yearned for land I could call my own as my husband has. He doesn't mean the front and back yards of our neighborhood home. My cowboy longs for a wide-open ranch—and forget mowing and weed-eating. Don't ruin Keith's picture with some fancy mansion either. My man's dream home is a cabin with a tin roof. In his imagination, his land is meant to remain wild and untamed . . . a little like its owner.

I don't think Keith is alone in his inner longing for land. I think maybe God slipped it into a hidden sleeve of a man's soul where it secretly drives everything he puts his hand to. I believe men on the crowded streets of New York City yearn for land. For many, subduing the sod has simply been replaced with subduing office challenges, making business conquests, and lassoing deals. The societal trend toward city-worlds doesn't make office work bad. It just makes it less than what a man's cowboy soul secretly wants. A few weeks ago our family was in the mountains hiking through a path in the snow, and out of the blue my son-in-law said, "You know, Ma'am, a man can't find his soul on the sidewalk." I grinned and thought of today's lesson.

Visual person that I am, when Keith speaks of his dreamland, I see us walking its perimeters much like Abram walked "through the length and breadth of the land." The images don't entirely line up. Ours has a lot of dogs running the "length and breadth" until their happy tongues drag the ground. However, our choice of where to stake our tents would be similar to Abram's.

Where does Genesis 13:18 tell us Abram moved his tents and "went to live"?

_____

A little land and a lot of trees. That'll do. "So Abram moved his tents and lived." Note the hint of contrast. The word "tents" speaks to us as temporary while the word "lived" suggests greater permanence.

Note parallels between this verse and Paul's wording for our bodies:
Genesis 13:18	2 Corinthians 5:1
_____	_____
_____	_____

Christians are called to be a blessing to this world.

No, this world is not our home. We, too, are looking for "a better country" (Heb. 11:16), but while we're here, we have some living to do. As the spiritual seed of Abraham, we Christians are called to be a blessing to this world. Take your tent and live today like earth has no tomorrow. Find a little shade under a big tree for a respite from the heat, but sow spiritual seed on this planet with everything you have ... for this is God's will.

Now read today's text: Genesis 14:1-16. What does this passage describe?

_____

This chapter of Scripture is unique in the patriarchal narratives. Certainly this is the only time we see Abram engage in military activity. God never wastes words, so He has a point to make; let's see if He'll reveal it to us as we consider these verses. The math in verses 1 and 2 is simple enough for me: four kings against five kings.

List those on each side:

_____ VS _____

_____ _____

_____ _____

_____ _____

_____

Shared enemies produce peculiar allies. We see that principle at work today. I'm not one to feel picked on and conspired against as a believer in America, but even I can't help but think that the entertainment industry often allies with political agendas to make Christians look like idiots. In this nation's battle for what is nobly tagged as "tolerance," Christians sometimes seem to be the only entity not tolerated. The only reason I don't lose heart over the opposition against holders of conservative biblical values in this nation is because I know Who has already won this war. Christ's kingdom will come and "the government will be on his shoulders" (Isa. 9:6).

What caused the war according to Genesis 14:4?

_____

What was the outcome of the war according to Genesis 14:11?

_____

Not all the kings hold significance for us, but allow me to point out a few. Three locations are probably familiar to you: Shinar, Sodom, and Gomorrah.

Review Genesis 11:1-4. What happened on a plain in Shinar?

_____

Genesis 10:10 also confirms that Babylon is in Shinar. Now take note of the names of the kings of Sodom and Gomorrah. *The New International Commentary of the Old Testament* tells us that, "*Bera* is apparently related to the verb *rā'ā'*, 'be evil,' and means 'in evil.' *Birsha* may be related to the verb *rāša'*, 'be wicked,' and means 'in wickedness.' "[9]

What vested interest do we have in Sodom at this point in our patriarchal narrative (Gen. 13:12; 14:12)?

_____

I note an important difference in the terminology of both the NIV and the KJV regarding Lot's proximity to Sodom in Genesis 13:12 and 14:12.

In Genesis 13:12 Lot "pitched his tents _____ Sodom."

In 14:12 Lot was taken captive "since he was _____ _____ Sodom."

In my estimation, near and in are two different things. That's the trouble with pitching our tents near something persuasive. If we're not careful, we tend to move on in. And when we move in, we soon fall captive to the captors of our environment. That's what happened to Lot.

Enter Abram. We couldn't have blamed him if he assumed the attitude that Lot had gotten himself into this trouble and Lot could get himself out. After all, hadn't they separated? F. B. Meyer writes:

"The men who live the life of separation and devotion towards God, are they who act with most promptness and success when the time for action comes. Lot being in Sodom, could neither elevate its morals nor save it from attack. Abraham living among the hills is alone able to cope successfully with the might of the tyrant king. Oh, do not listen to those who say you must live on the level, and in the midst of worldly men, in order to elevate and save them."[10]

From Meyer's statement above write a moral that you can share with your children, family, or a friend.

You don't need to hang with them, they need to hang with you (I cor 10:12)

In fact, living in the midst of carnality and worldliness can weaken us so we lack the power to walk ourselves out of the mess, much less carry others to freedom. Abram's strength in this narrative was in his separation.

My favorite F. B. Meyer statement about the relationship between separation and sanctification is: "Faith makes us independent, but not indifferent."[11]

"Faith makes us independent, but not indifferent."

 What do you think this statement means?

_____

_____

Give an example from your experience.

_____

_____

_____

_____

 Look carefully at Genesis 14:13. What is Abram called? _____
" " 4:25,26

The description given to our patriarch in this verse could hardly be more significant. He is called "Abram the Hebrew." We began our search of Genesis 14 in hopes of uncovering God's point in Abram's single appearance on the battlefield. I believe the entire theme of today's text is summed up in Abram's distinction as "the Hebrew." After the rebellion at the tower of Babel, God instituted nations, separated peoples, and chose to make one group entirely distinctive. He first described that distinction in Genesis 12.

Read Genesis 12:2-3 as the backdrop for today's text.

In Genesis 14, how does God demonstrate His faithfulness to these promises?

_____

Abram was a wanderer not a warrior, but he wisely trained men to protect his people, flocks, and herds. Even so, they should have been like blind mice scurrying before such allied forces.

Romans 8:31 offers a New Testament explanation for their victory. What is it?

_____

God's side is the only safe place to be. The original promises in Genesis 12:2-3 offer the immediate Old Testament explanation. "I will bless those who bless you and whoever curses you I will curse." For years my daughters and I have enjoyed a little Bible-based humor by reducing circumstances and experiences under two headings: 1) A blessing. 2) Not a blessing. (Sometimes abbreviated A.B. and N.A.B.) For instance, Mexican food would fall under the A.B. category while mosquitoes fall under the N.A.B. category. To us, all things either are—or are not—a blessing. I believe that Lot's capture fell under Abram's N.A.B. heading. True to His covenant promises, God withheld blessing from Lot's captors and, instead, they were certain to end up with A.C. (A curse).

On the other hand, the recipient of the blessing "recovered all the goods and brought back his relative Lot and his possessions, together with the women and the other people" (Gen. 14:16). Beloved, through the blessing of God all can be recovered. Never forget it.

> *Abram the Hebrew.* _____ (your name) *the Christian.* **Blessed to be a blessing. Set apart to step in.**

On the battlefield of Genesis 14, God drew the delicate balance between separation and relation. Abram was called to be separate—not so he could be detached but so he'd have the God-strength to help. Like us, Abram was affected by the world around him. Our planet is small. We the people of God are called to be sanctified and separate so we can have the strength to rise up and help. Abram could not ignore the political climate that surrounded him. Nor can we. We must remain alert, informed, trained, and willing.

After all, each of us knows a Lot in Sodom.

> **Write a prayer for a Lot you know. Ask God to deliver him or her and make yourself available for the Lord's use in the task.**

_____

_____

_____

_____

_____

Day Five
God Most High

As I begin our lesson today, my heart burns with fresh passion for God's Word. The Scriptures you and I are about to study together are heavy with treasures. Will you pause and ask God to absolutely delight you with His Word today? Psalm 119:16,18 says, "I delight in your decrees; I will not neglect your word … Open my eyes that I may see wonderful things in your law." God, grant us "the Spirit of wisdom and revelation" (Eph. 1:17) that will cause Your Word to jump off the page and into our hearts. Lord, let it be!

According to Genesis 14:17-24, who was Melchizedek? (More information is supplied elsewhere, but I don't want us to consider it yet.)

Why wouldn't Abram accept anything from the king of Sodom?

What title for God is introduced in this segment? _____

Does verse 19 offer you insight into the title's meaning? ❑ yes ❑ no If so, what?

How about verse 20?

I love the mysterious side of God. Mind you, I'm free to love that side of Him only because I find ample security in the side of Him I know and can understand. Without an element of *security*, *mystery* is scary to me. I am convinced that the totality of everything God has told us about Himself in His Word and in nature is little more than a hint. He is the master of surprise who exults in unveiling revelations.

If we could only grasp that the most ingenious and creative thoughts of man are mere whispers of God's abilities. Surely you've read mystery novels or suspense thrillers with twists and turns and jumped when something unexpected came out from behind a curtain. When you turned the last page of the best of them, haven't you marveled, "How in the world did the author imagine such a plot?"

A smile spreads across my face as tears sting my eyes. Beloved, don't you see? Man's vast creativity and capability to spin a tale or unveil a mystery is just another part of how humans are created in the image of God. He is the master storyteller, weaving a thousand story lines together over the course of 66 books and many centuries. True stories! With every story the plot thickens and the veils thin. Different beginnings toward a perfect end. Bad guys lose. Good guys win. But not until we've bitten our fingernails to the quick, wondering if the villain will prevail and the hero will fail. Our souls are fitted for excitement and intrigue, and though we sometimes scream and shut our eyes, we will one day get off the roller coaster and shout, "What a ride!"

All because we were created in the image of God. By Him. For Him. The late Mike Yaconelli puts his own spin on it. "The God of the Bible is the master of surprises: frightening clouds of smoke and fire, earthquakes, windstorms and firestorms, donkeys that talk, pillars of salt, oceans splitting apart, using a little boy to kill a giant, the Messiah in swaddling clothes and dying on a cross. No one can follow God and be comfortable for long."[12]

Admit it. Too much comfort too long bores a God-fashioned soul.

Enter Melchizedek, born in the mind of God who created him and no doubt grinned as He scripted his name on the page. Melchizedek is a shadowy figure stepping from behind a veil for only a moment, leaving us to wonder who he is or why God bothered to introduce him but reveal little of his background information. Questions are good. They leave lots of space for God to fill in the blanks far beyond our imaginations.

The first question that might occur to us regarding Melchizedek is: How in the world did a priest of God show up out of nowhere in the pages of Genesis 14? Wasn't Abram the only thing God had going? Dear One, what we see with our eyes and understand with our minds is never the only thing God has going. Furthermore, Genesis 14 doesn't begin to explain the peculiarity of this figure like Hebrews 7:3 does.

What does Hebrews 7:3 tell you about Melchizedek?

_____

Bizarre, isn't it? Can I explain it? Ah, 10 years ago I would have explained it to you confidently based on my best doctrinal sources. I would have wrapped old Mel right up and stuck a bow on the end of his nose. But I've gotten a little smarter since then. Smart enough to know that I don't have a clue. Melchizedek simply was. God makes the rules of nature and can break the rules of nature any time He pleases. As long as you're in Hebrews 7, go ahead and read the more extensive story written in Hebrews 6:19-7:17.

After you read the segment, explain what Melchizedek has to do with Christ.

_____

_____

One way we know Melchizedek wasn't a preincarnate appearance of Christ is the comparison Hebrews draws between the two of them. For instance, Hebrews 7:3 says of Melchizedek, "*like* the Son of God he remains a priest forever" (emphasis mine). Melchizedek's peculiar priesthood was somehow a foreshadowing of Christ's. I referred to Melchizedek as a shadowy figure in God's mystery novel, but maybe I should have said he's fore-shadowy.

Since most of us doing this Bible study don't have the privilege of Jewish ancestry, we probably miss one argument the writer of Hebrews is settling. His intention in this segment is to explain how Christ could be a high priest of God without coming from the priestly tribe of Levi which was established much later. The writer's point is that the priesthood existed long before Levi. I love the line, "when Melchizedek met Abraham, Levi was still in the body of his ancestor" (Heb. 7:10). God made up the priesthood. He can bring it to completion in Christ through any line He pleases.

Look back at our original references introducing Melchizedek in Genesis 14:18-20. We tend to be most intrigued by the tithe Abram gave to the priest of God. Our assumption is that Abram understood the high office the priest represented and gave him a tenth as a way of offering it to God. Any time I put a check in an offering envelope at my church, I am essentially practicing the same sacred action. My gift is to God, but since I can't place it directly in His hands, I give it to Him through offerings to organizations representing Him on earth. However, I am not most intrigued by the tithe.

What did Melchizedek "bring out" according to Genesis 14:18?
❏ gold and silver ❏ bread and wine ❏ plunder

This captivates my imagination most. Why bread and wine? Sure, they could be nothing more than physical provisions, but I doubt it. The fact that we already know that Melchizedek's priesthood foreshadowed Christ and that Christ instituted the new covenant (Luke 22) with the bread and the wine makes the chances of a simple provision in Genesis 14 a little slim. Under the new covenant, the bread represented Christ's body and the wine Christ's blood. Surely access to the Most High God (the priest's ultimate purpose) is granted no other way than through the broken body and spilled blood of Christ—whether foreshadowed in the Old or fulfilled in the New Testament.

Genesis 14:18 introduces us to a name far superior to the shadowy priest's. *El Elyon*: God *(El)* Most High *(Elyon)*. The title "Most High" or *Elyon* by itself is used far more often in the Word of God than the full title "God Most High," but the general reference remains consistent. The Name of universal superiority was aptly proclaimed first in the Valley of Kings (the meaning of "Valley of Shaveh"). The kings of the earth will cast their crowns at the feet of the God Most High.

The subtitle on the cover clearly states the goal of our study. What is it?

_____

One masterfully creative way God invited Abram, Isaac, and Jacob to get to know Him was by introducing Himself through various names. In those names we see a glorious paradox. God took Abram out of the worship of many gods by introducing him to One God by many names. One alone suffices because He is the sum total of all authority: the possessor of every chief title and office. The CEO and CFO of all creation. No matter what your need, God holds a title that meets it.

 At this season in your life, what is your greatest need?

Wisdom, the word, Peace, happiness, refuge

Somewhere in His Word, God is known by a name that meets that need. If you already know it, what is it? _____ (This is not a doctrinal test. Just answer with the best of your understanding.)

If you don't already know the name of God that meets your need, trust in advance that He holds that title. You will likely stumble onto it in our study of Genesis 12–50. Expect us to note each title introduced in Genesis as it comes. The frequency of new names for God in the Book of Beginnings implies their great importance in getting to know the One they represent. Though the full meaning and expression of each name has yet to be revealed, the context surrounding them hints volumes.

The first time an important term appears in Scripture often reveals critical information. Case in point, the first description the Bible offers after the first mention of "God Most High" probably holds the most important key to understanding the title.

Fill in the following according to Genesis 14:19.
"Blessed be Abram by God Most High,

_____ ."

Hopefully you also noted it on the first page of today's lesson when I asked you if Scripture noted any additional information.

While the NIV and HCSB use the wording "Creator of heaven and earth," the KJV and NASB use the wording "Possessor of heaven and earth." Which is right? As we'll often discover upon deeper research, both are right. Be encouraged to know that each of the major versions has substantial grounds for the translations they've made. The differences come from varying opinions about which ancient manuscripts are the most reliable. You and I might fail a seminary exam on hermeneutics if we don't share the exact interpretation as the professor, but, rest assured, most of the major translations offer what you and I pursue: a sound and lively opportunity to know the one true God of Scripture.

hermeneutics
the study of the methodological principles of interpretation.

In essence, *El Elyon* represents exactly what it implies in its English translation. He is God Most High. Above all others. None can touch Him. None can rival Him. He is transcendent over all things and all titles. He is the Creator and Possessor of heaven and earth. He is one God for all people. No serious student of the Book of Genesis can miss His universal outreach. One man and one nation were chosen so that all nations could be blessed.

The following are just a few of many Scriptures referring to God as the Most High. Record anything these verses imply about the holder of that title.

Daniel 4:17 _____

_____

Psalm 21:7 _____

These two Scriptures make balancing bookends to the volumes that could be taught on this title. Consider Daniel 4:17 the first bookend. The title Most High God points to God's absolute sovereignty.

I can think of no Scripture that expresses God's sovereignty more aptly than Psalm 115:3. How does that Scripture make you feel?

_____

If the verse makes you uncomfortable, bare your heart before God and try to tell Him why. Don't fear what He'd do if He saw hues of distrust in the depths of your heart. He knows why they are there better than you do. You might consider asking Him why His sovereignty scares or unsettles you. Perhaps the reason is a missing bookend on one side of the volumes you know about God Most High. Recall Psalm 21:7. God's sovereignty can terrify us only to the extent that we are uncertain of His love. You and I are never childish or unwise to remind ourselves daily how much God loves us. Only to the extent that we abide in His love can we be comforted by His sovereignty.

> **Imagine titles for two books that might answer your hardest questions. Put the titles on the two book spines below. (One of mine would be, *Why Children Sometimes Suffer*.) Beloved, all questions will one day be answered. Until then, we have a God Most High who refuses to separate His sovereignty from His love.**

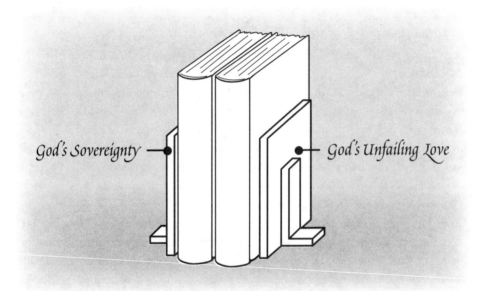

God's Sovereignty — God's Unfailing Love

Notice our difficult questions always fall between the bookends of God's sovereignty and His unfailing love.

[1] Victor P. Hamilton, *The Book of Genesis: Chapters 1–17* (Grand Rapids: William B. Eerdman's Publishing Company, 1990), 363.

[2] Bruce Feiler, *Abraham: A Journey to the Heart of Three Faiths* (New York: Harper Collins Publishers, 2002), 39.

[3] Hamilton, 365.

[4] F. B. Meyer, *Abraham; or, The Obedience of Faith* (New York: Fleming H. Revell Company, 1904), 20-1.

[5] Hamilton, 381.

[6] Meyer, 38.

[7] Spiros Zodhiates et al., eds., *The Complete Word Study Dictionary: Old Testament* (Chattanooga, TN: AMG Publishers, 1994), 113.

[8] Hamilton, 394.

[9] Hamilton, 401.

[10] Meyer, 60-1.

[11] Ibid., 60-1.

[12] Michael Yaconelli, *Messy Spirituality: God's Annoying Love for Imperfect People* (Grand Rapids: Zondervan, 2002), 43.

Leave Your Country

Book of Genesis - In the beginning
Chapter 15

Psalm 81:10

1. God ordained Abra(ha)m to be both __patriarch__ and __prophet__.

2. Those God __uses__ greatly seem to greatly __battle__ __fear__. Therefore, we may battle fear but we must not __let__ it __win__.

   false evidence appearing real (FEAR)

3. The Hebrew word for *count* means "to __score__ (to __mark__ with a __tally__.)"

4. On the basis of biblical re-emphasis, God does not mean for us to miss that Abraham __believed__ the Lord and it was __credited__ to him as __righteousness__.

   Romans 4:23-24

   • Genesis 15:6 records the __first__ __mention__ in Scripture of any form of the word __believe__. Let's make our goal to one day see the words

   " __Karen__ __believed__ __God__ " in His handwriting.
   (Your Name)

   • The word *credited* means "to count, impute, __esteem__."

   • We can __act__ without belief, but we cannot __believe__ without __acting__ (Isa. 7:9).

   when was the last time something good happened?

5. Elements of the Covenant Ceremony:

   • The Hebrew terminology for "made a covenant," *karat* means "to __cut__, cut __off__; to make a covenant."

   • Each animal and bird God required in the ceremony was later listed among the __acceptable__ __sacrifices__ under the Levitical __laws__.

   • Since God could __swear__ by no one __greater__, He swore by __himself__. *Psalm 139*

   Jeremiah 34:17-20
   Hebrew 6:13-15

   • The birds of prey represent __foreign__ __attack__.

   • The word for "passed" is *avar* or *abar* meaning to __cross__ __over__.

   God crossed over so we could *Deuteronomy 31:1-3*

The Approaching and Approachable God

We began our first week of study with the call of Abram and the covenant promises God made him. We saw evidences of fulfillment almost immediately. Ultimately, God's promise to bless all nations through Abram is Messianic. It will only be completely fulfilled in Jesus Christ the Messiah. According to 2 Corinthians 1:20, Christ is the "yes" of all of God's promises, and none were more significant than those made to the founder of His chosen nation. Our appreciation for God's wonderfully stubborn commitment to covenant—or more importantly to the people of covenant—should escalate considerably over week 2. The wonder of grace is not so much in God's commitment to keep His promises as God's commitment to keep His promises to stubborn, faithless people. This week, please keep an eye out for the answers to the following principal questions:

Day One
The God Who Sees Me
Day Two
The Covenant of Circumcision
Day Three
No Longer Sarai
Day Four
Anything Too Hard
Day Five
Smoke Rising

This Week's Principal Questions

Day 1: Through what questions did God dialogue with Hagar (Gen. 16:8-14)?
Day 2: According to Genesis 17:2, what had the Lord come to Abram to do?
Day 3: What blessings were specifically spoken over Sarah in Genesis 17:15-16?
Day 4: What very specific prophecy did Sarah overhear in Genesis 18:10?
Day 5: How does Ephesians 4:18-19 partially explain the condition of Sodom?

Day One
The God Who Sees Me

I have known God since childhood, yet I still have moments of utter astonishment over His revealed activity when all that will come to my lips is Psalm 8:4, "What is man that you are mindful of him, the son of man that you care for him?" Though the thought of our invitation to approach God amazes me, I am at times almost stricken face-to-the-ground when I realize afresh how readily, how willingly, God approaches us. In the manifold operations of running the universe, not only is He ever with us but also He interrupts us at times with an unexpected revelation of His pure pursuit of us.

Indeed, what is man that He is mindful of us? I shake my head with wonder. We are not an afterthought to God. We are the point of His involvement with this planet. He does not just tolerate us, He pursues us. Indeed, He *seeks us* though we are never out of sight. "Oh, the depth of the riches of the wisdom and knowledge of God!" (Rom. 11:33).

Please read all of Genesis 16 to retain the context, then we'll discuss the text in two parts. After reading, concentrate on Genesis 16:1-6.

We might entitle this portion of Scripture "The Trouble With Helping God." And believe me, it always leads to trouble. Satan capitalizes on this portion of our femininity. God has wired us in wonderful ways. By nature we tend to be nurturers, straighteners, fixers. To want to help is part of our original wiring. Remember this portion of Genesis 2? "But for Adam no suitable helper was found. So the LORD God ... made a woman ... and he brought her to the man."

Today's Treasure
She gave this name to the LORD who spoke to her: "You are the God who sees me," for she said, "I have now seen the One who sees me."
Genesis 16:13

Anything you have to manipulate to get is rarely yours to keep.

Where do we think our drive to advise originates? Most men don't have an affinity for hearing other people's problems, but women often thrive on it. Why? Partly because we enjoy telling people what to do with their lives. It's in our wiring. Clearly Sarai got her wires crossed.

Satan prides himself on tangling our wiring until the outcome is a knotted counterfeit of God's wiring. Help tangles into manipulation with the slightest rerouting. Recently I was preparing for a Sunday school lesson when a related sentence came into my mind that seemed to come from the Holy Spirit: "Anything you have to manipulate to get is rarely yours to keep." I sat before God recalling instances in my life which support such a statement. Sometimes I knew I was being manipulative. Other times I sincerely convinced myself that I was just trying to help and wanted what was best for everybody. (I know this is shocking to all of you who are like me, but wanting what is best is not always synonymous with knowing what is best.)

I can remember trying to manipulate certain relationships and interests for my husband, my children, or myself. Although such manipulations sometimes got off to a promising start, they never "kept." With enough thought, other examples came to mind about positions or opportunities I tried to "help" bring about that never lasted.

How about you? Have you ever manipulated something that you didn't get to keep? If you're comfortable sharing it, do so briefly.

_____

_____

I don't doubt for a minute that my womanly wires would have gotten crossed in a dilemma like Sarai's. Then again, who can imagine coming up with Sarai's method of childbearing? What wife in her right mind would hand her husband over to another woman? A younger woman? Let's make two quick observations. First of all, desperation can make an otherwise lucid person do outrageous things. Wouldn't you agree? Secondly, the custom of acquiring an heir through a maidservant was practiced in parts of the ancient world.

The New International Commentary quotes four ancient texts that suggest practices similar to the one Sarai offered to Abram. "An Old Assyrian marriage contract" included this instruction: "If within two years she has not procured offspring for him, only she may buy a maid-servant and even later on, after she procures somehow an infant for him, she may sell her wherever she pleases"[1]

God never adjusts His commands to fit the customs of nations, no matter how deeply ingrained they are. Furthermore, His immutable standards prove right every time—and for each party involved. History has yet to record a single nation completely free of oppressive or unjust customs. God never oppresses people. People oppress people.

Carefully study the dialogue between Sarai and Abram. Does either of them ever call Hagar by name? ❏ yes ❏ no

How do they refer to her? _____

Any time we seek to use, oppress, abuse, or remove others, we first invariably disconnect from their individuality (name, personal rights). For instance, Hitler systematically brainwashed his governmental leaders to view the Jews as animals and to assign them numbers instead of names. On a much smaller scale, any of us are far more successful in nursing our prejudices if we can avoid knowing our target group personally and seeing them as individuals with value. Hagar's personal rights and choices were never figured into Sarai and Abram's alternative plan. Hagar was just a "servant," a "her," a "she."

No wonder Hagar "began to despise her mistress" after she realized she was pregnant (Gen. 16:4). Such a change in attitude invariably happens in relationships God doesn't ordain. God's instructions regarding how we engage in relationships and how we treat one another are meant to simplify and bless our lives. Every time I've departed from God's will for my relationships (meanwhile trying to rationalize or spiritualize), they ended up souring. Have you noticed the same thing in your own relationships? Hagar's reasons for despising Sarai were probably as complex and tangled as the feminine wires that had gotten crossed.

Let's admit it. Pregnancy is physically and emotionally challenging under the best of circumstances; then factor in the resentment aggravated by hormones and discomfort. Women seldom have one feeling at a time, so complicate the matter even further with Hagar's feelings of superiority over Sarai. Hagar the maidservant completed what Sarai the respected wife started, concocting a perfect formula for disaster.

What does Proverbs 30:21-23 say about Sarai and Hagar's strange arrangement?

———————————————————————————————————————

No doubt the earth under Abram's feet trembled as Sarai announced, "You are responsible for the wrong I am suffering" (Gen. 16:5). Instead of falling to his knees, Abram responded passively, "Do with her whatever you think best" (16:6). For crying out loud, no one was thinking well, let alone *best*!

Glance once again at verses 7-15. By the time we catch up with Hagar, she has traveled quite a distance and is obviously on her way back to Egypt. Try to crawl into Hagar's character for a moment. If you were she, what would you have planned to do once you arrived, and what would you have told your relatives?

———————————————————————————————————————

———————————————————————————————————————

———————————————————————————————————————

Of all the things we might imagine Hagar felt, surely the intensity of aloneness was almost unbearable. The last thing she expected was to encounter God. Don't you suppose she assumed Yahweh was Abram and Sarai's God? Not an Egyptian maidservant's. No, Hagar wasn't looking for God. God was looking for Hagar.

God's sudden revelation through the angel of the LORD is stunning. "The phrase 'angel of Yahweh' appears 58 times in the OT and 'angel of God' 11 times."[2] Scripture doesn't allow us to categorically assume every occurrence of these phrases depicts God Himself or a preincarnate revelation of His Son. Many of the instances equate the angel with deity, but others separate the two. When the angel of the LORD or the angel of God proves himself distinct from deity, we can still assume the utterly miraculous and profound. Check the context in Hagar's encounter.

Do you think the angel of the LORD in this context was God Himself or a powerful messenger sent by God? Support your answer with Scripture.

_____

_____

The only evidence raising any argument against Hagar's encounter with God Himself is the terminology in verse 11 "the LORD has heard of your misery." However, this evidence doesn't tip the scale against the evidence in favor of her having encountered God Himself. Very likely God referred to Himself in third person to make sure she knew His identity. I am convinced this glorious Intruder in Hagar's plan was God Himself. Verse 7 stirs my heart deeply. God *found* Hagar. And yet, God the Omniscient—infinitely aware—knew where she was all along. The intention of the wording is to make sure the reader knows God sought Hagar, the Egyptian maidservant. Do you think she glanced over her shoulder to find someone else He was surely seeking? Aren't we like that sometimes? We have difficulty imagining God would bother with such a grand revelation for us alone. Are you far more likely to associate God's presence with a corporate gathering of believers or with your pastor or Bible study leader? Do you think He would bother for you alone?

 Through what questions did God dialogue with Hagar (vv. 8-14)?

_____

Do you think God already knew the answers? ❑ yes ❑ no

If so, why do you think He asked them?

_____

Dear One, very often God initiates intimacy with us by raising fresh questions. Hard questions. Even questions that have no earthly answers. But the search leads us to heaven's door. God often causes us to search ourselves, asking us to articulate what we're feeling and why we're making some of our present choices. In 1 Kings 19:9 God asked, " 'What are you doing here, Elijah?' " In John 20:15, Christ asked Mary Magdalene, "Woman, why are you crying?" Countless times in various circumstances I've felt the Holy Spirit say to me, "Beth, why are you doing this?" or "Why are you sad?"

Beloved, would you be bold and risk intimacy with God as you answer the questions He whispers to your heart?

From where have you come?

_____

Where are you going?

_____

You may not be in a negative place, but can you identify your path—both behind you and immediately in front of you? A lump wells in my throat as I consider that by God's grace He has a plan even when we leave it. God didn't call the baby "that maidservant's child." He called him by name: *Ishmael* meaning "Yahweh has been attentive to your humiliation."[3] Read these words as often as you must to absorb them into your own belief system: "Yahweh has been attentive." To you, Dear One, to you!

To me, even in the humiliation I brought on myself.

God knew the Ishmaelites would exist as surely as the Israelites. Their existence was their manifest destiny. You no doubt noticed that the news concerning Hagar's son was not altogether lovely. God stated the prophetic description of Ishmael as a matter of fact, not as a curse or a compulsion. Then something happened in Genesis 16:13 that is unparalleled in Scripture. Hagar gave God a name. No other character in the Old Testament, male or female, ever does such a thing. Only Hagar, the Egyptian maidservant.

🐪 What name did Hagar give God (16:13)? _____

In Hebrew, *El Roi*. Ours, Dear One, is the God who sees. Is there any particular reason why that name means something special to you right now?

_____

_____

Hagar's next statement is equally moving. "I have now seen the One who sees me." The sentence could more literally be translated from the Hebrew as a question: "Have I really seen the back of Him who sees me?"[4] A Hebrew word for "back" is articulated in the original language.

Why might Hagar seeing God's back make sense in reference to Exodus 33:20-23?

_____

_____

The divinely initiated encounter between God and Hagar began with these words: "The angel of the LORD found Hagar near a spring in the desert." How like God to become her Spring in the desert. *El Roi*. He sees when no one else cares to look. He sees through the smile we wear when we're dying inside. He sees our hurt when we're mistreated. He sees us when we cry into our pillow because we feel unloved. He sees beyond our sin into the depth of our need. He sees when we're hiding. Running. He sees when we continue to sow the seed of His Word even in the floodplain of our grief.

Sometimes we don't realize we've encountered God until our vision clears. Maybe that's what seeing His back means. He is the God who sees *you*.

Can you identify your path — both behind you and immediately in front of you?

Day Two

The Covenant of Circumcision

I wonder if Hagar looked different when she returned. Had her face changed? Her demeanor? How can a person be unchanged after a divine encounter?

She had seen the "back" of the One who saw her. *El Roi*, the God who seeks and finds. Were Abram and Sarai glad to see her? Relieved? Were they still convinced her child was their only chance of an heir? Or did Sarai hope her poor judgment was forever buried in the desert?

The curtain comes down on Genesis 16 with these words. "So Hagar bore Abram a son, and Abram gave the name Ishmael to the son she had borne. Abram was eighty-six years old when Hagar bore him Ishmael."

Who gave Ishmael his name according to this passage? _____

Hagar must have shared her divine encounter with Abram, whether face-to-face or through her mistress Sarai. Only Hagar knew what to name the child according to God's instructions. Can you imagine how shocked they must have been by God revealing Himself to an Egyptian slave girl? Or could they possibly have looked past the mistaken superiority of their own chosenness to the landscape of the promise, "all peoples on earth will be blessed through you"?

So Hagar bore Abram a son. We all speak the same language when we come into this world: wails and gurgles. And normal mothers, whether slave or free, rich or poor, love their babies and search their tiny faces for glimpses of what they'll be when they grow up. When Ishmael pitched a fit for his dinner, do you imagine Hagar remembered the words, "He will be a wild donkey of a man"? When he pushed away unwelcome kisses like any toddler would do, do you think Hagar recalled, "his hand will be against everyone"? Perhaps she grabbed him close, squeezed him tightly, and laughed, "Not your mother, Little One."

Read the first verse of Genesis 17. Compared to the conclusion of the previous chapter, how much time had passed? _____

Take care not to confuse God's silence in Scripture with inactivity. Taking into account the relatively small size of the Creator's entire written expression to man, He obviously doesn't waste words on descriptions of events that were of great importance to the participants but did not fall under the priority of divine inspiration intended for the rest of us. Think as broadly as you can as you consider this period of silence.

What kinds of experiences or changes do you imagine filled these years for any of the four individuals involved? I've listed some categories to spark your imagination:

Physical: _____

Emotional: _____

Spiritual: _____

The time with no further word from God profoundly underscores the significance of the fresh revelation to Abram. He could easily have assumed that his lapse of faith resulting in transgression with Hagar forfeited the fulfillment of God's promises to him. Ironically, the only way Abram knew God was still talking was through the testimony of an Egyptian slave girl. Humbling, wasn't it? Abram couldn't fathom God's absolute and unyielding determination to keep the covenant as surely as He made it. By the time we finish this journey together, we will not be at all surprised that one of the first definitions of the Hebrew word for covenant, *berit*, is "determination."[5] God, Dear One, will keep His promises in spite of us.

We don't cross the threshold into Genesis 17 without being introduced to another Hebrew name for God. If possible, recite from memory the names of God previously introduced in our study and any descriptions you associate with them.

To this auspicious list add another of great significance: *El Sadday,* or in English, God Almighty. (*El Shaddai* in the more familiar spelling.) Ancient interpretations differ over the name's meaning, but the common denominator of unparalleled, unassisted might reaches across the board. Some scholars believe the name may somehow imply *mountain.* "Jewish rabbis believed that the term meant the 'One who is self sufficient.'"[6] A common understanding of the name is "all sufficient God." While researching Genesis 17:1, I came upon a very intriguing—at first almost troubling—cross-reference.

What does Exodus 6:3 tell you in reference to the revealed names of God?

_____

_____

At first this statement may seem contradictory since God appears as YHWH or "the LORD" as early as Genesis 2. Note that most of the references to God by this title are directed to the reader rather than to the participants. In those cases Moses as narrator simply could have been using the divine name introduced to him in Exodus 6.

In the cases where the characters in Genesis use YHWH, another idea may be intended. Perhaps "God" or *El* before many of God's titles keeps the blessing to all peoples through Abram in the forefront. YHWH undoubtedly emphasizes the covenant role of God with His chosen nation and in particular the *keeping* of the covenant even more than the making of it. The wording, "make myself known," in Exodus 6:3 implies a more intimate knowledge most often by participation. Thus God is not saying that Abraham never knew the covenant name of God. Rather God says that in the events of Moses' time YHWH is revealing Himself uniquely by fulfilling the promises of the covenant made to Abraham. These differences make sense in light of God's distinct agenda in the period of the patriarchs versus the time of the Exodus. The former is more panoramic, the latter a more intentional tight shot on the covenant relationship developing between God and one people.

After introducing Himself afresh to Abram as God Almighty, what powerful commandment did God issue Abram (Gen. 17:1)?

_____

_____

If you're reading from a *King James Version*, the commandment is daunting: "Be thou perfect." The word translated *perfect* in *King James* and *blameless* in the *NIV* doesn't mean sinless. It means whole, entire, or complete.[7] I believe God was saying something much like this to Abram: "I am God, huge and powerful. I don't need you. You need me. Now, take every step with the keen awareness that you walk continually before My gaze. I want all of you—not one person behind closed doors and another in the open. I want your mind as well as your heart. I want your soul as well as your spirit. If you want to do this thing with Me, get all the way in." Can't we all relate with any temptation on Abram's part to retain some independence? Don't we tend to want all God has for us while we give Him only half of us?

 Read Genesis 17:1-14. What had the LORD come to Abram to do (v. 2)?

In God's lengthy discourse to Abram, what was Abram's one act of response?

Take a look at Genesis 12:1-3, God's first statement of promise to Abram. What additional dimensions appear in Genesis 17:1-14?

> *God breathed Himself into Abraham.*

You undoubtedly noted the name change. Abram means "exalted father" while Abraham means "father of many." Poor Abram. Even his name had mocked his insufficiency. We tend to desire praise, don't we? God's intention is not to promote us, however. He intends for us to bear much fruit, showing ourselves to be His and bringing Him glory (John 15). "God changes Abram's name by adding something to Abram. He adds to Abram's name the Hebrew letter *he*, the repeated letter among the four letters of the Tetragrammaton. It is a sound in the Hebrew language, like the letter *H* in the English language, that is made by breathing out. The Hebrew word used for the Spirit of God is the word *Ruach*. It means literally 'the outbreathing.' He breathes Himself into Abram and makes him Abraham, Father of Multitudes. The new syllable of Abram's name is placed in its center. Abram, with [Jehovah's breath] within him, becomes Abraham."[8]

So, what happened to Abram? Inhale and blow a deep breath onto the palm of your hand. What you just did to your palm, Jehovah did to Abram. The difference? His breath brings life. "I have made you a father of many nations" (Gen. 17:5). Bask in the past tense of the statement. God had made Abraham a father of many nations before Abraham had glimpsed a single descendant. Beloved, I wonder what God has already made you. Things that perhaps you've not even glimpsed. Believe God! Give Him your entire being and walk one step at a time before His knowing gaze and with His sufficient strength.

I was just telling the Lord I needed Him to breathe on me like that—I asked Him to make me "Be he eth."

What would your name be if God breathed a "he" (the Hebrew letter He added to Abram's name) into it?

Do you understand that God does exactly that when we receive Christ as our personal Savior? He breathes His Holy Spirit into our lives, and we become fit to bear much fruit.

> I hope you noted Abram's link to royalty: "kings will come from you" (Gen. 17:6). I only want to whet your appetite for now, but what glorious three-person royal link do you discover in Matthew 1:1?

_____

God breathes the Holy Spirit into the lives of believers.

The most prominent addition in Genesis 17 is the command that Abram and his descendants "undergo circumcision" as "the sign of the covenant between" God and His people. The practice of circumcision is so ancient that researchers have been unable to trace its origin. Various peoples even in Abram's day practiced circumcision while others (like Abram's family) did not.[9] The uniqueness of this circumcision resides in the purpose (a sign of the covenant God made with them) and the timing on the eighth day. Even in ancient days, circumcision was timed at around 13 years of age to mark manhood. God's command to circumcise infant males was at least in great measure to emphasize the blessing of offspring and lineage over the egotism of celebrated manhood and self-sufficiency.

God's obvious intention was that men in this chosen line (and "every male among [them]") would be marked. If I may tread sensitively but instructionally, they were to be marked in their manhood, in their closest association with virility, strength, and procreation. God doesn't blush over these kinds of things. We do. This wasn't a matter of sexuality. This was a matter of spirituality. God meant for this practice to be significant in every way. He could have commanded Abraham and his descendants to pierce their ears, making large holes like some ancient tribes or to brand themselves with hot irons on their chests like others. The mark God had in mind for them was strictly private as a reminder to the man himself that he belonged to God and that his strength, virility, and ability to bear much fruit rested in the blessing of God Almighty.

The great significance of Abraham's circumcision will become very clear over the coming chapters. In his 99th year Abraham immediately obeyed this commandment by God. We will see him celebrate his son's birth within one year of his obedience. Considering a nine-month pregnancy, the promise was quickly fulfilled after circumcision. The point? Before circumcision, Abraham was unable to produce anything except by human planning and manipulation. After circumcision, Abraham experienced the divine miracle.

🐫 **The New Testament emphasizes a circumcision of the heart (see Rom. 4:9-12; Gal. 2:15-21). Can you see any parallels for our lives? Share them below.**

_____

> You and I may need to "put off" or even figuratively "cut off" something from our lives so we may bear much fruit. Is God speaking to you? If so, use this space to write your response to Him.

_____

_____

The consequences of Abraham and his descendants' obedience to this command are clear. What consequence is stated in Genesis 17:14?

_____

The wordplay is unmistakably clear. God's point to Abraham and his descendants was this: you can be cut ... or be cut off. You decide. The Hebrew word for "cut off" in verse 14 is the same word inspired for "cutting covenant."[10]

Nothing else marks a man as a man like godliness—the true circumcision of the heart. I laughed with a group of women recently over the significant numbers of average-looking godly men with gorgeous women at their side. Why? Since you're not here, I'll answer my own question: because Christian women think nothing is stronger or more virile than a man who loves God. That's manhood to us. Long before we got a clue, that was manhood to God. "I am God Almighty; walk before me and be blameless."

Day Three
No Longer Sarai

Today's Treasure

God also said to Abraham, "As for Sarai your wife, you are no longer to call her Sarai; her name will be Sarah."

Genesis 17:15

Recently my praise-team leader wrote a letter in preparation for a weekend conference. He ended the letter with the lyrics of an old hymn, "Savior, Savior, hear my humble cry. While on others Thou art calling, do not pass me by." With all my heart I pray for God to reveal Himself magnificently through this teaching and speaking ministry. The team and I pour out everything He's given us and beg Him for more. But at the same time, like everyone else, this feeble pound of flesh has her own needs, fears, concerns, pains, and deep desires. While on others Thou are calling, please, Lord, do not pass me by! What a nightmare I'd have if I got so busy telling others to look at You that I missed You myself!

Perhaps the thoughts reflected in the old hymn explain my tenderness toward the words unfolding our text today. Genesis 17:15 reads, "God *also* said to Abraham, 'As for Sarai your wife, you are no longer to call her Sarai; her name will be Sarah. I will bless her.'" While on others God was calling—Hagar, Abraham—He did not pass Sarah by. Oh, how thankful I am for the phrases "God *also* said," (emphasis mine) and "as for _____ ..." I wonder whose name you'd write in that blank today. Does someone you know seem overlooked—perhaps, humanly speaking, for understandable reasons? Maybe he or she proved foolish. But haven't we all? Haven't we all been desperate for a name change? An identity change? Plenty of "alsos" and "as fors" remain for those desperate for His touch. Go back and write in that blank the name of someone who fits the need—even if it's yourself; turn the Scripture thought into a prayer for a fresh work toward a new identity in Christ.

Read Genesis 17:15-27. Recall from our previous lesson God's forthright commandment to Abraham and his descendants concerning the covenant sign of circumcision. How quickly did Abraham obey God according to verse 23?

_____

Obedience. Swift. Sure. We will not escape the role of obedience through our journey with the patriarchs. Keep it ever before you.

🐫 **Now, describe the blessings specifically spoken over Sarah's life.**

_____

_____

What were Abraham's responses to God's direction? Mark any that apply.
❑ He fell on his knees.   ❑ He cried out.
❑ He fell facedown.   ❑ He laughed.

Where do you see glimpses of Abraham's strong feelings for Ishmael?

_____

What did God promise He'd do for Ishmael?

_____

Yes, Ishmael would be blessed, but God promised Abraham a son through Sarah. This was the son of whom God promised: " 'I will establish my covenant with him as an everlasting covenant for his descendants after him' " (Gen. 17:19). What was Abraham to call him? In Hebrew, *Yishaq* which means, "he laughs."[11] In the first three contexts in which Isaac's name appears, he is associated somehow with laughter. If you think about it, laughter is a relieving outburst expressing any number of inner emotions.

Name several kinds of emotions we use laughter to express or even mask.

_____

_____

I have always been a laugher but certainly not always because life was funny. Thinking back on my younger years, I remember often laughing with my siblings until our sides ached, and many times we laughed about things that weren't particularly funny. In fact, on a number of occasions our laughter was over the pure absurdity of a situation.

One of my most bone-chilling memories involves the hideous sound of a mentally-ill adult's mean-spirited laughter. I doubt any sound has ever terrified me more than that adult's laugh. Rather than remaining trapped in fear, I've learned that God's healing now allows laughter from within me and around me to spring far more often like a fountain from a well of joy or delight.

When you were asked earlier to name several different kinds of emotions we use laughter to express or mask, you probably began with the most honest form. We laugh when we think something is hilarious. You might have named sarcasm, surprise, nervousness, and meanness as prompters for laughter. Others exist as well.

What do you think was behind Abraham's laughter (Gen. 17:17)?

_____

_____

Abraham's laughter on Sarai's behalf may have had to do with God's message. Let's focus on Sarah and the promises God made regarding her. Note God chose to announce the name change and blessings concerning Sarai to Abram rather than directly to her. God's revelation to Hagar dismisses the idea that He preferred not to speak to women. (Thank goodness.) Likewise, I don't believe God was avoiding Sarai to punish her for foolish decisions. Goodness knows Abraham made plenty. God may have wanted Abraham himself to view Sarah as blessed, changing how Abraham—as her husband—identified her.

Possibly Abraham thought Sarai was the obstacle to the fulfillment of God's promises. Obviously, Ishmael proved Abraham still had the ability to sire a son in the years immediately following the promises. Sarai was the holdup. Whether or not Abraham consciously deducted such, his attitude suggests that he believed Sarai's barrenness was more powerful than God's promises. That's why he kept suggesting other ways of helping God fulfill His promise, not the least of which is found in Genesis 17:18, "If only Ishmael might live under your blessing!" In his wildest imagination, Abraham did not think God could use Sarai. She was, after all, _un_fruitful. Unable. Unusable.

That very well may be why God spoke Sarai's blessings into Abraham's own ears. Abraham needed to stop seeing his wife as the hang-up and start seeing her as the "how." We can look back at the narrative and see how absurd Abraham's deductions were, yet we so often encumber ourselves with similar thinking. We think to ourselves, _____ _____ is the reason why God is not freed up to work in my life. His or her unbelief, unresponsiveness, unhealthiness, uncleanness, unwillingness to tithe (for crying out loud), or total unawareness ("He doesn't have a clue!") is the problem. He or she is unbalanced, uneducated, unyielding, unchurched, uncooperative, or unbroken. God can't fulfill His promises to me because of my pastor's, my employer's, my business partner's, my children's, my parents', or my spouse's "uns." Yep, everybody else's "uns" are my problem. Atomic uns. So powerful they break God's promises.

What if I told you that at one time I believed my husband Keith's "uns" would surely nullify the fulfillment of God's calling over my life? Would you like to know how the situation turned out? God has used virtually nothing as powerfully as Keith's "uns" to mold and shape me into a more humble, pliable woman. In a strange sort of way, like Sarai the impossible vessel, Keith the impossible vessel also became God's miraculous "how." After God conceived His plan—my own Isaac—in my life, He began the glorious undoing of countless "uns." Nothing has made me appreciate what God has done any more than the sheer impossibility of such glorious works.

🐪 **Who or what do you tend to believe holds up God's full blessing to you?**

_____

List as many of the "uns" involved as you can.

_____

_____

Beloved, you may very well have just come face-to-face with your Sarai. Your holdup may well turn into your how.

Sarai's name change is nothing less than remarkable. "As for Sarai your wife, you are no longer to call her Sarai; her name will be Sarah" (Gen. 17:15). No one knows for certain what the name *Sarai* meant, but the new name *Sarah* means "princess."

What was to be Sarah's connection to royalty (Gen. 17:15-16)?

_____

"Abraham, don't call her Sarai any longer. Her name will be Princess."

Don't hurry past. Take it in.

Aren't you glad we don't know what her original name meant? The fact that it's unidentified leaves it wide open for our application. You see, what the name *Sarai* meant makes no difference. God can change anyone—no matter what she's been called—into a princess.

Please write Genesis 17:15 in the space below.

"As for _____ your _____, you are no longer

to call her _____; her name will be *Sarah* I will bless her."

"Savior, Savior, hear my humble cry. While on others Thou art calling, do not pass me by."[12]

Day Four
Anything Too Hard

Today's Treasure
"Is anything too hard for the LORD?"
Genesis 18:14

Allow me to begin today's lesson by scribbling the immense, mind-bending doctrine of divine sovereignty in first grade words on a Big Chief tablet: Being God means He gets to do what He wants. "Yes," devoted believers might say, "as long as it's right and perfect." True. But try not to think of God's perfection as His confinement—as if to say He can "only" do what is perfect. Rather, God is free from the confinement of all imperfections. In other words, His perfection does not limit Him. It frees Him.

Among the things God surely must enjoy doing, He can choose to reveal Himself any way He wants. His revelation doesn't have to make sense to us. We don't have to worry ourselves to death trying to get the Hebrew sentence structure to work for us. We don't have to debate it in seminaries (though we can). And we don't have to automatically accept a brilliant scholar's attempt to take the mystery out of it. God can reveal Himself through flames of fire from within a bush, through a water-gushing rock, through a commander of an army, or through a voice out of a storm. If I may be so bold, I think He rather likes the variety. So today why don't we just sit back and enjoy it?

Join me near the great trees of Mamre and take a load off. The weather's too hot to do anything more strenuous than eavesdropping, so lend Genesis 18:1-15 a careful ear.

Be blessed by the echo (v. 3) of the chorus from the old hymn we talked about in our previous lesson: "Do not pass your servant by."

> **Read Genesis 18:1-15. Record everything you find peculiar or especially intriguing in this wonderful segment of Scripture; ask God any corresponding questions you wish you could hear Him audibly explain.**

Peculiarities: Questions:

_____   _____

_____   _____

_____   _____

_____   _____

God not only reserves the right to reveal Himself any way He pleases, but He reveals Himself anytime He pleases. The first verse tells us He "appeared to Abraham ... in the heat of the day." Adam and Eve? "In the cool of the day" (Gen. 3:8). An all-occasion, all-weather God. Just the kind I need. Picture Abraham minding his own business at the entrance to his tent, drying the sweat off his centenarian brow. He looks up and three men are standing nearby. Abraham's reaction tells us he knew from the start that these were no ordinary men. He made haste and bowed before them ... then a fascinating pattern surfaces. The text begins to move like a river winding into three streams before finding its way back together again. Note the move from singular expressions regarding the visitation to plural, and then back to singular again.

> Circle each reference to the one or ones whom Abraham encountered in today's text:
>
> "The LORD appeared to Abraham ... "
> " ... three men standing nearby."
> "If I have found favor in your eyes, my lord, ... "
> " ... then you may all wash your feet and rest under this tree."
> " ... they asked him."
> "Then the LORD said, ... "

typology

a doctrine of theological types; esp: one holding that things in Christian belief are prefigured or symbolized by things in the Old Testament

The text begins unmistakably with a revelation of YHWH Himself and concludes with Him alone speaking. In between, however, are unrelenting references to all three visitors, leaving us to wonder is He one or is He three? I'm grinning just like you probably are. Yes, many scholars, particularly those who love typology, believe the three figures that seem to blend into one called "LORD" are hints of the Trinity. Others believe that all three are angels (or God's ambassadors) but none of them are God. Though the Lord's revelation includes them in this scene, He is unique from them and would actually constitute a fourth party. Others believe that two of the three visitors are angels and the other is the Lord revealing Himself. Though the thought of either possibility thrills me, for the little it's worth, I tend to lean toward the latter. I'll tell you why. Without moving ahead into our next lesson's story line, let's glance ahead strictly to see whether we can identify the figures.

What happens in Genesis 18:16,22?

_____

Now take a look at Genesis 19:1. How are the two now identified?

_____

I believe it's quite possible that the LORD, flanked by two angels, appeared to Abraham in a human form. A number of Old Testament passages tell us the LORD sits enthroned between the cherubim. Maybe He brought a couple of them along, one on each side. Abraham's recognition of the extraordinary visitation is obvious. After bowing "low to the ground," he spoke using a singular reference to one of the visitors calling him a word we're wise to learn. You'll notice in the NIV the reference to "lord" in verse 3 is not capitalized. The reason is because the English is translated from the Hebrew *adonay* which always refers to a superior but can also mean "sir."[13] LORD (appearing in all capital letters) is never used for anyone but God Himself, but forms of *adonay* can sometimes be employed as a title for God or men in some kind of position of honor.

Fill in these blanks *exactly* as the letters of each word appear in Psalm 8:1.

"O _____, our _____, how majestic is
your name in all the earth!"

The first title, with all capital letters, is the one we see most often in the Old Testament: YHWH. God alone is called by this divine name. It is most distinctly associated with His role as the covenant maker and keeper in relationship to man. The second title is *Adhon*, (singular form of *Adonay*) intended in Psalm 8:1 to refer to God alone. In Genesis 18, however, it is also used in reference to a man.

Check out Genesis 18:12. What did Sarah call her husband?

_____

While the *New International Version* translates the word "master" in this verse, the *King James Version* translates it "my lord." Sarah no doubt loved her husband of many years, but she didn't equate him with God.

Relish a quote in one of my commentaries regarding the mysteries of the encounter in Genesis 18. "Obscurity is story's way of telling us the truth about this God with whom we daily have to do, by reminding us of God's hiddenness, of the concreteness of God's revelation, and of the impossible possibilities that are open to all who believe."[14]

Impossible possibilities. Follow the story line with me. Abraham requested they stay, wash their feet, and rest as a meal was being prepared. He ran to the tent and told Sarah to throw a little homemade bread together "quick!" Any of us who make homemade bread know the guests might as well have caught up on their sleep under that tree. One resource pointed out that three seahs of fine flour would have made far more bread than these three visitors could have consumed, but Abraham's obvious intention was to lavish them.

You probably noticed that Abraham didn't eat a bite. "While they ate, he stood near them under a tree" (v. 8). While you and I may not have entertained celestial guests, perhaps each of us has shared a table with someone we respected so much we couldn't eat. I have a deep admiration for Anne Graham Lotz. Imagine my astonishment when she spoke in Houston several years ago and called ahead to my office to request that we meet for breakfast. I could hardly eat a bite. I wanted to pinch myself to see if I was dreaming. She could not have been more gracious, and every time she asked questions regarding my testimony I thought, "Who cares about me? Let's talk about you!" I felt this strange blend of extreme insignificance and yet honor to be at her table. My funny staff insisted that I call them the second I was back in the car. "How was it?" they asked, gathered around a speaker-phone. To their relief and mine, I was able to report that I neither spilled my coffee on her nor caught my foot in her purse strap, turning over the table as I left.

Of course, had I been in a restaurant where I saw one of my favorite teachers like Anne having breakfast with someone, I might have fallen over in my chair trying to ... how shall I say ... share the blessing? Not unlike Sarah in far more thrilling circumstances. "Where is your wife Sarah?" Genesis 18:9-10 tells us Sarah was "listening at the entrance to the tent, which was behind [Abraham]." Just imagine the wide-eyed expression of this needlessly concealed eavesdropper when she realized she'd been caught.

 What very specific prophecy did Sarah overhear (v. 10)?

_____

We see another association of Isaac and laughter. Why did Sarah laugh (v. 12)?

_____

Sarah was old in every sense of the word, but we don't have to be old to feel worn out. Do you ever feel too weary, worn, and beaten up by life to believe God can do anything wonderful and miraculous with you? Can you stack up all sorts of rational reasons why you feel you are past God's being able to use you? I have noticed a pattern in my relationship with God. Many times when He told me through His Word and prayer to believe Him for something very specific, over time the outlook on the matter dwindled from good to slim to utterly impossible before He brought it to pass. Keith and I are facing such a matter right now. In fact, this morning the situation seemed to hit the "impossible" category. While my stomach churned with concern, a smirk crossed my face as I thought, *it might be prime time for the God show.* He wants to make absolutely sure that we know He's the one who fulfills divine promises. We will rarely be able to conclude that any God-given destiny simply followed a natural course of events.

God fulfills His divine promises.

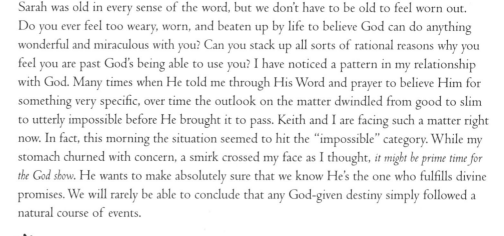 Dear One, may I ask you a blunt question? Do you believe in miracles? Whether your answer is yes or no, please explain why.

_____

_____

_____

The most important line in the entire encounter is the question the LORD posed to Abraham in Genesis 18:14. Place your name before the comma as if God is posing the question just to you. Please write the question on the line below:

"_____,

         (your name)

_____ ?"

The original word for "too hard" may be at the top of my list of favorites among the Hebrew words I've learned through the years. *Pala* means "to separate, distinguish; to be wonderful, do wonderful things; wondrous things, miracles." Used primarily with God as the subject, denoting the fact that he does things which are beyond the bounds of human powers or expectations."[15]

Beloved, is anything "too hard" for you right now? If so, you have the perfect setting for a miracle. Wonders come all sorts of ways, sometimes in the greater miracle that results when we don't get what we were so convinced we wanted and end up with something far more glorious. I do not hesitate to ask God for a miracle in circumstances and prospects that seem too hard—in one way or another—and rarely if ever has one not surfaced. God just as readily esteems what is "too hard" for you.

My young friend Rich told me a story that may provide a fitting conclusion. Several months ago God swept his beloved Mammaw home, leaving his Pappaw alone after 50 years of marriage. Recently, Rich and a friend went to see this dear grandfather for the night. The elderly man soaked in their lively company like parched ground begging for water. Just before bedtime he inquired what they might want for breakfast. Young, single, and rarely cooked for, Rich requested bacon and eggs. They all said good night and headed for bed. Right before Rich turned in that night, he decided to grab a glass of water. When he flipped on the kitchen light, the sight of a small kitchen table completely and lavishly set for breakfast moved him to tears. His grandfather so deeply anticipated the fellowship meal to come that he set the table in advance.

Describe a time when you deeply anticipated a time with God.

_____

_____

What part of time spent with the Father means most to you?

_____

_____

Are we as anxious as Abraham to have God at our table? Can you hardly wait to serve Him? In Revelation 3:20 Christ says, " 'Behold, I stand at the door and knock; if anyone hears My voice and opens the door, I will come in to him and will dine with him, and he with Me' " (NAS). Set the table, Beloved, and greatly anticipate the One who can serve a miracle for dessert. "Is anything too hard for the LORD?"

Day Five

Smoke Rising

Today's Treasure

He looked down toward Sodom and Gomorrah, toward all the land of the plain, and he saw dense smoke rising from the land, like smoke from a furnace.

Genesis 19:28

Please begin today's study with prayer. Our passages today necessitate that we study and discuss some difficult material. R-rated, you might say. We run into these kinds of subjects constantly out in the world, but we are not as accustomed to dealing with them in Bible study. Keep in mind that God wouldn't have secured their places in holy writ if nothing vital could be learned from them. Our God is unashamed to tackle any subject, and we do so today against the backdrop of His eternal wisdom and righteousness. After you spend a moment asking God to help you gird up your mind and grow you in wisdom, scan Genesis 18:16-33 (in preparation for session 2). Then read all of Genesis 19.

Several shocking things happen in Genesis 19. Please list them and add any questions or comments that would help you prepare for today's discussion.

_____

_____

_____

_____

_____

Good grief. Clearly, sexual dysfunction didn't originate in our generation. Obviously, it's been around a while. I'll tell you what occurs to me over and over, and certainly not only regarding others. Without God's constant help, intervention, and restraining Holy Spirit, our evil and dysfunctional human inclinations know no bounds. I can't count the times Keith and I respond to something we read in the paper or see in the news with the words, "God help us all." Man has a dark side, but take heart, Dear One, God most assuredly does not. "God is light; in him there is no darkness at all" (I John 1:5). Just in case you need to hear this, Beloved, you can rest assured God is emotionally healthy. Never confuse God with man.

OK, let's work through these passages. We witness a dimension of the miraculous as early as Genesis 19:1. What time of day did the angels arrive in Sodom?

_____

What general time of day did the angels arrive "near the great trees of Mamre" according to Genesis 18:1?

_____

Most scholars agree we are to assume both time segments involve the same day, meaning that a likely journey of 40 miles took place in a few hours. To say they must have flown might not just be a figure of speech.

Lot's hospitality begins impressively but ends excessively. He begins by insisting that the guests stay in his home but ends with risking his daughters in order to protect the guests. We'll deal with that unsettling issue later. For now let's discuss the demands of the "men from every part of the city of Sodom" as they surrounded Lot's house.

What have we already learned about these men (Gen. 13:13)?

_____

We're also told in Genesis 18:20 that " 'The outcry against Sodom and Gomorrah is … great and their sin … grievous.' " God's inclusion of the riotous scene at Lot's house helps us grasp the depth of depravity and the cause of judgment. *El Roi* is undoubtedly the One who sees—and not only the wanderings of broken-hearted victims. We never have to think for one moment that wickedness goes unpunished.

What made the men of Sodom desire the two angels in particular? We find a partial answer in the Book of Ephesians.

🐪 **Paraphrase Ephesians 4:18-19 and tell how these verses apply to today's text:**

_____

_____

Our enemy, the Devil, and our own flesh deceive us when we think that we can relieve our ungodly desires by momentarily giving into them. Our indulgence only awakens "a continual lust for more." The Sodomites had obviously given themselves over to such impurity that they wanted whatever they could get and whatever they hadn't had. "No" is a very dangerous word to cease saying to ourselves. Quite possibly the angels were also beautiful, and the townsmen were too ignorant and godless to discern the difference between godly radiance and human attractiveness.

We are appalled at the thought, but sometimes the churched can also take what is rightly a draw toward godliness and demean it into desires of the flesh. Case in point: Some years ago I was floored when I visited with a small group of young women at my church who were talking about how "gorgeous" a guest speaker was. Their comments crossed a line that indicated they saw him strictly through the lens of carnal eyes.

Needless to say, the far more appalling moment in the scene around Lot's house was the offer of his own daughters. Even if they hadn't been virgins, Lot's suggestion was outrageous. Several times I've heard that Lot was confident the girls would be safe because the townsmen sought a homosexual encounter. The explanation may be plausible, but the concluding pregnancies of both daughters by their drunken father suggest drastic family malfunction. Somewhere along the way, boundaries were horrifically blurred.

Let me stop and say something tenderly to those of you who share a background of sexual victimization with me—whether inside or outside the family unit. Years ago, I couldn't have studied something like this without feeling oppressed by the enemy, but the healthier I've gotten in Christ, the more I've learned that I can study a subject without wearing it. Unfortunately, the depravity and dysfunction we see in Genesis 19 is also a reality in our world. Considering such subjects in the safety of Bible study keeps them where they belong: framed in the Truth that exhorts us toward righteousness.

My earlier comments about Lot may seem to contradict 2 Peter 2:7. What does this verse say about Abraham's nephew?

_____

_____

We can't be altogether certain of the basis for this "righteousness" attributed to Lot. His faith in the God of Abraham (Rom. 4:23-24) and his torment over surrounding sins are obvious elements, but he undoubtedly made several very foolish moves. Even righteous people can be caught off guard by crisis and make horrible decisions.

As the time of judgment drew near, the angels (two men; Gen. 19:12) urged Lot to tell the young men pledged to marry his daughters to escape coming judgment.

How did Lot's future sons-in-law respond according to verse 14?

_____

_____

Do you ever encounter people who act as if the threat of judgment on a wicked world is a joke? What do you think of such a response?

_____

_____

_____

If Lot's young sons-in-law had a second of clarity when the first pelts of sulfuric fire fell from heaven, their last thought was the sobering reality that the judgment of wickedness is no joke. Take a look at 2 Peter 3:3-10 and note any comparisons.

_____

_____

What comparison does Scripture make in 2 Peter 2:6-9?

_____

_____

If we were watching these events on film, the most chilling scene in the aftermath would be Lot's wife turning into a pillar of salt as she disobeyed an urgent command not to "look back" or "stop anywhere" (Gen. 19:17). The prospect of turning to salt may seem fantastic to skeptics, but I have no trouble imagining that it happened just as the Word says. Consider the comparison one scholar makes between the fate of Lot's wife and the archaeological evidence of the destruction of Pompeii in A.D. 79.

"First, a volcanic gas settled over the city, asphyxiating many of the citizens while they slept. The city was then covered with heavy deposits of volcanic ash up to a depth of about twenty feet in which human and animal life was entombed. In the process of archaeological excavation, the excavators pumped plaster of paris into hollow places and encountered in the ashes numerous human and animal forms. The chemical content of the ash had apparently turned human bodies into some chemical substance that was sufficiently hard to allow the surrounding ash to retain a perfect cast of the bodies."[16]

Interestingly, Josephus, the ancient Hebrew scholar, wrote: "Lot's wife ... changed into a pillar of salt; for I have seen it and it remains at this day."[17] We don't know why Lot's wife looked back. Whether grief, curiosity, astonishment, or attachment caused her to look back, she was disobedient to a stern command at a time of raining judgment. Even though we don't know her motive, we are wise not to miss the potential application. I can think of few things more dangerous than looking back with attachment to an old life surrounded by wickedness from which God mercifully delivered us. After God delivered me from deep bondage to sin, I recall sensing a stern warning in my soul that in view of His mercy and grace, I'd be very wise never to entertain a single longing to go back. We may not turn into pillars of salt, but we can most certainly turn into monuments of the living dead.

Due to the nature of the ministry God has assigned to me, I know many people who are going through various 12-step programs to find support in breaking the cycle of addiction. Recently, I sat spellbound through a television program where counselors were lovingly but seriously confronting clients they suspected were on the fast track to relapse. It was not a Christian program, but several principles they taught could have come straight out of the Bible. One of the counselors confronted a woman in her willingness to let herself long for her old substance as if it had been a faithful friend. Until she can grasp that her addiction could hold death for her, she is headed for relapse.

🐪 **Can you think of a time when "looking back" was a grievous mistake? Share as discreetly as possible.**

_____

_____

_____

For whatever reason, Sodom was the death of Lot's wife. Strangely, it was also the death of dignity and propriety in Lot's daughters' lives. Rather than cherishing the lives they'd mercifully gained, their insistence on dwelling on what they had lost ("there is no man around here") weakened them toward heinous sin. As a young person, I saw sins one so young should never have to witness. I came into my adolescent years bitter and determined not to fall into the same kinds of sin. I didn't realize it at the time, but my chief reason for making those choices was not pleasing God. It was pride. I wanted to be better than "them." Because my intentions were not pure, my integrity was unguarded, and I ended up heaped in sins. Some were different from those I had observed ... but no less serious.

Lot's mistake on behalf of his family was pitching "his tents near Sodom" (Gen. 13:12). When believers are totally outnumbered and no one stands with us in godliness, few are strong enough to resist lowering the standard to relativity. Proverbs 23:10 warns us not to "move an ancient boundary stone." Somewhere along the way, an ancient boundary stone got moved on Lot's lot—even if not by him. No, the Lot family didn't participate in homosexual sin, but the line dividing right from wrong and healthy from unhealthy got blurred. When desperation came, alternatives that should have been shocking simply were not.

Few things are more dangerous than looking back to that from which God has delivered us.

Does this make sense? If so, say it in your own words or give an example.

_____

_____

_____

I'll never forget the advice a broken-hearted mother of college-aged kids gave me. She and her husband had modeled their parenting after the common philosophy, "no matter what your kids do or what they tell you, never, never act shocked." She had since come to the conclusion that the lack of apparent shock blurred the lines between the acceptable and the unacceptable in the eyes of their children. I was a mother of young children at the time. She looked straight into my eyes and said, "Sometimes nothing is more appropriate than pure, unadulterated *shock*."

Jesus gives us a pure motivation that results in effective loving.

Read John 14:23. Why does love for Jesus lead to obedience?

_____

_____

_____

----

[1] Victor P. Hamilton, *The Book of Genesis: Chapters 1-17* (Grand Rapids: William B. Eerdman's Publishing Company, 1990), 444.

[2] Ibid., 450.

[3] Ibid., 453.

[4] Ibid., 456.

[5] Spiros Zodhiates et al., eds., *The Complete Word Study Dictionary: Old Testament* (Chattanooga, TN: AMG Publishers, 1994), 57.

[6] Ibid., 113.

[7] Ibid., 125.

[8] Jennifer Kennedy Dean, *The Life-Changing Power in the Name of Jesus* (Birmingham: New Hope Publishers, 2004), 313.

[9] Leon R. Kass, *The Begining of Wisdom: Reading Genesis* (New York: Free Press, 2003), 313.

[10] Zodhiates, 57.

[11] Ibid., 51.

[12] Fanny J. Crosby, "Pass Me Not, O Gentle Savior," *Baptist Hymnal* (Nashville: Convention Press, 1991), 308.

[13] Zodhiates, 8-9.

[14] Victor P. Hamilton, *The Book of Genesis: Chapters 18-50* (Grand Rapids: William B. Eerdman's Publishing, 1995), 8.

[15] Zodhiates, 2354.

[16] Hamilton, 48.

[17] Ibid., 48.

SESSION TWO
The Approaching and Approachable God

I. Comparing verses 17-19 and 20-21. In the first discourse God is _____
  to _____, and in the second He addresses _____.

  The first discourse:

  • Beautifully demonstrates that God's _____ are perfectly consistent with
    His _____.

  • Positions Abraham once again in the role of _____ (see Amos 3:7).

2. The second discourse is undoubtedly intended to _____ _____
  with Abraham. God has deliberately _____ _____ in an anthropomorphic
  _____ throughout Genesis 18. *Anthropos*—_____ or _____;
  Morphe—_____ or _____.

3. God invited Abraham—a mere man—to walk _____ _____ so that He could teach
  Abraham how a man can walk _____ _____.

4. Can _____ trust _____ (v. 17) and can _____
  trust _____ (vv. 23,25)?

  • The affirmative answer to the first concern results in Abraham's being cast in a second role:
    _____ _____ (Jas. 2:23).

5. Our comfort can be this: what is not sorted out _____ and _____ is sorted out
  _____ and _____.

WEEK THREE
Triumphs and Tests

Cultures may change from generation to generation, but each is tied to the other with threads of common colors. Whether today or a thousand years ago, the same silk threads that make life a tapestry also tie us in knots. The week before us is ecstasy and agony. We can, however, take the pulse of the entire patriarchal narrative through the accelerated heartbeat of Abraham. Let this quote stir you and prepare you for the week ahead. "Late Monday night, November 23, 1654, Blaise Pascal, mathematician, naturalist, skeptic, and bon vivant, underwent a religious experience that profoundly changed his life. On a piece of parchment, later found sewn into his clothing, he wrote: 'From about half past ten in the evening until half past midnight. Fire. "God of Abraham, God of Isaac, God of Jacob," not of the philosophers and scholars. Certainty, certainty, heartfelt joy, peace.' "[1]

Day One'
Not That Again

Day Two'
Laughing Out Loud

Day Three'
God Heard

Day Four'
The Eternal God

Day Five'
To Mourn for Sarah

This Week's Principal Questions

Day 1: In Genesis 20 you have the first of four revelations from God through dreams in the Book of Beginnings. What was the basic message of the dream?

Day 2: What does Genesis 18:11 explicitly tell you?

Day 3: According to Genesis 21:8-11, what was the cause of Sarah's drastic change in temperament?

Day 4: What did Abraham give Abimelech in Genesis 21:28,30 and why?

Day 5: What does Abraham tell the Hittites he needs?

Day One'
Not That Again

A dear Bible teacher once shared with me her frustration with a particular senior adult women's class. Though they were faithful to attend and were thoroughly involved in the weekly lessons, she found most were too set in their ways to let God's Word continue to transform them. Thankfully, many senior adults are exceptions and rise up in stark contrast to that small group. Most of my favorite letters through the years have come from women in their 70s and 80s who still seek and serve God, letting Him change them "from glory to glory" (2 Cor. 3:18, HCSB).

I'll never forget the woman in her 80s who wrote me to say she was determined to "break free" in Christ—even if it killed her. Countless letters have come across my desk from small Bible-study groups, letting me know about a dear sister in her glory years who had studied God's Word practically to her last breath. I have no greater respect for anyone than someone who continues to study and serve God until the end of life. That's what I want to do. Don't you?

Today we'll discover that we never grow too old to sin or deceive. Those who continue to apply God's Word until their last breath are wise indeed. If God were finished changing and conforming us to the image of His dear Son, we'd be face-to-face with Him right now.

Today's Treasure

For a while he stayed in Gerar, and there Abraham said of his wife Sarah, "She is my sister." Then Abimelech king of Gerar sent for Sarah and took her.

Genesis 20:1-2

Please read all of Genesis 20 and complete the following:

Glance back at Genesis 12:10-20 and draw a few comparisons. What sounds familiar to Genesis 12:10-20?

_____

_____

 Genesis 20 relates the first of four revelations from God through dreams in the Book of Beginnings. What was the basic message of Abimelech's dream?

_____

Contrast Abimelech and Abraham.

_____

_____

Sarah was 65 years old when Abraham deceived the Pharaoh about the true nature of their relationship (Gen. 12). In Genesis 20 Sarah clocks in at an amazing 90 years old which may explain the absence of Abraham's flattery as found earlier, "I know what a beautiful woman you are. When the Egyptians see you, they will say, 'This is his wife.' Then they will kill me but will let you live' " (Gen. 12:11).

We might wonder why the king of Gerar pursued a woman of such years. We can't rule out desirability because a much younger earth and different era probably had a drastically different effect on aging. We learn from history, however, that love and desire were often among the least of the motivations for marriage among heads of states. Politics and protection often motivated alliances. Don't forget that "Abram the Hebrew" and his men defeated a powerful alliance of kings in the Valley of Shaveh (Gen. 14). Word gets around. If Sarah had only been Abraham's sister, she would have been a shield for Abimelech and perhaps a charm of sorts to the superstitious.

You might be interested in a few additional facts about the people of Gerar. "Gerar was the capital of a race of men who had dispossessed the original inhabitants of the land, and were gradually passing from the condition of wandering shepherd life into that of a settled and warlike nation; afterwards to be known to the Hebrews by the dreaded name, Philistines: a title which, in fact, gave to the whole land its name of Palestine."[2]

Let's consider some of the life lessons that can be drawn from Genesis 20. First, note God's attention to the nations. God willingly revealed Himself through a dream—not to Abraham—but to this king of a heathen nation. We must not lose sight of God's world vision: "all peoples on earth will be blessed" (Gen. 12:3). The very first mention of the important word *prophet* appears purposely in the context of Genesis 20.

Look at Genesis 20:7. What is the first role associated with a prophet of God?
❑ interceding ❑ rebuking ❑ warning
❑ preaching ❑ foretelling

While these five roles can be identified through the actions of various prophets of God through Scripture, we might be blessed by the first priority of interceding prayer. " 'Now return the man's wife, for he is a prophet, and he will pray for you and you will live' " (Gen. 20:7). Prophets of God were meant to care. Not curse. Surely in this strange way Abraham was forced to deal with the seriousness of the position in which he placed not only his wife but a king and his people.

> **Imagine God telling you to get on your knees to pray for someone you had placed in a bad position. How would you feel about the command, and how would your feelings affect your praying?**
>
> **I would feel** _____
>
> **Therefore, I would pray** _____

When my family or staff goes through a challenge on my behalf that has nothing to do with sin, I often sob my way through prayer over feeling responsible. Imagine God saying to Abraham, "Pray for Abimelech and his people, Abraham, that they don't die as a result of what you did. Cry out for their lives." Assigning me the responsibility of praying for the people I hurt or placed at risk would have a dramatic effect on me. How about you?

> **God holds us responsible for marriage. Read the verses in the margin and fill in the following:**
>
> **In verse 3 God stated, "You are as good as dead because of the woman you have taken; she is a _____ woman." In verse 6 God further states, "Yes, I know you did this with a clear conscience, and so I have kept you from sinning _____ _____."**

" 'You are as good as dead because of the woman you have taken; she is a married woman.' "
Genesis 20:3

" 'Yes, I know you did this with a clear conscience, and so I have kept you from sinning against me.' "
Genesis 20:6

God takes sins against marriage personally. He is merciful and forgiving, but the seriousness of such sins and their consequences should ignite a fresh wave of godly fear in us. I feel our culture's habit of attaching little importance to marriage will meet God's strong disapproval.

Let's focus now on the repetition of Abraham's earlier sin. You couldn't have missed Abraham's explanation to Abimelech in verse 13.

> **According to Abraham, what agreement had he asked Sarah to make and when?**
>
> _____

We have no way of knowing whether Abraham was telling the whole truth since honesty was not his star quality at that moment. Let's assume he was honest about the early agreement he and Sarah made. We see between chapters 12 and 20 no mention of Sarah claiming Abraham strictly as her brother everywhere they went, so the plan was obviously for sticky situations with other nations. Perhaps the plan fell into the "just in case" category. We can relate. At one time or another, how many of us have thought to ourselves, *I would really hate to have to . . . but I can if I must. This is the plan just in case.* We sometimes scheme what we'd do if we got caught in this or that situation. Or if we simply got *caught.* We'd hate to have to lie, but *just in case* we have a plan. Premeditated sin. Serious stuff.

Or possibly, Abraham and Sarah simply defaulted into an old pattern of handling a crisis situation. Let's imagine that their deceit might have been more of a reaction than a forethought plan. I can easily react to a crisis by flipping frantically through my mental file for a previous predicament and reacting similarly. After all, over time the consequences of that past reaction didn't seem so bad. In fact, maybe in retrospect that decision was worth it. Abraham left Egypt 25 years earlier a very rich man, but don't for a moment discount the emotional and mental torment and marital distress that resulted from his poor decision. Abraham probably didn't remember how much it had hurt until he experienced the pain of the decision again.

🐪 **Can you relate? Has time ever dulled the difficulty of a poor decision, lulling you into making a similar decision? What did you learn from the experience?**

_____

_____

I don't suppose anything has caused me more pain than repeating an old folly. The fact that I knew better and knew God better added a self-loathing that was as difficult to get over as the foolish decision. I was in my early 30s and already on my way to healing before I realized how askew my thinking was and how broken my emotions had been. God drove home to me the biblical point that freedom would come only through the renewing of my mind (Rom. 12:1-2; 2 Cor. 10:3-5; Eph. 4:23).

When I started waking up to the pain that my self-destructive thinking had caused and realized its potential to destroy my future, I became somewhat like Peter. When Christ wanted to wash his feet, Peter said, "Then, Lord, not just my feet but my hands and my head as well!" (John 13:9). I decided that I not only needed my conscious mind renewed, I needed my subconscious mind renewed. In fact, I began to pray, "God, invade my dream life, my thoughts when I sleep, and every closet in my brain! Put Your truth in the innermost places of my mind, even those I don't know exist." (This is still a constant prayer of mine, by the way.)

While I was teaching the video sessions for *Living Beyond Yourself*, God led me to discover the Greek word *horme* as I researched various passions and their power to motivate. According to the *New Testament Lexical Aids*, "*Horme* is an impulse or urge, a strong and forceful movement toward something, and connotes the ideas of thrusting, propulsion, and suddenness. It is not unlike a sudden thought, whim, or dictating inclination."[3] After praying that God would invade every part of my thought life, I added this new dimension to my prayers: "God, fill me so completely with Your Holy Spirit that even my reactions and sudden impulses are godly!" I want to be like Peter when he saw Jesus on the shore and impulsively jumped in the water and swam to Him with all his might! (See John 21.)

Abraham and Sarah defaulted to an old pattern when they met the crisis in Gerar. The threat was not in their imaginations. They realized that when they were in a king's territory, he could take from them what he wanted, and if they resisted or showed any ownership, he could kill them. You might say the circumstance propelled them with the dictating inclination of deceit as illustrated by the Greek word *horme*. We have defaulted to old patterns as well. Under stress or sudden crisis, our first reactions at various points may be fleshly and selfish. *What if* we began attentively and repeatedly praying for the Holy Spirit to invade and renew us so richly and deeply that even our impulses were godly? That even our "default" response was sanctified?

Describe a specific difference this could make in your life.

_____

_____

What if through the power of the Holy Spirit we developed godly reactions and not just responses? Impossible? No. Challenging? Yes! Perfection is out of our earthly reach, but "through and through" sanctification is not (I Thess. 5:23).

If you desire for God to invade every part of your mind and heart, thoughts and impulses, write a prayer in this space and tell Him so.

_____

_____

_____

Day Two
Laughing Out Loud

Today's Treasure
Sarah said, "God has brought me laughter, and everyone who hears about this will laugh with me."
Genesis 21:6

Nothing on earth rivals the ecstasy of experiencing a heavenly promise fulfilled. God's appointment of time in between the word of promise and its fulfillment can tempt us to ridiculous thoughts like, *"I'm going to fool around and die before God remembers to bring this to pass."* And as if waiting for God's time isn't hard enough, God fills the waiting with tests like a clerk who shoves grapefruits into a bulging grocery bag. Room for one more ... and maybe another ... and, look, there's a little space for another small one. When the bag grows heavy like "time ... fully come" (Gal. 4:4), the breakthrough erupts and fruit rolls.

Sarah knew the feeling. Her wait, like ours, was about what God wanted to birth and maybe even what God wanted to kill (all other options).

Before I get too excited and teach the whole lesson in advance, hasten to Genesis 21:1-7 and record the promise God fulfilled:

_____

When the three visitors stopped near the great trees of Mamre for a divine appointment with Abram, the Lord announced that He'd return to them "at the appointed time next year and Sarah will have a son."

The wording is rich in Genesis 21:1. Fill in the blanks according to the NIV:

"Now the LORD was _____ to Sarah as he had said."

The word *gracious* is translated from the Hebrew *padaq* meaning "to number, count; to call into account; to look after."[4] The word has a wide range of meanings in the Old Testament and can be used in either a negative or positive context. The occurrence in today's passage is its first use in Scripture. "A strong undercurrent in the meaning of *padaq* is a positive action by a superior in relation to his subordinates."[5] *The King James Version* translates *padaq* beautifully. Read it in the margin.

> The LORD *visited* Sarah as he had said, and the LORD did unto Sarah as he had spoken.
> Genesis 21:1, KJV
> (Emphasis added.)

Circle both the phrases beginning with the word "as" in this verse. What can you conclude from these two phrases?

_____

_____

Nothing could be more gracious of God than to visit His child with His Presence. The divine visit referenced in Genesis 21:1 could relate either to the time of supernatural conception between Abraham and Sarah or the miracle of the child's birth. Though the miraculous nature of this pregnancy and birth is inarguable, please don't confuse it with the miracle of Christ's conception (Luke 1). Christ had no biological earthly father. God was and is His only Father. Abraham was undoubtedly the biological *pater* of Isaac, who was born out of a loving physical union that took place between Abraham and his elderly wife. God's visitation lent the supernatural power to conceive and deliver.

Valentine's Day is just around the corner as I write. I won't kid you. I love love. Think about this for a moment: we tend to consider the best love stories in terms of how they began: romantically … adventurously … against all odds. Our society has proved we have no trouble beginning love. However, we are tragically deficient on enduring love and ending love well at the close of a lifetime.

If you'll allow me room for a little extra boldness, God's plan necessitated Abraham and Sarah fanning those flames of passion again. We don't know that they didn't nearly laugh their heads off at the thought of God's marvelous plan. Isaac's name could encompass endless motivations for laughter. Loving couples who have been together a long time enjoy priceless moments of private joking—not the least of which concern physical intimacy. I've gotten tickled recently by a contest on our local Christian radio station. In honor of Valentine's Day, husbands or wives call in with their "love handle" or pet name by which their spouse calls them. If the mate hears the name on the radio broadcast, he or she is to call in and claim the name to win a weekend getaway. In many cases I fear the winning couple might need to stay way more than a weekend to let their friends get over it.

For all we know, Abraham and Sarah had pet names for each other and laughed all the way to their graves over the child God enabled them to conceive in their senior years. I can picture Abraham pretending to flex his muscles for Sarah while the skin hung down unenthusiastically from his upper arm. Then I can picture Sarah laughing until she cried … or had a coughing fit. Ways we uniquely communicate with one another are God-blessed dimensions of marriage. Marriage is often difficult, and sharing tender moments like these eases the difficult and mundane seasons with bouts of delight.

Do you know a senior-adult couple who still seem to be in love? Describe something about them that makes you smile.

_____

With new romance infused late into their relationship, picture Abraham and Sarah somewhat like the couple you mentioned. We'll miss a tremendous blessing if we spiritualize the human aspect out of their story.

Genesis 21:2 states, "Sarah became pregnant and bore a son to Abraham in his old age, at the very time God had promised him." Any of us who have had children know good and well that plenty happens between conception and delivery. Had God inspired Moses' wife to write Genesis instead of Moses, we might have been privy to significantly greater detail. This we know: God "visited" Sarah and enabled her to become pregnant and bear a child. We have no Scripture to support that she and Abraham knew they'd had a visitation and that they were suddenly expecting a baby. In all likelihood, time had to tell.

🐫 **Go with me here, Sister, because the woman in me finds this part fascinating. Just think: Sarah didn't have a monthly cycle to give her early signs that she was pregnant. How do we know? What does Genesis 18:11 explicitly tell you?**

_____

That's a nice, biblically correct way to say that Sarah had already gone through menopause. I'm blessed to know she never killed anyone. However, Hagar might say that Sarah didn't get to that point without considerable mood swings.

🐫 **How do you think Sarah finally figured out that God had fulfilled His promise and she was expecting Isaac? Share your thoughts.**

_____

_____

I'd love to join your small group and get into the rich kind of discussions that we women like to have. We should be scholarly in our study of God's Word, but we should also enjoy meditating on Scripture from our gender perspective. The combination makes the process of studying the Bible all the more real and applicable.

We probably answered the previous question with several of the same assumptions. Sarah was looking for the pregnancy, so she very likely jumped to accurate conclusions at the first sign. On the first morning or two she felt nauseated, she may have assumed it was Hagar's bad cooking ("I knew she was trying to poison me!"), but after a while, she would have figured out she had one of our least favorite symptoms of pregnancy: morning sickness. Weeks later she might have lain flat on her back to see if her tummy was changing.

Can you imagine the care Sarah took of herself once she realized she was expecting? Even though she had a God-given guarantee that she'd carry the baby to term and deliver a healthy bundle of boy, surely Sarah made some of the same careful adjustments that many of us did with our first babies. Take a look at a similar pregnancy account in the first chapter of the Gospel of Luke.

We should also enjoy meditating on Scripture from our gender perspective.

Read Luke 1:5-7 and describe this couple.

_____

What happened in Luke 1:11-13?

_____

Read Luke 1:24-25. What did Elizabeth do according to verse 24? How long?

_____

Why do you think she did such a thing?

_____

_____

If we believers could grasp that we are vessels of Christ's Spirit, we'd realize our inestimable value!

We have no way of knowing for certain, but it's possible Sarah protected herself and remained under great care during the first months of the pregnancy. (Or while she was waiting to develop the nerve to tell her friends). Sarah may have reacted in a manner similar to Elizabeth. I never valued my own life more than when I was expecting my babies. In my thinking, the cargo I carried made me valuable. Oh, dear ones, if we who are believers could only grasp that we are vessels of the very indwelling of Christ's Spirit, we'd realize some of our inestimable value!

After being obsessively careful the first several months, the second half of a normal pregnancy isn't as worrisome in at least one respect: you can feel the baby's activity inside of you. Imagine. About midway through Sarah's pregnancy she began to feel Isaac kick. At first she wasn't sure. The feeling was like the flutter of butterfly wings or a tiny bubble popping. But after another month or two, her abdomen heaved with the swift kick of a lively baby boy practicing sports.

Then "Sarah … bore a son" (Gen. 21:2). Much like many of us, she may have been expecting the baby to arrive for weeks, but several false alarms taught her she'd have to wait until the pains took a definitive pattern. Historical records of practicing midwives reach far into antiquity. We can accurately imagine at least one other woman right beside Sarah, coaching her through labor and delivery. Harder for us to imagine is a one-hundred-year-old man pacing back and forth, kicking up the dust as the minutes stretched into hours.

Then there Isaac was, red face tightened into an angry knot and cord still attached, reminding Sarah that all babies are miracles. Her gray hair lay soaked with sweat while tears ran like tiny rivers through the crow's feet around her eyes. Those aging eyes had witnessed volumes of life but never a more precious moment than this. Slippery. Squirming. Screaming. Son of Abraham. Child of promise. Genesis 21:6 says it perfectly: "God has brought me laughter." Yes, with a capital "L." Suddenly, the wait was worthwhile. Isn't that how it goes?

I'm amused at the lack of mention of Sarah's old age in the text. Abraham's alone is mentioned—and twice, in fact, but who's counting (vv. 2,7)? After all, who could keep from admiring Sarah as she labored courageously and brought forth a son, nursing him like a twenty-year-old mother might do?

Abraham was beside himself. He believed God, so he knew that he would have a son. But for the life of him, Abraham didn't know how he'd feel. Words are assigned to the smaller things, after all. Bigger matters are too sacred. You can't describe them. If you're wise, you just sit a spell and soak your weary, wandering feet in them.

I am tender to those of you who may find today's lesson bittersweet, even painful. Perhaps your marriage has long outlasted a sense of passion or your womb remains empty—though you've prayed and prayed for a child. Was there any reason this was a difficult lesson for you (beyond the annoying teacher)?

_____

Take heart, Dear One. This lesson may have been for you more than anyone. If Isaac's birth says anything at all, surely it says that nothing is too difficult for the Lord. Among thousands of other things, God can perform miracles in marriages long past their prime. He can give offspring (using doctors, physically, by adoption, spiritual children—whatever the means)—to the barren. What may be a little more unsettling is the thought that both marriage and birth miracles could happen to the same couple!

That's what happened with our Abraham and Sarah. I feel as if we stopped by their home today. In fact, the thought occurred to me what kind of gift I might have brought. I think a fun ending to today's lesson is to muse over the gift we'd bring for Sarah or baby Isaac if we were invited to a party in honor of Isaac's arrival. You're welcome to think in terms of today's kinds of gifts—keepsakes or modern conveniences—but conclude with a specific item that you'd give for such a special occasion. Oh, lighten up and do it! I'll make sure to include my gift idea in the leader's guide so I can share mine at small group, too.

What gift would you choose? _____

You're such a good sport. Thanks for letting me study with you today.

Day Three
God Heard

When I was a little girl, my family lived just outside a small Arkansas town in Ouachita Hills. Tall pine trees towered over our tiny home. My favorite part of the wooded yard was a burlap-bag swing my daddy hung from a sturdy branch on one of the pines. Some days I swung back and forth on that bag until my skinny legs were burlap-raw. As a woman, who dearly loves her gender, I've been swinging back and forth ever since. I think I'll go ahead and 'fess up. Today's lesson could give males all the ammunition they need to prove that female moods swing wider than a bag on a long rope.

I'd like to point out that the opening scene in today's Scriptures happened several years after Isaac's birth, but I know my gender well enough to know that the kind of emotional swing we're about to study can also happen in the same day. Or the same hour. I started this lesson in a good mood, but suddenly I feel like taking a trip on that old swing.

Today's Treasure
God has heard the boy crying as he lies there.
Genesis 21:17

🐫 Glance at the Scriptures we studied yesterday, then hop on the swing for today's first text: Genesis 21:8-11. What caused Sarah's drastic change in temperament?

_____

Have you ever noticed how family celebrations filled with high expectations have an uncanny way of bringing out less-than-desirable family dynamics? I think we are safe to say that by the end of this merry day, no one had a good time.

Ishmael figured he'd rather be in the spotlight for bad behavior than be forced out of it altogether. The Hebrew word *tsachaq* translated *mocking* in verse 9 means "to laugh outright (in merriment or scorn); by implication to sport: laugh, mock, play, make sport."[6] The form in this verse "signifies 'to laugh malevolently' rather than merely to play innocently."[7] Picturing a young teenage boy teasing and picking on his 3-year-old half brother is no reach. Something stronger, however, is implied in this scene. Ishmael suddenly posed a threat Sarah could not tolerate.

The Hebrew version of Genesis 21:8 suggests an interesting play on words. The word for "mocking" in this verse is a participle "of the verb *sahaq*, from which the name 'Isaac' is formed. Thus, Sarah observes Ishmael playing or sporting and 'Isaac-ing.' "[8] The next time you get really tickled, try thinking of your actions as Isaac-ing. Aren't you intrigued by the role laughter plays in the accounts surrounding Isaac and his birth? We might sum up Sarah's feelings toward Ishmael with this: *You can laugh with us, but think twice before you laugh at us.*

Our Scripture passages today contain very little description concerning Isaac. We only know that he's old enough to have just been weaned—customarily up to 3 according to ancient practices. I can't think of a more lovable age. Nothing has the potential to be more delightful (or more frightful) than a 3- or 4-year-old. Most of us have been around children this age through family or friends.

Briefly describe a few things about a typically precocious little boy of 3.

_____

If Isaac ever lived up to his name, surely he did at this age. A very prim and proper friend of mine had quite a spitfire on her hands when her daughter was about this age. My friend came to say goodbye to me after an aerobic class I'd taught, and the little one looked straight up at me and quipped something like this: "Miss Beth, did you know you sweat like a little piggy?" My proper friend nearly had a coronary while this Mrs. Piggy squealed with laughter all the way home. I favor my grandmother who used to say of herself, "I'm drunk on young 'uns."

Picture Isaac as delightful and unpredictable as any other 3-year-old. He was his mother's only child and the apple of her eye. Sketch a half-brother into the scene, picking on Isaac and making fun of him at his own party. It's a wonder Ishmael didn't get smacked in the head with Isaac's new sippy cup. Any of us might be angry in a similar situation involving our own children, but when Sarah rose to the occasion, she went over the top. In my opinion, a feast of celebration on weaning day has a mother at a decided disadvantage. That kind of timing could send any woman out to the burlap-bag swing.

Once again Sarah refused to use Hagar's name. "Get rid of that slave woman and her son" (Gen. 21:10).

What conclusions can you make from Abraham's response (v. 11)?

_____

_____

We can only imagine Abraham's heartache. What we may be tempted to call *folly* Abraham called *son*. Surely Ishmael bore the image of his father in *this* expression or *that* habit. How Sarah must have hated the reminders. Worse yet, the arrangement had been her idea. For better or for worse, Ishmael was Abraham's flesh and blood, and the old man grieved the threat spit from the mouth of bitter conflict. I feel for him. Have you ever dearly loved two people who could not abide one another? Sarah was Abraham's wife and the matriarch of the promised line, but Ishmael was his son. Abraham knew if Ishmael left, part of his heart would leave with him.

Please read Genesis 21:12-13 and record the gist of God's response to Abraham.

_____

God may not have approved of Sarah's severity, but He allowed her plan because, though neither Hagar nor Ishmael knew, it would put them on the road to His greater plan. The sovereignty of God will remain a consistent silver thread in the fabric of Genesis, weaving in and out of sight like stitches in a hem. If we're willing, it will be our comfort. If we're not, it will become our nagging question. Trusting that God knows all things and that He works out circumstance for our good can be an emotional lifesaver (see Rom. 8:28).

How does Ephesians 1:11 speak to the conflict in Genesis 21:8-13?

_____

How does Ephesians 1:11 speak to a present challenge in your life?

_____

_____

God's sovereignty weaves in and out of sight like stitches in a hem.

I love the *New International Version* wording. Ours is a God who "works out everything." Unless your situation or mine is an exception to "everything," God can handle it and work it out within the context of His plan. Yes, even if someone has treated us harshly as Sarah treated Hagar and Ishmael. *The New International Commentary* suggests, "Ishmael loses property but gains a nation."[9] Hagar and Ishmael could not have seen past the immediate horror of the prospect into the promise fulfilled. In His infinite mercy, God scheduled a visit to remind them personally.

From your point of view, what is the most tender moment in Genesis 21:14-21?

_____

Genesis 21:14 won't be the last time we'll see the phrase "early the next morning" in reference to the timing of Abraham's actions. The early hour suggests prompt obedience, and it may also suggest an inability to sleep. Surely every time Abraham closed his eyes he pictured Hagar and Ishmael out in the desert, exposed to harsh elements and thieves on the lookout for defenseless travelers.

Imagine the old man's brokenness as he gave Hagar the food and water, "set them on her shoulders and then sent her off with the boy." He would never see them again. Do you think he watched them as long as he could as they disappeared into the distance, or do you think Abraham closed himself in the tent because he couldn't bear to watch?

Which would you have done had you been Abraham? (No right or wrong answer exists. I just want you to join them on the page as much as you can.)

"She went on her way and wandered in the desert of Beersheba" (v. 14). The Hebrew verb used for "wandered" suggests uncertainty, loss of direction, and even hopelessness.[10] Let's try to relate in modern terms. Imagine that you are a single mother. You've been thrown out of the only home you know in a remote town in Arizona, and you have no hope of returning. You are given transportation, but you only have enough gas to last a few hours. You have no map. You've driven and gotten nowhere; you're almost out of gas. Reality creeps up on you with a wave of nausea: you are lost with no civilization in sight. The sun bakes the cracked ground, and the water bottle is empty. Your child is terrified and asks what you are going to do. Desperation disintegrates into hopelessness.

Take the car away and you can begin to see what Hagar and Ishmael faced. We are not told the number of days they journeyed, but clearly they traveled long enough for Ishmael to reach the brink of death. Once they ran out of water, the desert heat and lack of vegetation hastily dehydrated their weakened bodies. Imagine Hagar trying to keep Ishmael moving while he grew increasingly weak. At his age, he was nearly as big as she, yet he had all the fears and emotions of a child. We might wonder why a young teenage boy neared death faster than his mother. Surely the answer is in the iron will of a mother determined to take care of her child.

Hagar assumed the obvious: Death was imminent. Putting Ishmael under a bush to die seems strange to us, but her actions were intentional. Most certainly the bush was thorny, and she was protecting her son's body from predatory animals ... particularly the kind that don't wait until you're dead. I'm sorry to be so graphic, but this was their reality. Consider the Hebrew verb used in the phrase "she put the boy." "When used with a human being as its object, the verb almost always refers to lowering a dead body into its grave, or the lowering of a person into what will presumably be his grave."[11]

Then comes the part of the story I find almost too painful to picture. After Hagar tucked the weakened body of her son under the bush and kissed his fevered face, she stayed close enough for Ishmael to know she was near but far enough away to hide her eyes. In her hopeless state, whether or not to watch her son die was the solitary choice left to make.

Meditate on a more literal translation of verse 16 offered by the *New International Commentary on the Old Testament*. "Then she went and sat down by herself opposite him about a bowshot away, for she said: 'Do not let me see the child die.' Sitting down opposite him, she started to sob."[12] The words were spoken as a prayer. Note the description in the previous translation: *by herself*. Desert or no desert, nothing is more isolating than grief.

No one loved Ishmael like Hagar did. She alone carried him in her womb, birthed him through pain, nursed him to health, and tucked him into bed. She'd met his every need as any mother would … but she could not meet this one. "Do not let me see the child die. And … she began to sob."

"God heard the boy crying" (v. 17). Did Ishmael cry at the sound of his mother's sobs? Or was he afraid? In pain? God alone knows because God alone heard. Human ears could not have heard the whimpers of a weakened boy over the wails of his broken mother. God's ears, though, hear "groans that words cannot express" (Rom. 8:26). God heard the sobs as if they were prayers without words. The psalmist eloquently expressed a similar thought, "Out of the depths I cry to you, O LORD" (Ps. 130:1).

What was the divine interruption to Hagar's sobs?

_____

What did the angel of God tell her to do (v. 18)?

_____

"Lift the boy up? Oh, God, that I could! He has no strength and I can no longer carry him" (see Gen. 21:18). Would God make us a promise without giving us the provision to see it fulfilled? "Then God opened her eyes and she saw a well of water" (v. 19). Ah, yes. Sometimes God brings a woman to a well, and other times He brings a well to a woman. "So she went and filled the skin with water" (v. 19). Trembling, don't you imagine, as a flash flood of hope filled her own frail skin? See Hagar in your imagination, filling the canteen made of animal skin as fast as she could for fear Ishmael might die before God's promise was fulfilled. Picture her running, water splashing, toward the bush where she'd left him. No need to worry about waste. God Himself dug the well; it would not run dry.

Now picture Hagar kneeling beside Ishmael, oblivious to the prick of thorns. Imagine her lifting his head, heavy with the nearness of death, as she insists, "Ishmael, open your mouth!" She pours. Her trembling hand tips as much over his face as into his mouth, leaving streams through the dust on his ashen cheeks. "So she … gave the boy a drink" (v. 19). God was their oasis in their desert.

"God was with the boy as he grew up. He lived in the desert and became an archer" (Hebrew: *qassat*). Perhaps now the earlier terminology doesn't seem so out of place as we're told that Hagar moved about a bowshot (Hebrew: *qeset*) away so as not to watch Ishmael die. Even the distance Hagar removed herself to sob over his death whispered Ishmael's destiny. Are we surprised to learn God was with Ishmael as he grew up? Not if you have a background like mine.

At last Hagar is called *mother* (v. 21) and rightly so. Ishmael had been born to her twice it seemed.

Conclude by writing your own thoughts or meditations.

_____

_____

Day Four

The Eternal God

Today's Treasure

Abraham planted a tamarisk tree in Beersheba, and there he called upon the name of the LORD, the Eternal God.

Genesis 21:33

In our previous lesson God brought a well to a wandering, desperate woman. In today's lesson a well becomes a matter of dispute. With the common thread of a well in mind, read Genesis 21:22-34. The name "Abimelech" should be familiar. Glance at Genesis 20 to refresh your memory.

What history have Abimelech and Abraham shared?

_____

Whether for protection, intimidation, or simple protocol, Abimelech brought Phicol "the commander of his forces" with him to meet Abraham. The name "Phicol" means "the mouth of all" or "mouthful."[13] Big mouth might be a better way of saying it. Not that the name makes me squirm, but let's just say I'm glad Mom named me Beth. Some might say Phicol would have been more fitting.

Three or four years have passed since Abraham's previous encounter with Abimelech. In Genesis 20 Sarah was not yet expecting Isaac. By this point in Genesis 21, Isaac was already weaned. Since Abraham was living in the land of the Philistines, Abimelech no doubt kept tabs on him. He knew this: "God is with you in everything you do" (v. 22). The thought first dawned on him through the power of Abraham's prayers.

What happened as a result of Abraham's intercession (Gen. 20:17-18)?

_____

As the years passed, proof of God's presence with Abraham must have stacked up until Abimelech knew he needed Abraham's favor. He asked Abraham for something that becomes vital in the study of God's Word. In Genesis 21:23 Abimelech asked Abraham to show him "kindness." The Hebrew word *hesed* is one of the most important words in the Old Testament. It shows up first in Genesis 20:13 and is translated love in the NIV.[14]

Read Genesis 20:13 and explain its context.

_____

The first two occurrences of *hesed* show up in contexts that offer excellent clues to its meaning. In Genesis 20:13, though Abraham took wrong advantage of the concept and relationship, *hesed* is viewed in the context of the marriage covenant. In Genesis 21:23, *hesed* is viewed in the context of an oath and covenant (*beriyt*, translated here as *treaty* in v. 27) between two peoples. In the shortest definitions possible, *hesed* is covenant kindness and loyal love. It is the expression of love, favor, or kindness based on a covenant relationship. Covenant kindness could also be shown outside a covenant relationship as if to say, "I will show you the kindness of someone in covenant to you, though I am not." *Hesed* was the ultimate mercy. The concept of *hesed* is undoubtedly most attributed to God.

What phrase is repeated throughout Psalm 136?

Why would God allow such a profound concept to be illustrated first through the lacking relationships of man? To teach the unknown through the known. The ancient world understood the binding oaths of covenant kindness and loyal love. As God revealed Himself through the annals of history as YHWH, the covenant God, He suggested His otherwise unfathomable mercy and tender love as the ultimate extension of *hesed*.

As I have studied the concept of *hesed*, I've come to the stark realization of something so difficult for me to grasp that I can hardly teach it: Through the covenant relationship we've entered by the blood of Jesus Christ, the God of all creation is loyal to us. *Loyal.* Can you fathom it? The sovereign Most High has pledged His loyal love to us. As drastic inferiors in this relationship, *hesed* would make more sense to us if we were bound by covenant to be loyal to God rather than the other way around, but the humbling truth is that God bound Himself by covenant to be loyal to us. Paul expresses it beautifully in 2 Timothy.

In your own words, explain what 2 Timothy 2:13 says.

Because God signed His Name to this covenant with the blood of Jesus Christ, He will remain faithful to it no matter what happens. After staking His Name on it, He'd have to disown Himself to be unfaithful. I shudder with the implications of such a binding covenant. The reality of God's loyalty does not make me comfortable. In a way I cannot explain, it drives me with urgency to be faithful in return. He staked His Name on our relationship. Realizing that, how could we do anything but cleave to Him with our whole hearts?

Abimelech's request to Abraham reminds us that God's presence and blessing over our lives give us not only security but also responsibility. In essence, Abimelech said to Abraham, "Since God is so obviously with you, I request the following from you."

🐪 **Has someone who doesn't know Christ requested something of you because God seems to be with you? Think about it, and share an example.**

The heathen king of Gerar knew something by instinct that Abraham had failed to display in past years: since God is with you, I should be able to trust that you will not deal falsely with me and that you will show me covenant kindness. I learned in a commentary that Abimelech's request took 21 Hebrew words, but Abraham's response only took 2: *I swear.*[15] Some decisions take lengthy deliberation and many words. Others are black and white. In this case, Abraham met a "just do it" moment.

If Abraham and Abimelech were to deal rightly and truthfully with one another, all the issues at hand needed to be on the table. What matter did Abraham bring up to Abimelech?

_____

The western world has no real appreciation for the life a well brings to a dry and thirsty land. A few hours ago, at the turn of a knob, I took a nice hot shower after a winter walk. A little while later, I threw a load of towels in the washing machine and turned the dial to "heavy load." Before I sat down to write, I poured four more cups of water in my automatic drip coffee pot and ground a handful of dark roast coffee beans.

Meanwhile, I have two friends, one an American and the other an African, who spend every drop of energy and every dime they have raising money to drill wells in Africa. One tells me that the anticipation of hitting or missing water as a drill pounds into the earth is unlike anything he's ever experienced. The scene we've stepped into today is not just the stuff of ancient history. Right this moment somewhere in the world two groups of people are fighting over the same well.

 What did Abraham give Abimelech in Genesis 21:28,30 and why?

_____

The word "witness" (v. 30) also means "testimony." The Hebrew term behind it is "used only of things affirming permanence and unequivocal facts, such as ownership, a contract, or a covenant with God."[16] In a strange sort of way, every baa of the seven ewe lambs bore witness that Abraham owned the well. Abimelech's reception of the lambs testified his reception of Abraham's claims as "unequivocal facts." "So that place was called Beersheba, because the two men swore an oath there" (Gen. 21:31). A very possible play on Hebrew words occurs in the name given to this place. "Beersheba" can mean "well of seven" or "well of oath." The Hebrew word for _seven_, a very important number often symbolizing completion or perfection, is the same as the Hebrew word for "oath": _saba_.[17] God's oaths—and therefore any made in His Name—are to be kept perfectly and completely. Countless times the life of a lamb bore witness.

What did Abraham do after Abimelech and Big Mouth departed (Gen. 21:33)?

_____

Abraham was a tree man. His first stopping place in Canaan was by a tree (Gen. 12:6). He later built an altar at Mamre by a tree (Gen. 13:18). He entertained the three visitors under a tree (Gen. 18:1) and lived near trees (Gen. 14:13). In a land of little shade, he planted a tamarisk tree as a special place—perhaps to meet with God. There he called upon the LORD by a very profound name: the Eternal God (Gen. 21:33).

As a student, I often drove my teachers crazy with the question, "Why?" My relentless pursuit of making sense of things has at times almost been the death of me. Needless to say, the wells I dug in the process often came up dry. Other times, however, the digging pursuit of _why_ led to fountains of living water. As I studied the end of Genesis 21, I wanted to know why Abraham planted a tree then called the Lord by the name Eternal God. The Hebrew name *El Olam* is introduced in this very context. By practice we've learned that the context of a name introduced in Scripture tells us something important about it. The name always fits the context, so why doesn't it seem to this time?

I searched one commentary after another and came up dry, then I decided to research trees in my concordance. I don't know if I'm onto something, but I want to share with you what I found.

Read Isaiah 65:22. What comparison does God make to a tree?

_____

A sturdy, healthy tree long outlives a man. Some trees live so long that some of those still green and fruitful in the Holy Land could possibly have shaded our Savior from the noon heat two thousand years ago. Abraham was very old when he made the treaty with Abimelech. The promise God made to him for an heir was already fulfilled. For all Abraham knew, death was imminent. A stranger in a land far from the familiar, I wonder if Abraham sought to plant something as a memorial that would remain long after he was gone. His reference to the LORD as the *eternal* God suggests to me that something about the moment spoke to him regarding *time*.

Few people seriously long for the end of life. Most fight to live with astonishing tenacity. I'd like to suggest that our resistance to the end of earthly life originates neither in worldliness, selfishness, nor a lack of faith. I believe it originates in our makeup.

Please read Solomon's words in Ecclesiastes 3:11 in the margin. This verse makes references to time and to eternity. What does it say to each:

Time: Eternity:

_____   _____

_____   _____

> He has made everything beautiful in its time. He has also set eternity in the hearts of men; yet they cannot fathom what God has done from beginning to end.
> **Ecclesiastes 3:11**

All references to time in God's Word pertain to created things and, most pointedly, life on Planet Earth. We know that the Trinity (God the Father, Son, and Holy Spirit) have always existed and will always exist. They are *olam*, eternal. Out of their glorious fellowship they desired to create humans to share in holy relationship. According to His master plan, our eternal God created this thing called time and placed us—indeed all of creation—within it. Here is the intriguing part: though God set us in "time," He set eternity in our hearts. (The word "eternity" in Eccl. 3:11 is also *olam*.) In other words, our bodies are subject to time, but something in our hearts resists the temporal and longs for eternity.

Every time we think, *surely there is more to life than this,* we hear the hint of eternity in our hearts. Every time we learn the cancer has returned and we're willing to go through another treatment, our drive to hang on to life is the hint of eternity in our hearts. Every time our love outlasts our loved one's life, we hear eternity's murmur. Everything in us that cries out in resistance to an end comes from an innate sense that we were meant to be without one. Haven't we all noticed that something seems wrong and painful about "endings"? We resist them furiously because a longing for "always" is set in our hearts.

Surely you have heard hints of eternity from your own heart at one time or another. Share an example.

_____

_____

Though our bodies are temporal, our souls are eternal, and our hearts testify continually to "forevers." This is true for the redeemed and unredeemed alike. All normal people long for a life without end and a love that doesn't end. For those who trust in Jesus Christ, the end of earthly life means only a change of wardrobe, from an earthly tent of flesh to a body fit for eternity. Our longing hearts will find their fulfillment in Christ. When at last our grip is peeled off the tree limb, we'll wonder why we ever hung on. Strangely, we hang on to this life in our hidden longing for the next. *El Olam* set eternity in our hearts.

Day Five
To Mourn for Sarah

Today's Treasure
She died at Kiriath Arba (that is, Hebron) in the land of Canaan, and Abraham went to mourn for Sarah and to weep over her.
Genesis 23:2

Genesis 22 carries the most critical implications in the entire patriarch story, so I will save that chapter for video session 3. I want to work through it with you face-to-face rather than on paper. Our study today will center on Genesis 23. I'll have you read it in a moment.

Permit me to get something out of my system. Between two very sober subject matters is a paragraph that provides at least a grin. Glance ahead to Genesis 22:20-24, verses naming Nahor's sons (Abraham's nephews). I'd hate for you to miss the first two. Their names were Uz and Buz. I'm sorry, but that's more than I can pass up. Somehow in the midst of names like Pildash, Jidlaph, and Bethuel—all of which drive my spell check crazy—Uz and Buz are a tad unexpected. They remind me of my older daughter's cat named Bill. Once God instituted the rite of circumcision, ancient Hebrews through the ages named their sons on the eighth day. What in the world would make a father look in the face of a tiny, squirming infant and announce proudly and loudly, "His name is Buz!" Must have been the haircut.

Believe me, you'll be glad to have had a moment's respite when you see our subject matter. Please familiarize yourself with Genesis 22, so you'll keep the narrative in chronological order. Then carefully read Genesis 23, our Scriptures for today.

What is the subject matter of Genesis 23?

_____

_____

 Many of us have buried loved ones. Which part of this scene sparks a memory that causes you to relate? Why?

_____

_____

Keep that question and your answer in mind as we explore these verses. The conclusion of yesterday's lesson provides a fitting backdrop to consider Sarah's death. We read that Sarah lived to be 127 years old. She enjoyed 37 years of life after Isaac, her laughter, bounced into the world. What more could Abraham have asked? And, yet, when her labored breathing grew shallow and then still, he grieved with everything in him. Eternity was set in his heart, making such an end feel unnatural and painful, even after so long. I have come to the conclusion that length of marriage makes a spouse harder rather than easier to lose.

My beloved mentor, Marge Caldwell, and her dear husband, Chuck, will both turn 90 this year. They have been married for nearly 70 years. Can you even imagine? I have never known a couple more in love and better suited for one another. I've had the joy of sitting next to them in many church services, and one of the memories I'll cherish forever is their partnership in worship.

You see, some years ago physicians diagnosed Chuck with macular degeneration. All who love him were devastated because his life was still so full of physical activity. He was a student of God's Word and often joined Marge in speaking and teaching. He was a great golfer with the energetic gait of a much younger man. He dearly loved to read. I feel sure this degenerating disability has been excruciating for him, but I can't tell you for a fact because he's courageously taken it in stride. He hears for Marge, and she sees for him. Marge and Chuck insist on coming to contemporary worship—no small commitment considering many songs are unfamiliar, and he can't read the screens. No matter. Marge simply reads him the lines, and then he sings them. I'm about to cry picturing it. Mind you, the delay keeps him singing about a line behind, but who around him can be anything but blessed?

I've tried to picture which one of them should go first. Do you ever do anything so ridiculous, as if the decision is up to us? Thankfully, it's not. I can't picture either of them without the other.

> **Do you know a couple who have been together so long you can't picture them apart? Share who they are and something special about them.**

_____

_____

As we study Genesis 23, we don't see a man exercising mere cultural practices and rituals of mourning. We see a man who is grieving.

> **In the margin, underline the two things Abraham went to do.**

> **Wouldn't you agree that weeping is just one expression of mourning? Think about it for a moment. What are some other expressions?**

_____

_____

She died at Kiriath Arba (that is, Hebron) in the land of Canaan, and Abraham went to mourn for Sarah and to weep over her.
Genesis 23:2

You may be familiar with ancient practices like rending garments, but I'm not talking about rituals. I'm talking about honest to goodness compulsory grief. Not something we plan. Something we just *do* because we can't help ourselves. As Genesis 23:2 tells us, Abraham's mourning involved various bouts of tears. You know the kind. You cry until you're certain you have no more tears and then a few hours later, they wash over you like a flood. You wonder where on earth they're coming from. Abraham's mourning also meant staring out into space, experiencing moments of nothingness ... of meaninglessness ... even though a son nearby would have begged to differ. In the early moments of loss, nothing we have can quite make up for what we've lost. Only time and healing can bring back our realization of all we have to live for. Early grief steals our world as if nothing and no one else ever existed.

Part of Abraham's mourning surely also involved a loss of appetite. Picture his relatives standing over him saying, "You haven't eaten a bite in days, Abraham. You've got to keep up your strength." And the bereaved wants to respond, "Why? Why should I?" As old as Abraham was, he probably wondered why he wanted to live. Another part of his mourning was probably getting angry with someone ... anyone. Maybe even the weather. After all, have you ever felt like the only appropriate weather after a death should be rain? How dare the sun come out! And how dare someone laugh in the next room? Then one of the relatives probably tried to comfort Abraham, and he thought to himself, "Oh, please. You never even liked her. Don't act pious now."

But Abraham wouldn't have been nearly as hard on the relatives for any mistreatment of Sarah as he would have been on himself. She'd put up with so much, after all. You and I know this drill all too well, don't we? We think of every thoughtless and ugly thing we've ever done when a loved one dies. Abraham couldn't have been an exception. Don't think for a moment he didn't replay the scene when Sarai hugged her family goodbye and followed him out of the only home she'd known in Ur. She probably sobbed for days. Don't think he didn't replay the inexcusable risk he took with Sarai when he insisted she tell the Pharaoh she was Abraham's sister.

Then there was that whole ordeal with Hagar. Have you ever covered your ears to stop hearing accusing voices, but you can't silence them because they're in your own head? I imagine when Abraham's mind turned to the scene of this sin he did something just like that. Yes, an heir through Hagar had been Sarai's idea, but wasn't it because she was desperate and felt like such a failure? *Shouldn't I (Abraham) have refused the plan but embraced my wife for her willingness to step aside as the obvious hindrance?*

Can you think of other dimensions to Abraham's mourning? If so, please share.

_____

_____

The many faces of mourning. The human heart and mind are as complex emotionally as they are physiologically, and nothing makes them more vulnerable than grief. A good reason supports the common counsel to make as few big decisions as possible at a time of grief: the bereaved are painfully easy to take advantage of. Look back at the scene, and we'll see further proof that Abraham wasn't just going through the motions of ritual mourning. Reread verses 3 and 4. Can you almost hear the panic?

 What does Abraham tell the Hittites he needs?

_____

Sarah's death could not possibly be the first in their clan since reaching Canaan. Over 60 years have passed. They have undoubtedly lost loved ones as well as trusted servants and employees. Forgive my crudeness, but up until now any dirt would do. Not for Abraham's Sarah, however. Not for the Princess.

"The Hittites replied to Abraham, 'Sir, listen to us. You are a mighty prince among us. Bury your dead in the choicest of our tombs.' " (Gen. 23:6).

Prince. Perhaps God's words echoed in Abraham's mind, " 'As for Sarai your wife, you are no longer to call her Sarai; her name will be Sarah. I will bless her and will surely give you a son by her' " (Gen. 17:15-16). God appointed Abraham the task of telling Sarai she had a new name. Perhaps she asked what it meant, or maybe she already knew: princess. Sarah was the most beautiful woman Abraham had ever seen. He was so captivated by her beauty that he obsessed with fear that someone would kill him to have her. Despite their every faithless act, God proved faithful.

Finally, Sarah's middle rounded with promise, and Laughter was on his way. Abraham remembered how scared he had been that she wouldn't live through the birth, but God strengthened her to deliver. Now she was gone. Genesis 23:3 could suggest he held her close trying to keep her body from growing cold. Then a realization hit him like a lightning bolt: "I have no place to bury her!"

Abraham wanted a burial site. Not a hole in the ground. He wanted something worthy of a princess. Yes, God had promised his descendants the land, but Abraham did not personally own an acre of it.

Fill in the blanks according to Genesis 23:3-4.

"[Abraham] said, 'I am an _____ and a _____ among you. Sell me some property for a burial site here so I can bury my dead.' "

His first description, *alien,* means what you might imagine: foreigner or sojourner. The second word, *stranger,* has a more vivid original definition: "settler, inhabitant, foreigner, emigrant. Essentially denotes a squatter who could not possess land, a sojourner in a foreign country where he was not naturalized."[18] As wealthy and respected as Abraham was in the land, at the moment he felt like a squatter with nothing to call his own and nowhere to bury his dead.

What was the amazing response of the Hittites (vv. 5-6)?

_____

At the Hittites' suggestion, Abraham remembered a piece of land with a cave that would be fitting for Sarah's burial. The land belonged to Ephron who initially told Abraham he'd gladly give him the land. Perhaps Ephron was honorable, or perhaps he knew that Abraham would never consent to receiving the land gratis.

Glance back at Genesis 14:23-24. What was Abraham's basic attitude about receiving something free of charge?

_____

Abraham had a reputation for refusing gifts from pagan nations. His honor as a husband was also at stake in the manner by which he'd pay his last respects. (Emphasis on *pay*.) This burial site would be his final gift to his princess. Should it cost him nothing?

Though the Hittites as a whole were honorable to Abraham, I tend to think Ephron gambled that the old patriarch's emotions would forbid him to accept the gift. My basis? He immediately turned around and quoted Abraham a worth of 400 shekels of silver, an exorbitant price. I believe Ephron played with Abraham's emotions when he said after quoting the price, "But what is that between me and you?" Translation: "Rich man that you are, Abraham, surely you'd spend such pittance on your beloved wife." In her commentary on *The Message of Genesis*, Old Testament scholar Joyce Baldwin writes, "Ephron did well out of the deal, and probably enjoyed telling generations to come how naïve Abraham was over money."[19]

You see, ancient never means irrelevant. In many respects Solomon was right when he said "there is nothing new under the sun" (Eccl. 1:9). How many grief-stricken loved ones have accrued a mountain of debt because their emotions talked them into paying their last respects exorbitantly? Four hundred shekels of silver did not leave Abraham in debt, but his obvious willingness to pay far more than the land's probable worth offers a relevant application for us today. Perhaps a fitting summation might be the following: the higher the emotions—for whatever reason—the deeper the need for counsel.

At the conclusion of Abraham's story, we'll find that this piece of land with the burial cave constitutes the only bit of property Abraham actually possessed as personal owner. Eventually, he, Isaac, and Jacob would all be buried there, but on that sad day, Abraham left his princess bride there alone.

---

[1] L.E. Goodman, 1996. Preface to *God of Abraham*. New York: Oxford University Press.

[2] F. B. Meyer, *Abraham or The Obedience of Faith* (Grand Rapids: Zondervan Publishing House, 1953), 116.

[3] Spiros Zodhiates et al., eds., *The Complete Word Study Dictionary: New Testament* (Chattanooga, TN: AMG Publishers, 1992), 1059.

[4] Ibid., 113.

[5] Ibid., 2355-56.

[6] Ibid., 2358.

[7] Bruce K. Waltke, *Genesis: A Commentary* (Grand Rapids: Zondervan, 2001), 294.

[8] Victor P. Hamilton, *The Book of Genesis: Chapters 18-50* (Grand Rapids: William B. Eerdman's Publishing, 1995), 79.

[9] Ibid., 81.

[10] Ibid., 83.

[11] Ibid., 83.

[12] Ibid., 83.

[13] Hamilton, 86.

[14] Zodhiates, 2317.

[15] Hamilton, 89-90.

[16] Zodhiates, 2347.

[17] Hamilton, 92.

[18] Zodhiates, 2380.

[19] Joyce G. Baldwin, *The Message of Genesis 12-50: From Abraham to Joseph* (Downers Grove, IL: Inter-Varsity Press, 1986), 95.

SESSION THREE
Triumphs and Tests

1. Our _____ have our _____ on them (v. 1). The Hebrew word

   for *tested* means "to test, try, _____, ... Generally carries the idea of testing the

   _____ of someone or something through _____ _____."

   Possible meaning for *Moriah:* My _____ is _____.

2. Our _____ tests involve our _____ _____.

   The Hebrew word for *love* means "to love, desire, to _____, ... Implies an ardent

   and _____ inclination of the _____ and a _____ of

   affection at the same time ... a strong emotional attachment for and a desire to _____

   __ or be in the _____ of the object of love."

3. We are not _____ in our tests. _____ we take them is _____ _____

   to _____. The Hebrew *na* is called the "particle of _____" and is used by

   God only in issues of _____ importance often defying "_____

   explanation or _____." Abraham's only recorded words to God in the chapter:

   "_____ I _____" (Heb. 10:7).

4. _____ is not the hardest part of our most trying tests. _____

   the _____ can be hardest of all.

5. Like Abraham, we're likely to discover that the _____ the _____,

   the _____ reaching the ramifications (vv. 15-18).

   • The Gospel was _____ beforehand in the promise and _____

   beforehand on the mountain.

   • The place was commemorated by the name "The _____ Will _____."

   • The Hebrew word for "provide" also means _____ _____.

   The Vulgate: In the mountain the LORD _____.

   Septuagint: In the mountain the LORD is _____.

WEEK FOUR
Eyes on Isaac

Our fourth week of study offers a brief reprieve from last week's emotional roller coaster. For the most part it captures the gentler side of family. This is a good time to remind you that the study of the patriarchs is for everyone. You may be married, widowed, single, or childless. On the other hand, you may be the old woman who lived in the shoe with so many children she didn't know what to do. Let God speak to your heart even at times when the Scriptures highlight a relationship you don't share. We will undoubtedly behold romance in our journey through Genesis but even if your life lacks romance, God can still speak volumes to you. Let's not cut ourselves off from the study of anything we feel we're missing. You and I don't want to develop hardened hearts. Let's stay alive to all things life. You never know what God may have awaiting you in the future. As you study, keep an eye out for answers to these principal questions:

This Week's Principal Questions

Day 1: What sign did the servant request according to Genesis 24:12-14?

Day 2: In what ways do you see a typical big brother expressed in Laban's actions?

Day 3: What blessing was spoken over Rebekah as they sent her on her way?

Day 4: What does a comparison of Genesis 15:15 and 25:8 suggest to you?

Day 5: What occasion was Isaac and Ishmael's last recorded encounter (Gen. 21:8-10)?

Day One'
A Jar on Her Shoulder

A crucial shift takes place in our study today. Scripture makes numerous references to the Lord as *the God of Abraham, Isaac, and Jacob*. As our subtitle *Encountering the God of Abraham, Isaac, and Jacob* suggests, our chief goal in exploring the lives of the patriarchs is to deepen our relationship with the One who calls Himself their God. Throughout our first three weeks of study, the spotlight has shone on Abraham. Today the emphasis shifts to events concerning the second patriarch: Isaac, beloved son of Abraham and Sarah.

One of the most appealing elements God used to draw me to the patriarch story was the emphasis on family. I am a family person. My guess is that you probably are as well. We don't have to be married with children to love family. Some of the most family-oriented people I know are single adults deeply involved in their parents', nephews', or nieces' lives. My friend Lisa Weir is a great example. She is a gifted assistant principal at a middle school; between her sister and brother she has six nieces, and you'll often find at least one of them in her arms. I see them as often with their Aunt Lisa as I see them with their parents.

We also don't have to come from particularly healthy families to place a high premium on family relationships. Part of the draw of Abraham, Isaac, and Jacob's family saga will be our ability to relate to their complexities, weaknesses, and even dysfunctions. You and I can be glad and relieved that God is willing to associate His great name with individuals and families that clearly don't have it all together.

Today's Treasure

Before he had finished praying, Rebekah came out with her jar on her shoulder. She was the daughter of Bethuel son of Milcah, who was the wife of Abraham's brother Nahor.

Genesis 24:15

Day One'
A Jar on Her Shoulder
Day Two'
This Is from the Lord
Day Three'
He Loved Her
Day Four'
Longing for a Better Country
Day Five'
Ishmael and Isaac

Before we get into our text today, quickly glance at Romans 15:13. What is God called in this passage?

_____

Hope always points to the future. This title of God assures us that in Him our future can always be dramatically different from our past.

Today we get to bask in the beginning of a peculiar love story that will bill Isaac as our leading man in the next stage of our drama. Genesis 24 is the longest chapter in the book of beginnings—67 verses. We'll spend three full days exploring its subject matter.

Read Genesis 24:1-9 and note Abraham's concern below.

_____

How do Abraham and his servant swear their oath?

_____

"I will make you into a great nation and I <u>will</u> <u>bless</u> you."
Genesis 12:2

Abraham was now old and well advanced in years, and the LORD <u>had</u> <u>blessed</u> him in every way.
Genesis 24:1

The Jewish Study Bible suggests that the unfolding of Genesis 24 "functions as Abraham's deathbed scene" in certain ways, "recapitulating the promise that impelled him on his course."[1] Be blessed by a comparison of verb tenses.

Read the verses in the margin, paying special attention to the underlined words.

Will bless. Years later, *had blessed.* The Lord our God will always prove faithful. If He promises to bless, bless He will.

🐫 **Beloved, how does Ephesians 1:3 relate the concept of blessing to you?**

_____

I believe that as it did in the life of Abraham, obedience to God causes many of those imputed blessings to become imparted blessings in our walk here on Planet Earth. As we walk in obedience to God, our final testimonies will prove that we have been blessed in every way. Without exception, every area of my life has been affected positively by a growing intimacy with God. When we seek to be fully His, blessing overflows the walls of our compartmentalized lives.

Now let's consider the peculiar sign of the oath the servant swore to Abraham. In both Genesis 46:26 and Exodus 1:5 the Scripture uses the Hebrew word *yarek* which our English translations render as *descendants. Yarek* means *thigh.*[2] This wording explains the action ratifying the oath between Abraham and his servant. Descendants were said to come from the thigh of a man as a generalization encompassing the obvious.

When Amanda was two and a half, I explained to her that I was carrying a new baby "in my tummy." The expression was a kinder and gentler generalization that helped me avoid more literal anatomical terms. *Thigh* is used much the same way in the ratification of an oath concerning offspring.

The word translated *servant* in Genesis 24:2 is *zeqan*, literally meaning *old*, hence *senior*. In contrast, the Genesis 22:13 reference to the servants that accompanied Abraham and Isaac to Mount Moriah comes from the Hebrew *nearim* meaning *young*. [3]

> **Put yourself in Abraham's position and list several reasons why you might prefer an older servant to a younger one to choose a spouse for your child.**

_____

_____

Abraham was determined that Isaac marry a Semite woman or, more pointedly, an Aramean as opposed to a Canaanite. *The Jewish Study Bible* contends that "intermarriage with the Canaanites" would present a "lethal threat to Abraham's identity and destiny."[4]

> **Now read Genesis 24:10-28. What did the servant take "from his master" (v. 10)?**

_____

> **What were among those "good things" (v. 22)?**

_____

The 10 camels and all sorts of luxuries including jewelry served as part of the *mohar* or *bride price*. The New Testament refers to Christians as the Bride of Christ.

> **According to Ephesians 5:25 what bride price did our Groom pay?**

_____

Christ paid the ultimate bride price with His very life. He also lavished us in spiritual gifts (1 Cor. 12). The wedding and marriage imagery is as stunning as a radiant bride in both the Old and New Testaments. In our present study alone we should be impressed that God inspired no fewer than 67 verses about the union between Isaac and Rebekah.

> **What sign did the servant request from God (Gen. 24:12-14)?**

_____

This was no small request, mind you. Each camel could drink 25 gallons of water. The servant requested something highly unlikely as a sign from God.

> **According to Genesis 24:15, how soon did Rebekah appear in the scene in answer to the servant's prayer?**
> ❏ just after he finished
> ❏ before he finished praying
> ❏ before he started the prayer

Oh, for the words *before he had finished praying* to apply to some of our own requests! Could any of us ask for more wonderful timing?

What does Isaiah 65:23-24 say relating to our passages today?

_____

Beloved, God hears the prayers of His children. Please note something very important. In the scene at the spring between Abraham's servant and Rebekah, not only did the answer come, but the action fulfilling the answer also came. I believe far more often than not God answers our prayers immediately though we may not see the fulfillment with our own eyes until much later. We sometimes ask, "God, why won't You answer me?" Often He has answered, but the fulfillment is still on His "items yet to be completed according to His sovereign and wise plan" list. If we could only find peace and security in knowing that God is good for His word! Though the action tarries, it shall come.

How does Genesis 24:16 describe Rebekah?

_____

I so wish I had been a virgin when I married. God meant virginity to be a precious gift. Because of my history of both victimization and sin, I did not at all feel beautiful on my wedding day. Keith hates for me to say such a thing, but I remember vividly the emotions I felt that day. Perhaps you have a similar past or maybe, though you remained pure, you struggle with feeling beautiful. Dear, Dear One, Christ answers both of those needs. Through His glorious forgiveness, redemption, and refinement, we can joyfully be presented as "virgins" (2 Cor. 11:2). Emotionally, mentally, and spiritually, my virginity has undoubtedly been restored as one of the sweetest works of God's redemption in my life. I feel an innocence and purity now that was totally foreign to me even in my elementary school years. And what about feeling beautiful?

Look at Ephesians 5: 26-27. How will Christ present us to Himself?
(Check all that apply.)

❑ wealthy ❑ without wrinkle ❑ without blemish
❑ holy ❑ skilled ❑ young
❑ radiant ❑ without stain ❑ blameless

You see, Christ makes us beautiful. I love Eugene Peterson's paraphrase of Ephesians 5:26 in *The Message*: "His words evoke her beauty." Sweet sister, even as you sit and study this lesson today, God's words are evoking your beauty. As you stare into your Bible and take in what He says, the light of God's Word reflects off your face and you become radiant. Imagine Christ looking at His Father right this moment and saying, "Isn't she gorgeous?"

Instead of thinking, "He couldn't possibly," why don't you choose to take the compliment you've overheard personally and say out loud, "Thank you"? Perhaps about now you're wishing others could see some of that beauty. They will if they haven't already! Ecclesiastes 8:1 says "wisdom brightens a ... face and changes its hard appearance." You will never have a beauty secret with more visible results than the study of God's Word. Let His word evoke your beauty daily.

Let's conclude with a last glance at Genesis 24. How did Abraham's servant assume Rebekah was the one for Isaac? (Hint: the requested sign)

_____

Imagine the servant's joy. Don't you know he could hardly believe his eyes? Try to remember the last time you felt you'd come face-to-face with answered prayer. What a glorious spiritual high! The servant's eyes beheld God's answer. She was the one! Rebekah is the subject of 11 action verbs in these verses. The servant's answer from God became action indeed.

Today's segment of Scripture (Gen. 24:1-28) concludes with two touching scenes. Describe the servant's concluding actions (vv. 26-27).

_____

Describe Rebekah's concluding actions (v. 28):

_____

I wish we'd been invited into the scene between Rebekah and her mother's household. Since Rebekah's father appears to be alive, according to a later reference in the chapter, Scripture's emphasis on her mother's household may suggest that Rebekah couldn't wait to tell the women in the family. Her mother's household may have included any sisters, aunts, and female servants in the family in addition to her mother. (Why she wouldn't want to run with the news straight to Uncles Uz and Buz just isn't that hard to understand.) Let's face it. Women like the enthusiasm of other women. It's that pep-squad mentality.

Day Two
This Is from the Lord

Much of the second segment of Genesis 24 we'll study today is the servant's recap of earlier events. We'll read those verses momentarily. The recap affords space in our lesson to muse a little further over our introduction to Rebekah in day 1. Let's begin today's discussion with a quick review.

Glancing back at yesterday's text, what was the sign the servant asked God to grant him to affirm the choice for Isaac's bride?

_____

The sign the servant requested would be a sure indication of hospitality. No doubt the senior servant wanted to pick a bride who seemed a perfect fit with the courtesy of his own master. We ourselves caught a glimpse of Abraham's hospitality in his reception of the three visitors (Gen. 18). I believe the servant sought the character of his master's household

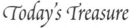

Today's Treasure
Laban and Bethuel answered, "This is from the LORD; we can say nothing to you one way or the other."
Genesis 24:50

minimalist

one who expends the least possible effort to achieve a desired goal

in a prospective bride. Having no idea who the servant was or what was at stake, Rebekah served far beyond the normal expectation.

Earlier today I encountered a frustration I'm beginning to think God may have allowed to remind me how much God values excellence. I am concerned that the maximum-load mentality of our culture could potentially turn us into minimalists. We're growing too exhausted to go the extra mile. Sometimes we do only what we must to get by on a project because we have 15 other projects nipping at our heels. We're pushed too hard and too fast to go the extra distance excellence demands. Even in church work we are often thrown into so many activities and responsibilities that we don't take the time to allow the Holy Spirit to develop our spiritual gifts.

Do you ever feel like a minimalist? I do! Name two ways you could realistically incorporate balance in your life.

_____

We aren't in danger of becoming minimalists because we want to. We're in danger of becoming minimalists because maximum overload causes minimum effectiveness. Who can take an extra step with the loads we carry? In the spirit of Genesis 24, we're balancing 10 jars on our shoulders instead of one, and each jar holds an ounce of water. Had Rebekah been like us, the scenario might have gone more like this:

The servant hurried to meet her and said, "Please give me a little water from your jar."

Rebekah answered, "Which jar? If you could count, you'd know I have 10. And, anyway, each of them has only a few drops. If I give you a drink, what am I supposed to have left?" (Drama escalates.) "You're killing me here, buddy. Trying to drain me to the dregs? Take, take, take! That's all people like you want to do! Well, I have more to do than wait on you, you old coot. I've got to get back to camp and juggle jars. Make yourself useful and give me a ride to my tent on one of those camels. My back is killing me."

Somehow I think our culture's Rebekah would have returned to camp with one less nose ring, having no idea that the greatest opportunity of her life was on the other side of that extra mile. I'm just having a little fun with you while offering some food for thought. Minimalists are among the very last things you and I want to be as followers of Jesus Christ.

Proceed by reading Genesis 24:29-51. Who is Laban?
❏ Rebekah's father ❏ Rebekah's brother ❏ Rebekah's uncle

 This is our first introduction to Laban. He will soon play a major role in our story line. In what ways does Laban express …

typical big-brother actions? _____

less than typical actions for a big brother? _____

Let's first take a good look at Abraham's servant in action. As you can see, most of today's Scripture segment is the servant's recap of the events that brought him to Laban's home. No one can accuse the old servant of being a minimalist, that's for sure. His example of excellence in his task is well worth a few notes. Consider how Abraham's servant …

Took on his master's burden as if it were his own. In today's vernacular, the servant "owned" the task, performing it as thoroughly and excellently as he would have for his own son. Through the narrative of Genesis 24, you and I are able to watch the servant in his master's absence. He remained true to his master's call in every detail.

Prioritized the matter with fervent prayer for success. Success meant finding the right bride for Isaac, and the servant respected that God alone knew who she was.

Please note the added description of the servant's prayer in verse 45. According to the NIV, how did the servant pray?

_____

> Before I finished praying in my heart, Rebekah came out, with her jar on her shoulder. She went down to the spring and drew water, and I said to her, "Please give me a drink."
> **Genesis 24:45, NIV**

The wording "in my heart" suggests that he prayed silently and deeply. Don't pass over the detail quickly. The servant knew "the God of [his] master Abraham" could read his thoughts and had the power and willingness to answer the prayers of his heart as readily as the prayers of his mouth. In a polytheistic world, the servant had to have known there was no god like Abraham's.

The servant possessed remarkable enthusiasm for the success of his master's mission. After a long and difficult journey, the servant refused the food spread out before him until he could recount every detail (v. 33). In our me-centered society, how often do we become completely enthused about a project that is not essentially about us? The old servant wasn't looking for a wife for his own son. He had nothing to gain from the mission except to please his master and keep his oath.

Me-centeredness is so powerful and prevalent in our society that if we don't deliberately fight it we will undoubtedly live it. Our church work and various expressions of personal ministries will be no exceptions. John Maxwell doesn't believe in something the world calls business ethics. In his opinion, we can't turn ethics on and off in our personal and business lives. We either have ethics or we don't. I think he's right; if he is, our attitudes out in the secular world also permeate our attitudes in our serving life. If we're me-centered in our business and personal lives, we'll be me-centered in our serving lives—no matter how hard we try to keep ourselves cloaked in false humility.

If you're not practicing this approach already, I'd like to challenge you to do something God has made a priority for me in recent years. He directs me to sow seeds of active prayer, physical service, and giving in several ministries and service organizations that have nothing to do with me. A big world surrounds us with many needs and countless faithful ministries. I have to ask myself, "Am I only enthusiastic and giving to efforts that involve me?" Deliver me, Lord!

In what ways has God placed you in a position to move outside "me-ism" and serve unselfishly and enthusiastically like Abraham's servant?

_____

For the remainder of the lesson, let's take a good look at Genesis 24:50. I hope Laban's response caught your attention when you first read it. Paraphrase his response in your own words.

_____

Genesis 24:50-51 says, "This is from the Lord; we have no choice in the matter. Rebekah is here in front of you. Take [her] and go" (HCSB).

Sometimes God reveals His will so dramatically and obviously that all we have left to do is bow to Him. Opinions don't matter. Votes are inappropriate. God has revealed His will, and that's that. Any of us who have any lengthy history with God have most likely experienced occasions when God clearly revealed His will. The most memorable times probably involved a revelation of God's will that might have painfully differed from our own. Let's not minimize the personal cost of the marriage to Bethuel's family. Certainly they wanted Rebekah to marry and to marry well, but certainly they would have preferred to keep her nearby.

In hopes of jogging your memory concerning one of your own Genesis 24:50 moments, I'll tell one of mine. Just last night I shared a story about my older daughter with someone who sweetly pointed out I'd shared it the day before. She then said, "You must miss her so much." I quickly excused myself before I burst into tears. Yes, I do miss her. As I shared earlier in our video sessions, Amanda and my beloved son-in-law Curt are serving in ministry in the United Kingdom for five months. Frankly, it may only be the first of many opportunities to send them or our other daughter abroad. In the weeks leading to their departure many people asked, "How do you feel about Amanda and Curt leaving?"

Long before I studied this chapter of Scripture, I had a Genesis 24:50 moment: I just didn't know exactly how to word it. I didn't give myself room to have an opinion. We didn't sit down and take a family vote. My son-in-law is a mature believer who hears from his heavenly Father. God made His will clear. The only position Keith and I were to take was that of bowing in obedience; our only words were to be words of blessing. As Christians, we simply had no other choice than to be obedient. God also made clear that He meant for Keith and me to be joyful about their service—even in our tears.

> **One of my recent memory verses is Psalm 40:8. You might find it useful as well. Write it on a card and begin to memorize it.**

I want my children to do God's will even if their obedience takes them far from their mother's arms, and I want to send them forth guilt-free. I've never been prouder of Amanda, and if she can leave the comforts of everything familiar to her, the least I can do is support her. Amanda has been a great joy to me, and I had the privilege of working with her every weekday here at Living Proof. The sense of her absence is constant. God is teaching me, however, to rejoice in placing this small sacrifice before Him as a way to love and serve Him. It is my (painful!) privilege.

How about you? Describe your own Genesis 24:50 moment, and be prepared to share it in your small group if you're willing.

_____

A revelation of God's will can spark a serious integrity issue when our personal preferences are at stake. A good friend is on a committee that is searching for a new pastor. From its beginning the entire committee pledged to be unanimous in their vote for the pastor they would recommend to their church. The committee is made up of both genders, and their ages and personality types vary. Their commitment did not require that they prefer one candidate unanimously but that they come to a unanimous vote concerning what appears to be the revealed will of God. To keep their commitment, several of the committee members will have to exercise the integrity to say, "I believe this is the man even if my personal preference leans another way."

In a world of endless options, all of us long for God to make His will crystal clear. But today's lesson is a reminder that certainty doesn't always erase difficulty. I am so honored to serve you, Dear One. Let's keep bowing even when we're bawling.

Day Three'
He Loved Her

I so wish we could watch today's scenes on video together. I'd personally pop the corn and pour the Coke®, but you'd have to keep the remote control or I'd push pause every few seconds for discussion. The narratives in God's Word are as rich and captivating as any great novel. The authenticity of these stories makes them all the better and proves—at least to me—that God Himself is a romantic.

We will study the remainder of Genesis 24 today, but let's read it in two parts to let the drama build. First read Genesis 24:52-60. Many scholars believe the senior servant Abraham sent on this mission was Eliezer of Damascus who is mentioned in Genesis 15:2-4. If so, how special had he been to Abraham based on a review of those verses?

Whether or not the senior servant in Genesis 24 was Eliezer, his age indicates he'd been in Abraham's service for many years. I am touched by the depth of his own relationship with the Lord and the worship he demonstrated in Genesis 24:52.

How did the old servant respond to God after Laban and Bethuel agreed to let Rebekah become Isaac's wife (v. 52)?

The Hebrew word *hawah* means *to prostrate oneself . . . worship.*[5] As you picture this scene, imagine the old man going to his knees, perhaps even to his face. Surely the God of Abraham was also the God of the servant. I daresay God esteems the worship of no one more than that of a devoted servant, particularly one who is cloaked in anonymity and who is known only as *his Master's.*

After worshipping his faithful God, Abraham's servant presented the family with a lavish dowry. A celebratory dinner took place and all turned in for the night. Can you imagine Rebekah getting a wink of sleep? She knew nothing about the man she would marry except that they came from the same "stock" as my grandmother might say. The custom of marrying someone sight unseen has been practiced widely. Still, I can hardly imagine it. I fear my mind would be inundated with *what ifs.*

Today's Treasure

Isaac brought her into the tent of his mother Sarah, and he married Rebekah. So she became his wife, and he loved her.

Genesis 24:67

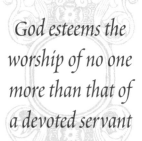

God esteems the worship of no one more than that of a devoted servant

How about you? List several *what ifs* you would have in Rebekah's position.

_____

_____

_____

I couldn't agree more! And I could add a few! *What if* he doesn't like dogs? *What if* he has no teeth? *What if*—this is a big one, girls—he snores? I already loved Keith before he started waking the dead with his snoring. I don't know if I could have stood it from the first night. Don't you wish we were chatting face-to-face about this right now? What fun we'd have!

Speaking of fun, get a load of Genesis 24:54-55. Abraham's servant awakened with a one-track mind: "Send me on my way to my master." After all, Abraham was old, and the servant wanted to present this new bride to him and relish his master's joy. Every true servant lives to hear, "Well done!"

Instead, after the initial response with submission to God's will, what request appears in verse 55?

_____

Look carefully for the key to the change of heart. According to verse 55, who entered the picture?

"Her brother and her _____ replied … "

The mother! She obviously decided they needed to keep Rebekah for another 10 days or so. I love the "or so" part. I'm a mom who can picture this moment vividly. I loved planning for Amanda's wedding and having our own Cinderella Ball the evening she and Curt were married. I didn't even mind sending them off for their honeymoon, but when they returned I suddenly developed an unexpected feeling. I felt like she should come back home for a while. We'd grow her up a bit more, wait until we were tired of her, and maybe—in 10 days, 10 years *or so*—give her back to Curt. A mama needs a little time! How much, a man may ask? A little bit more.

Please note who cast the deciding vote according to verses 57-58.
❑ Bethuel, the father ❑ Laban, the brother ❑ Rebekah, herself

This point is important. From the time Abraham first issued instructions to his servant, coercion was clearly out of the question. If the woman did not want to come with the servant, Abraham clearly stated that the servant was released from the oath (24:8). Remember how important "firsts" are in the study of God's Word. We will witness Isaac and Rebekah's imminent marriage as the first in the line through which God chose to bless all nations. Abraham and Sarah were already married when God called Abraham. I believe we see a conceptual precedent God set through the direction of His "friend," Abraham. Prospective wives were to be respected and asked. If they said "no," they were to be released. If they said "yes," the wives were to be blessed with treasures (in our application, chiefly of the heart) and treated as God's chosen gifts for their husbands—not treated as possessions.

I have a man who sees me as God intended. If you're married, I deeply hope and pray that you do, too. If you do not, go to God right now. Ask Him to change your spouse's heart and attitude toward you. Also ask what changes your heart needs for healing to come. Do not cease to ask until you receive such healing! Cry out for your marriage, Dear One!

What blessing was spoken over Rebekah as they sent her on her way (vv. 59-60)?

_____

Rebekah's family meant this blessing literally, but we as God's family can make spiritual applications. Rewrite this prayer in spiritual terms as it applies for a New Testament believer (v. 60):

_____

_____

I think one of my most important prayers is for people to bear much fruit for God's glory. When we bring people into His family together, we build spiritual tenacity to possess the gates of their (our) enemies (the devil and his dark hosts). My lexicon tells me that the city gate was where people congregated for business transactions. You can be sure the enemy and his demonic forces congregate to make all sorts of seedy business transactions. Never doubt that he's a planner. Oh, that the offspring coming from our family lines would stand so firmly against our enemies that every demonic plan would be thwarted! Lord, let it be!

Sisters, let's stop right now and pray our physical and spiritual families will stand firm. When you have prayed, check this box and proceed. ❑

Now read the remainder of Genesis 24 (vv. 61-66). Surely you see some romance in these passages. What is your favorite part?

_____

Keep in mind that Rebekah, her nurse, the old servant, and his men traveled quite a distance to reach Abraham's homestead. Certainly they'd seen other people on their journey. These roads were well established and frequented, as long-distance travelers stayed close to rivers. Even though Rebekah's entourage met any number of people along the way, I believe Scripture strongly suggests what we might call love at first sight as they approached the field where Isaac stood.

If you don't like romance, you might consider stopping right here. On the other hand, reading on might do you some good! Let's not grow cynical. God is the author of pure romance. Let's enjoy the story and perhaps even invite God to change our own. If we have to already possess something to enjoy reading about it, how do we know what to hope for? Hope pertains not only to this world but to heaven where you will no doubt have the perfect Groom. But, let's get back to our story ...

Maybe Rebekah's heart leapt suddenly as she looked in the distance, feeling somehow that the approaching stranger might be Isaac.

What was Isaac doing when he looked up and saw the camels approaching (v. 63)?

_____

The word *meditate* could simply mean thinking or even roaming about, but it could also be a form of a verb that means praying. Keith's very religious grandmother went to her grave thinking her grandson and I met at church. We met at a fraternity party. After he told her I was a "good Christian girl," she assumed we met at church, and he never got around to correcting her for the remaining 20 years of her life. If Keith was "meditating" when I met him, the word meant "thinking" or "roaming about." It most assuredly did not mean "praying." Isaac, however, did not belong to a fraternity and might indeed have been in a prayerful state.

What did Rebekah do when she learned the man in the distance was Isaac (v. 65)?

_____

If you don't know already, you'll be blessed to learn the common custom of veiling a bride originates right here in Genesis 24:65.[6] I learned this when I researched wedding customs for Amanda. My heart tenders as I read with you that when Rebekah saw Isaac she "took her veil and covered herself." One of my coworkers shared this morning that her husband took their grandchildren to a public place yesterday and said to her later, "I was stunned over the way young women dress these days in public!" He was embarrassed and uncomfortable with his grandchildren growing up in such a world.

My friends in the contemporary Christian group "Point of Grace" have been wildly popular among young adolescent and teenage girls. Having been entrusted by God with such a platform, the group feels called to openly address the immodesty in our culture and God's plan for all things adolescent, from wardrobes to sexuality. One of the group's mottos has been "dress classy, not trashy." I like that! Some of the girls I see out and about offer a public viewing meant by God for their husbands alone. I am saddened to say that I at times dressed immodestly in my young, desperate, and self-destructive years. We must think of ourselves as treasures of God rather than giving ourselves away flippantly and cheaply. Where is the mystery in our culture's approach? Rebekah demonstrated the mystery of modesty. That's healthy, Sisters.

The concluding verses in chapter 24 grant us another characteristic of the first wedding we get to witness in God's chosen line. Isaac "loved her." The Hebrew word is strong, teeming with joy, protection, and demonstrative affection.[7]

Let's view Isaac and Rebekah as precedent-setters. From their example, what would you like to see adopted into godly marriages?

_____

Ideally, in our opinions Isaac would have chosen his own bride, but remember that Abraham insisted, "If the woman is unwilling to come back with you, then you will be released from this oath of mine. Only do not take my son back there" (v. 8). Abraham did not want Isaac,

We must think of ourselves as treasures of God

the child of promise, enticed by the old Mesopotamian culture. With that in mind, I see a number of precedents set by Isaac and Rebekah's example: the ideal of parental blessing, prayer and the leadership of God, mutual consent, a draw of hearts toward one another, and a growing love that outlasts the romance of first sight. From where I sit, the only thing missing is her mother. Imagine Isaac saying, "We'll send for your mother in ten days, ten years or so."

I have loved studying today's lesson with you. I hope you've enjoyed it, too. I'll conclude with a fitting quote from G. K. Chesterton on marriage. Meditate on it, and I don't mean "roam around" it!

"They have invented a phrase, a phrase that is a black and white contradiction in two words—'free love'—as if a lover ever had been, or ever could be, free. It is the nature of love to bind itself, and the institution of marriage merely paid the average man the compliment of taking him at his word."[8]

Day Four
Longing for a Better Country

Life goes on, or so we're told. When a catastrophe happens, we are certain the whole world must feel the quake. Awakening to a world undisturbed and still turning can send us swinging from thinking we are the center of the universe to despairing that we might as well be invisible. We'll see today that life went on for Abraham after he buried his beloved Sarah with all his fond memories and painful regrets. Before we focus on Abraham's life after the loss, I want to direct your thoughts to another individual who felt the pangs produced from Sarah's death. Glance back at Genesis 24:67.

> How do you think Isaac's marriage soothed the loss of his mother? (Be nice, girls! I don't want to hear a word about his laundry!)

_____

_____

The night before last I dreamed about the boy Keith and I raised from the time he was 4 until he was 11. The dream was so real, so comforting, and so pleasant that my thoughts nestled with the dream's images all day long. I felt so close to him in the dream, having held him in my arms and talked to him at length. Former conflicts and confusion evaporated, and everything seemed to mend before my eyes. In the dream he was not a day older than when he moved away. I think my subconscious revised the past for the present comfort of a few dear moments. Reality was unchanged, but for a sweet while the ache was gone. Warmth and satisfaction filled its place.

No human can fix my heart or take the boy's place. But the love of my daughter Amanda's husband Curt has brought comfort, joy, and a balm to the wound like no one else. If I may shift the words of Genesis 24:67 to apply to a totally different kind of relationship, "So he became my son, and I loved him; and I was comforted after my loss."

Today's Treasure
Then Abraham breathed his last and died at a good old age, an old man and full of years; and he was gathered to his people.
Genesis 25:8

Can you apply the same concept to your own situation? Has someone else brought love, comfort, or joy to your life after a loss? (Mine wasn't a loss due to a death but a dramatic change in relationship, so I welcome you to think broadly.)

Our reading picks up after Sarah's death and concludes with Abraham's death. Please read Genesis 25:1-11. Who was Keturah?
❑ the Merchant of Venice   ❑ Abraham's second wife
❑ the captain of God's army

For whatever reason, the terms *wife* and *concubine* are sometimes used interchangeably to describe the same relationship. This is true for both Hagar and Keturah. Notice that verse 1 refers to Keturah as a *wife* while verse 6 labels her as a *concubine* (First Chron. 1:32 refers to her only as a concubine). Likewise, though Hagar is most often called "a slave girl" or "servant" in reference to Abraham and Sarah, Genesis 25:6 implies that she, too, was a *concubine* while Genesis 16:3 clearly says Sarah gave her to Abraham as a *wife*.

We don't know when Abraham and Keturah married. Scholars offer endless conjecture. We know that Abraham was 138 when Sarah died and that he lived to be 175. The 37 years following Sarah's death provided ample time to build the family described in Genesis 25:1-4. We can't help but notice that Abraham had no problem fathering other children while the conception of Isaac, the heir to the promise, required much time, faith, and hardship.

We often think receiving what we've been guaranteed ought to be a cakewalk, but Scripture shows the opposite is more often true. The most profound things God promised were often fulfilled against the greatest odds and through the most difficult hardships. To God, faith is often the point—God does nothing cheaply. Perhaps the divine nature of a promise fulfilled guarantees its expense. We may receive a hundred unexpected things from God with delightful ease while the fulfillment of some of the things we believe He promised us proves virtually impossible. You see, the impossibility is what makes the fulfillment of the promise fall under the *God category*. God makes promises man simply can't keep.

To keep Abraham's descendants straight in our minds, please fill in the following family tree based on the information in Genesis 25:1-11 alone. I've already filled in some names for you.

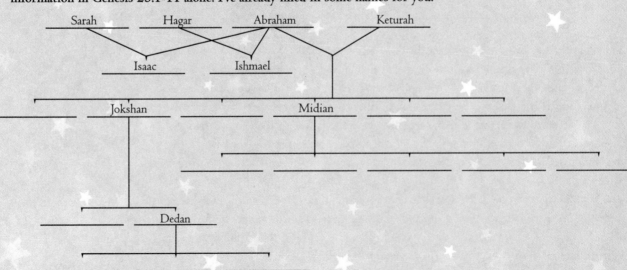

Reread verse 6. Record some reasons Abraham may have sent the sons of his concubines "away from his son Isaac to the land of the east."

_____

_____

"Altogether, Abraham lived a hundred and seventy-five years. Then Abraham breathed his last and died at a good old age, an old man and full of years" (vv. 7-8).

> Read Genesis 15:15. Check your context. Who is talking in Genesis 15:15?
> ❑ Abraham   ❑ the angel of God   ❑ the Lord Himself

🐫 What does a comparison of Genesis 15:15 and 25:8 suggest to you?

_____

Then Abraham breathed his last. My mother's last breath was a deep inhale and exhale as if she knew it would be her final taste of terrestrial air, and she didn't want to forget it. I wonder if Abraham did something similar.

> Look at Genesis 12:4 for a moment. Considering Abraham's age when he "set out from Haran" for the land of Canaan, how long did Abraham walk with God?

_____

No man is worthy of our worship, but some people are worthy of high esteem. Abraham is one of those. If man had written Scripture without divine inspiration, he would have made himself look good. However, God in His infinite wisdom made sure we saw weaknesses, frailties, and failures of those who walked with Him. God's approach guards our hearts and gives us hope. Maybe you and I haven't been terribly impressed with Abraham because we allowed several serious failures to characterize a century-long walk with God. I have had an active relationship with God for about 35 years. I'd be heartbroken for someone to characterize my entire relationship with Him based on several ugly seasons. Wouldn't you?

Whether or not we've been impressed with Abraham, I'd like to suggest that God has been. Want proof? Turn to Hebrews 11. Read the recap of Abraham's life like an obituary. Glance over the chapter and make a mental note of all the names mentioned in what is commonly called the Hebrews Hall of Faith. While each name is impressive, most of them are recognized briefly. A stunning 12 verses are dedicated to Abraham's faith. (Verses 13-16 speak directly of Abraham and also include those who accompanied or came from him.)

> Read Hebrews 11:8-19 very carefully. In the space below record every impressive detail concerning Abraham's faith-walk.

_____

_____

Try to think of an area of Abraham's life that remained unchallenged in his faith walk. He left his home, his extended family, and his occupation; he obeyed and went, even though he did not know where he was going. No man enjoys the out-of-control feeling of not knowing where he's going. Abraham's faith was tested in his marriage and so drastically in his parenting that I'm not sure I could have survived it. How about you? Hebrews 11:13-16 relates that Abraham may never have felt at home in Canaan. Something kept him "longing for a better country." (God has little intention of allowing His faithful followers to get too comfortable here.) Abraham may never have been quite sure he actually fulfilled his destiny.

We too often spiritualize the people God used mightily in His Word. As a result, we shrink back from our own callings. We picture New Testament people such as John, Peter, and Paul as spiritual giants who felt like spiritual giants. At this point in my life and ministry, I'm far more likely to picture them as insecure and unsure, scrambling at times to figure out what they were supposed to do next and wondering all the while if they were getting anything right. How amazed each of them must have been to realize in heaven that they—former flesh and blood, weak in their natural selves—had fulfilled their callings faithfully enough to receive a "Well done!" They may have tripped and wobbled along their race, but they made it across the finish line having done what they were called to do.

How did they remain so faithful? What does Hebrews 10:23 say?

_____

God is gloriously faithful, Dear One, even if at times He seems distant. When we walk with God, He affects our worlds, fulfills His promises, and births impossible Isaacs. How wise He is to hide our eyes at times from the full-range ramifications of our obedience! Who can stand an athlete or a talent once he highly esteems his own contribution? God's way is right. We are to boast in Him alone and leave the bragging on any human contribution to Him. God not only reserves bragging rights, but He also exercises them astonishingly. Before we conclude today, let's look at some bragging rights God exercised regarding Abraham.

Look up the following Scriptures and record what God said about Abraham. Three of the references include a descriptive phrase or title God gave him. Match the reference to the corresponding title. I've supplied the first answer.

Reference	What God Said	Match the Title
Romans 4:1-2	Might we say God gave Abraham credit for his faith?	Our forefather
Romans 4:18		The man of faith
Galatians 3:8-9		God's friend
Galatians 3:14, 29		
James 2:23 (Compare 2 Chron. 20:7)		

Abraham: the friend of God, the father of many nations. The one who "believed God, and it was credited to him as righteousness." And if we belong to Christ, we are Abraham's seed and "heirs according to the promise." God's eyes darted to and fro throughout the whole earth and fastened on a solitary man in a polytheistic culture. From a family with many "gods" came a man with One God ... who was many names. The LORD, *El Elyon, El Shaddai, El Olam.* His was *Jehovah Jireh,* the LORD of every provision.

Abraham is discussed as often in the New Testament as in the Old. John 8:56 tells us Abraham " 'rejoiced at the thought of seeing [Christ's] day; he saw it and was glad.' " In Christ's parable of the rich man and Lazarus, our Savior described Abraham alive and active in his eternal state. Christ painted a picture of the beggar after his death conversing at Abraham's side (see Luke 16). I often think of the wonderful conversations and timelessness that heaven will afford us—first and foremost with Christ and secondly with the faithful of other generations.

> Let's allow this exercise to provide a proper conclusion to our focus on Abraham's life: Should you find yourself sitting next to Abraham in heaven, what would you tell him you most appreciated about his story? Please be specific.

Day Five
Ishmael and Isaac

I purposely saved a very important piece of information in our previous lesson for our discussion today. For the first half of our lesson I'd like you to refocus on yesterday's segment so we can consider it from a different angle. Later we will turn our attentions toward the next segment. Reread Genesis 25:1-11. Do you recognize anything of importance that I failed to mention yesterday? Give attention to verse 9.

Who buried Abraham?
❏ Isaac   ❏ Ephron   ❏ Zohar   ❏ Ishmael   ❏ the Hittite

🐪 What occasion was Isaac and Ishmael's last recorded encounter (Gen. 21:8-10)?

Our safest assumption is that a messenger sent for Ishmael as Abraham's health began to fail. For all we know, Abraham may have asked to see him. As the end neared, Abraham's longing to gather his two oldest sons in his frail arms was probably almost as strong as death. I don't think we ever recover from parenting. No matter what kind of miles, years, or conflicts separate a parent from a child, if I may put it crudely, parenting is terminal. We take it to the grave, and at times we're fairly certain it will kill us. I used to tease my mom and tell her that her gravestone should read, "I'd like to thank my five children without whom I wouldn't be here today."

Today's Treasure
"His sons Isaac and Ishmael buried him in the cave of Machpelah near Mamre, in the field of Ephron son of Zohar the Hittite."
Genesis 25:9

Abraham loved Ishmael. The son of his unbelief became a hostile young man whose white-hot zeal burned wildly whether he was happy or angry. He never seemed to have a feeling that he didn't over-feel. The complexity of Abraham's own feelings for him probably twisted and turned in Ishmael's mind with a near obsession that never waned. Abraham loved him too much. He never loved him enough. Either way, between the Ishma and the El always dwelt the guilt.

Do you recall the agony of the boy's departure? Take a look back at Genesis 21:11 and fill in the blanks:

"The matter _____ Abraham _____

because it concerned his _____."

His son. Ishmael was the only son Abraham had for many years. He'd grown up before Abraham's eyes. The boy's father may have been old, but people still said from time to time how they favored one another. Abraham no doubt saw a change in Ishmael when the boy learned—as an adolescent—that Abraham was expecting a child through Sarah. The real son. The promised heir. Few only children handle the new baby on the scene particularly well. Imagine how the long-awaited miracle boy affected the adolescent. Hear the whispers among the servants. Sense the constant comparison. Feel the resentment rising.

By the time he was weaned, Isaac at his worst was little more than a spoiled brat, but Ishmael was old enough to bear dangerous feelings. Those feelings were betrayed by his actions at the feast and spied by the least sympathetic of all attendees: Sarah. Decades had passed when Abraham died, and Ishmael was an old man himself by our standards. By their apparent life expectancy, he was on the older side of middle age. We'd like to think all those old feelings had dissipated with time, but any of us who know someone old and bitter know better. Never forget that time by itself does nothing to heal.

Hagar and Ishmael endured a terrifying ordeal. How many times do you think Ishmael awakened through the years in a cold sweat, dreaming he was still under that thorn bush on the brink of death? How much food or water do you think he hoarded for years after nearly starving to death as a young man? Yes, his mother Hagar's divine encounter led to their miraculous rescue. And, yes, God promised to bless Ishmael and had. But how many young people do you know who have the maturity to focus on what God has done for them rather than on the injustices that they feel they suffered?

 Surely you've known someone blessed by God—even if in your mirror— who still focuses on the way he or she has been wronged. Without naming names, describe how this focus appears to affect his or her life.

_____

To say Ishmael grew old with a chip on his shoulder is probably a gross understatement. The patriarchal family was profoundly important in Ishmael's ancient culture. As you often see in God's Word, a person's entire identity was wrapped up in his or her father's. See for yourself in the following examples:

How is Joshua identified in Joshua 1:1? _____

How about Isaiah in Isaiah 1:1? _____

I can't resist asking you to look up Mark 15:39. How was the man who died

identified in this verse? _____

Let's get the feel of the ancient identity. We are usually identified by our fathers through our last or maiden names, but antiquity put an even greater emphasis on the relationship.

Personalize these blanks and imagine being known, introduced, and described exactly this way:

I am _____, daughter of _____.

Does this identity "feel" any different than simply being called by your first and last (or maiden) name? If so, how?

_____

_____

To me the difference is pretty distinct. Being called by my original (or maiden) name associates me with a family. On the other hand, being called "Beth daughter of Albert" associates me directly with my father, stirring up all sorts of emotions, and happily—at this point in my life—pleasant ones. If we did not have a good relationship or had relatively none at all, the identity would constantly knock the scab off an old wound.

Ishmael couldn't win. When his father was named, Ishmael was reminded of his absence. If his father wasn't named, Ishmael was reminded of his own anonymity. Abraham's renown reached all over the middle-eastern world. Ishmael could neither have him nor escape him. Like many sons of famous but absent fathers, Ishmael probably idolized and despised his father. Ah, one of the ironies of hostility is that it can't help but burn the vessel that holds it. As if the truth weren't bad enough, the passing years probably did little more than fan the flame. People we harbor ill feelings toward become overgrown and disfigured in our imaginations over time. Finally, they can become monstrous caricatures of their original selves.

Have you had such an experience? If so—again without naming or dishonoring the person—explain.

_____

_____

Then Ishmael stood before his elderly father's lifeless body. I remember the sobbing words of a woman who'd returned from her estranged father's funeral. "After all this time of hating him and loving him and building him up in my mind as a monster and an idol, there he was: small … lifeless." Neither dangerous as she remembered him nor glamorous as she revered him. Just innocuous. "My hatred drained from me like blood, and I stood there empty, missing the fullness of my old feelings," she said. Doesn't it seem that those who are bigger than life look all the smaller in their caskets?

As if Ishmael's grief over his dead father were not enough, Miracle-boy, Mr. Laughter, stood beside him. Let's allow our imaginations a little room here. Since we're not told how the half-brothers coped with one another's presence, let's imagine two scenarios: best- and worst-case. Most of us have been part of an extended family gathering over a central figure's death, so try to recall all the feelings—both good and bad—that tend to surface not only toward the deceased but toward one another.

Give several descriptions of what their time together might have been like ...

In the best-case scenario: _____

_____

In the worst-case scenario: _____

_____

In reality, the scenes over the days of Ishmael and Isaac's participation in their father's burial were probably an uncomfortable blend of all of the above. They probably went from competing over who felt worse and why to comforting the other as the bearer of deeper grief.

In conclusion and in preparation for video session 4, please read about Ishmael's sons on the heels of the segment describing Abraham's death: Genesis 25:12-18. So that you can experience a sense of irony, please fill in the following family tree based on the information in this segment of Scripture:

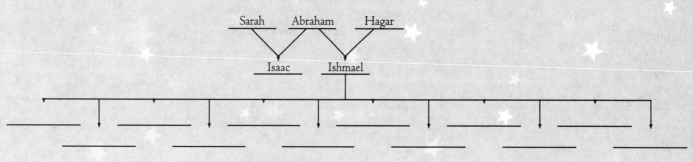

Ishmael had 12 sons. Tribal rulers, no less. At this point, Isaac, the heir from whom innumerable descendants were promised, had none.

This little piggy had roast beef, and this little piggy had none. And the one with none was the promised one. The strange, strange ways of God. Stay tuned for week 5.

[1] Adele Berlin and Marc Zvi Brettler et al., eds., *The Jewish Study Bible* (New York: Oxford University Press, 2004), 48.
[2] Spiros Zodhiates et al., eds., *The Complete Word Study Dictionary: Old Testament* (Chattanooga, TN: AMG Publishers, 1994), 52.
[3] Victor P. Hamilton, *The Book of Genesis: Chapters 18–50* (Grand Rapids, William B. Eerdman's Publishing, 1995), 138.
[4] Berlin and Brettler, 48.
[5] Zodhiates, 114.
[6] Anita Diamont, *The New Jewish Wedding* (New York: Simon and Scheuster, 2001), 81.
[7] Zodhiates, 2298.
[8] G. K. Chesterton, *The Defendant* (London: J. M. Dent and Sons, 1904), 36.

SESSION FOUR
Eyes on Isaac

The intention of our study today is to be _____ rather than _____.
Our biblical understanding, however, will lend insight to some of the political aspects of
"_____ _____" in our troubled world.

Genesis 25:12-18: Ishmael and his descendants:
- Ishmael's descendants became _____ nomads or _____.
- Ishmael had strong ties to _____ through Hagar (16:1) and his wife (21:21).

The Biblical Roots of Political Conflicts Involving Ishmael's Descendants:

1. Ishmael's _____: No matter how _____ we've been, our natural
tendency is to want the _____ we _____ _____ _____
(see Gen. 17:20). According to Dr. Ergun Caner, "The entire Islamic religion is based on making
Ishmael the _____ of the _____." Over 2200 years
after the events on Mount Moriah, Mohammed changed the character in the historical scene from
_____ to _____.

2. Ishmael's _____:
   A. Compare Genesis 16:11-12 and 25:18.
      - Genesis 16:12 reads: "And he will live in hostility toward all his _____."
      - Genesis 25:18 reads: "And _____ lived in hostility toward all _____
        _____."
   Time has an uncanny way of turning a _____ into a _____. We unearth an important
   application when we ask ourselves: What do we want our _____
   to _____ _____? Let's pursue _____ what we hope our
   _____ will _____.
   B. Islam's hostility toward Christianity.
      - Our belief system is _____ to them because they do not believe God can have
        a _____. Importantly, Mohammed also wrote in Sura (Chapter) 4:157-159 of the Koran
        that Jesus was never _____.
      - They believe Christians live in the "_____ of _____," chiefly
        because of the _____. In other words, they view us as a violent people.
        _____ individuals help break long-term _____.

We are the spiritual offspring of Abraham, and through Abraham _____ _____
are to be _____. Though nation may war with nation, individual Christians
can become part of that blessing by making our goal to _____ individual Muslims
to the _____ and _____ of Jesus Christ.

WEEK FIVE
The Heel Grabber

If you've studied any of the previous Bible studies with me, you know that we had ample time to develop strong attachments to protagonists like Moses, King David, the Apostle Paul, John the Beloved, and certainly Jesus, our One and only. The patriarchal narratives differ: they include four generations and embrace multiple characters. This week we meet the figure who will remain with us through the rest of our journey, inviting our attachment. Like many of our relational attachments, we won't always like him but we will always be intrigued by him. Meet Jacob, the grandson of Abraham. Plan to get deeply involved in his story line. If you're like me, you'll see yourself in him at times you least expect. The following principal questions will help insure that you are grasping the heel of our study this week.

This Week's Principal Questions

Day 1: What explanation did God give for Rebekah's difficult pregnancy (Gen. 25:23)?
Day 2: What fueled the rivalry between Jacob and Esau (Gen. 25:24-34)?
Day 3: How did the Lord introduce Himself to Isaac in Genesis 26:24?
Day 4: What were Rebekah's words to Jacob in Genesis 27:8?
Day 5: What impact does Hebrews 12:16 have on our understanding of Esau?

Day One
The Babies Jostled

I love nothing better than seeing a nursery worker pushing a bright red, heavy-duty, four-passenger "bye-bye buggy." With a plump-cheeked baby strapped in each seat, the buggy is a show-stopper. I don't care where I'm supposed to be or what kind of hurry I'm in, I come to a screeching halt and spill into pedia-speak. I cannot resist the sight of it. In all these years I've yet to see a baby cry in the "bye-bye buggy." They love it, and why shouldn't they? It's like an open-air school bus full of drooling peers. They're strapped in tight but acting like they've mastered a jailbreak and they're blowing the joint. They have no idea a nursery worker is pushing the cart. They think they're on their own.

Seeing that many babies overloads my maternal hormones, and I can hardly bear the joy. I say ridiculous things like, "Every last one of you come home with Biggies (my children's name for me) right this minute!" And right that minute I mean it. Then I go home to my middle-aged man where our biggest domestic demand may be deciding where to eat.

Babies galore. That's what our lesson is about today as we begin our fifth week of study with brand-new characters.

Please read Genesis 25:19-26.

What disappointment did Rebekah obviously have in common with Sarah?
❏ They both married older men.
❏ Other women were jealous of their beauty.
❏ Both were barren.

Day One
The Babies Jostled
Day Two
An Appetite for the Intermediate
Day Three
The Generational Impact
Day Four
Stolen Blessings
Day Five
Destructive Consolations

Today's Treasure
The babies jostled each other within her, and she said, "Why is this happening to me?" So she went to inquire of the LORD.
Genesis 25:22

What question prompted Rebekah to inquire of the Lord (v. 22)?

_____

When did you last wonder something similar?

_____

Either Abraham and Isaac and their wives had bad luck bearing children or a much bigger purpose was in play. Since we know that luck has nothing to do with God's people, let's explore the bigger purpose. In both Sarah's and Rebekah's lives, conditions arose that brought the fulfillment of God's promise into question.

God is drawing a map of a typical journey of faith before our eyes. Let's be willing to see it. Let's get out of our heads any expectation of receiving a promise and expecting it to be fulfilled in the same location and season! Far more typically the journey goes like this: We have to . . .

- Depart the place we received the promise.
- Travel through the land where the fulfillment of the promise is divinely tested and either humanly or demonically threatened.
- Tenaciously press through the obstacles to the place of fulfillment.

Now let's get visual with this concept. Draw your rendition of this "map" in the space provided, charting how a person typically gets from the place of receiving a divine promise to the place of its fulfillment.

If you've journeyed with God very long, you've probably walked this route several times. In Sarah's and Rebekah's cases, the fulfillment of God's promises involved bearing flesh-and-blood children. Your faith walk may also involve the desire for children, but we all share a conceptual similarity. The journey of faith most often involves God's revealed desire to birth *something* from us in the area of fruitfulness and purpose. You may be actively participating in such a journey. Go back to the map you drew and personalize those lands with your own example, adding descriptions or names to the various spots. We've all seen maps or diagrams that include a "You are here" point of reference. Mark on your map a point with the words "I am here" to help you identify where you are in terms of where you want to be. (They might happily be one and the same.)

How did God apparently encourage Isaac's spiritual participation toward the fulfillment of the promise of heirs (25:21)?

_____

Use your imagination and write a couple of sentences that you can almost "hear" coming from Isaac's mouth as he prayed "on behalf of his wife."

_____

_____

Isaac was 40 years old when he married. Surely as time and togetherness failed to bring forth an heir, he had his own share of self-doubts. "Should I have married earlier?" "Have I proved too weak of character?" "Too small of faith?" God's timing suggests a greater issue. I believe God intended to make crystal clear His participation in fulfilling the promise of heirs. God physically enabled the human race to procreate whether or not a couple knows or acknowledges Him. God wasn't about to let such an important promise seem naturally fulfilled. Had Isaac and Rebekah conceived the first year, they would have been tremendously less attentive to spiritual purpose and divine participation. In other words, they might have missed the God-gift.

 What has God given you in a way that you have no doubt who was the Giver?

_____

Once our prayer is answered, our tendency is to expect smooth sailing. Like Rebekah, we often encounter something altogether different. Rebekah conceived only to encounter a very difficult pregnancy. *The Beginning of Wisdom* translates Rebekah's question like this: "If it be so, why am I this?"

We might personalize the essence of her confusion as, "If the end result of this is

supposed to be _____, why am I _____?"
Go ahead and fill in those blanks if you're relating!

The same commentary also suggests that Rebekah's wording might be understood, "If there is at last to be an heir, why is there this struggle? Why is there not a smooth transition to the next generation?"[1]

Life offers many opportunities for similar confusion. You might have prayed for a godly spouse and God gave you one, but the marriage has been challenging. You may have prayed for a child you could raise to serve God, and He gave you a child. Years have passed, however, and that child still doesn't appear to have any interest in serving the Lord. God may have given you a ministry, but you were not expecting it to require such hard work. Somehow we never grow accustomed to the idea that pain and difficulties are part of the human experience. God is not going to exempt His children from life's difficulty. Rather, He highlights those very challenges to prove our faith is genuine. We have an infinite advantage over unbelievers, however, even in the here-and-now of our earthly experience.

Our difficulties are filled with meaning and far-reaching effects, leaving warm blessing on our earthly journey. Our lives are God's "I am here" tag on the map of humanity.

 What explanation did God give for Rebekah's difficult pregnancy (Gen. 25:23)?

_____

God's prophecy to Rebekah that the older would serve the younger is just one example among a long biblical list. David the shepherd boy seemed the least likely leader among the brothers. Peter, James, and John were simple fishermen. God simply doesn't make choices the way people make choices. He's looking for glory, explaining why He appears to have such an attraction to weakness.

Rebekah's difficult pregnancy was political and not personal. Perhaps we, too should not take every trial we face quite so personally. Certainly the challenge has something to do with us, or God would have chosen someone else. The higher purpose of a season of jostling may be our family as a whole, our workplace, neighbors, church, and, yes, at times our government. Don't dream for a moment that God is uninvolved in world politics. Nothing could be further from the truth.

Rebekah's twins would become nations destined for conflict. Let's hear again from the Jewish commentary, *The Beginning of Wisdom*. "The fertile womb, source of life, is also the breeder of conflict. More than one son guarantees rivalry."[2] I grin as I clearly recall insisting on a second child so my first one wouldn't be lonely. It cured her loneliness, all right. She always had someone to fight. Like you who have more than one child, I wouldn't have traded having more than one child for tranquility. Life is full of conflict. Sometimes we're better off learning how to handle it in the (ideally) safe environment of home. Consider a final quote from *The Beginning of Wisdom*: "But when leadership is contested between twins, preeminence can be had only by struggling against the person to whom one is naturally most akin. Can it be obtained without destroying one's brother, literally or figuratively?"[3]

In the weeks to come, we will discover the answer to that question. For now, let's conclude our lesson with the birth of Scripture's first recorded set of twins. What were they named? Why were they given those names?

_____

You saw that Esau was named for his appearance and Jacob for his actions? In that case I might have named Amanda "Bald and Darling" and Melissa "Precious and Screaming."

Think of a pair of siblings you've known since they were infants. Name the older one by his or her appearance and the younger by his or her early actions.

older: _____

younger: _____

Let's hope these are the last of the similarities our pairs share with Esau and Jacob. Prepare to learn volumes from them, Dear One. The map charted in Scripture to follow their faith walk is fascinating. I'll meet you on the road tomorrow.

Day Two

An Appetite for the Immediate

I recall when one of my children socked the other. Sweet little "other" had been begging for it for a long time. I was so stunned that I had to gather my wits about me before I could discipline the child. Time froze for an instant, and I stared back and forth at the two of them. They shared the same (albeit strange) parents and bloodline. I recall thinking what virtually every parent of two children thinks: "How can two children from the same womb who share the same father and the same gender be so opposed to one another?"

Thankfully, my girls are the best of friends as young adults, but let me assure you that we had our share of door slamming and hair pulling along the way. When I cried watching them say goodbye as one moved to another continent, I considered afresh how tangled my heartstrings are in the fabric of my children's lives. Seeing them show their love for one another is an unspeakable joy for me. No wonder Christ's heart cry to His own was " 'love one another!' " (John 13:34).

I'm no child psychologist, but I've parented long enough to observe that most sibling rivalry appears to be a vie for dominance. For the prime spot in the family. For—we might say—*the blessing*. Isaac and Rebekah never got to see their boys outgrow their rivalry. Jacob's story line is the most intriguing to me out of the patriarchs narrative. At times we will hardly be able to stand him, and at other times we won't be able to resist him. His saga begins today, intertwined around his brother's like knotted yarn.

Esau and Jacob not only came from the same womb, but they also occupied it at the same time. Yet the two of them could not have been more different.

🐫 Read Genesis 25:24-34. (If you missed video session 4, begin with v. 19.) Note in the margin every detail that surely fueled the rivalry between Esau and Jacob.

Surely you know a pair of siblings—whether young or old—whose differences are remarkable. Describe their variances without any dishonor to either one.

_____   _____

_____   _____

_____   _____

_____   _____

Differences don't always spark division and rivalry. Sometimes differences make two puzzle pieces fit. Unfortunately, we'll see a different kind of "fit" between Esau and Jacob. A few days ago I shared with you my mother's mock epitaph: "I'd like to thank my five children without whom I would not be here today." In their boxing ring, Jacob and Esau could have worn matching tee-shirts that said, "We'd like to thank our parents without whom we'd not be here today." As you noted the fuel for their rivalry, you couldn't have missed verse 28.

Today's Treasure
So Esau despised his birthright.
Genesis 25:34

How does that verse strike you?

_____

I can tell you how the verse strikes me. It makes me want to smack a set of parents. Keith and I were far from perfect parents, and our children were as different as night and day, but we were wild about both of them. I can't fathom loving one of my girls less than the other or being loved by my parents less than my siblings. Though parental partialities are devastating, they are not unusual. If a parent is drawn to love one child more than another, he or she needs to seek godly counsel to work through the reasons. Sometimes deeply-rooted issues are to blame. Other times, one child is simply easier to love than his cloudier, temperamental sibling. Wise parents, however, will not accept partiality.

I have been told many times, "Beth, I cannot change the way I feel." But we can change the way we think which will lead to a change in the way we feel. That's the essence of the "renewed mind" (see Rom. 12:2). As long as we keep thinking the same old thoughts, we'll keep feeling the same old feelings.

Describe some "same-old-thoughts" that parents who show partiality might think.

_____

_____

I'll throw in a few: "Who could help loving this child more? She (he) does what I ask and wants to please me." Or "we have so much more in common. We can't help being drawn to one another." We've just stumbled on the Isaac/Esau and Rebekah/Jacob problem.

Fill in the following blank based on verse 28.

"Isaac, who had a _____ for wild game, loved Esau, but Rebekah loved Jacob."

I think it was all about taste. Not so much taste in food as taste in type. I think Esau was Isaac's type: He was his father's taste in sons. Isaac liked the "wild" and the "game" in Esau. A skillful hunter, Esau was manly.

Do you see of a possible motivation? Isaac couldn't conceive a child with his beautiful young wife until he was 60 years old while Ishmael, the slave woman's son, sired a dozen. In Esau the outdoorsman Isaac saw enough masculinity for 10 sons. Esau was one big bundle of testosterone: perhaps Esau's masculinity reassured his father of his own manhood.

Jacob, on the other hand, was his mother's favorite. He was a "quiet man" (25:27). The Hebrew word translated _quiet_ in this verse can also be translated _wholesome_ even _blameless_, but these are questionable interpretations in context with the heel-grabber's scheming. According to the _New International Commentary_, the Hebrew "may mean, by semantic development, 'domesticated' or 'homebody.'"[4] This interpretation makes much more sense in contrast to Esau's description as an outdoorsman and in context with Jacob's actions. For what it's worth, I'll give you my own interpretation: I think Jacob was a mama's boy. In fact, I believe Rebekah was at the heart of all Jacob's scheming.

Look back at Genesis 25:22-23. Who is the only person who heard God's prophecy over the twins first-hand?

❑ Rebekah   ❑ Isaac   ❑ The Senior Servant   ❑ Laban

I think Rebekah had been trying to help God keep His word all Jacob's life. If you understand what I mean, say it in your own words:

_____

_____

Before the babies were born, God told Rebekah that the older would serve the younger. So Rebekah made sure she kept the younger by her side, positioning and conditioning him to make his move. What she didn't understand is that we don't have to steal, cheat, and lie to get what God promises us. God is the move maker. The same One who makes the promises fulfills the promises—without our manipulation. Jacob would have risen as the prominent brother and the next patriarch without the conniving.

Perhaps you'll find a play on words as interesting as I did. Look again at verse 29. The word used for *cooking* and in other translations *preparing* is "most frequently translated in the RSV OT as 'act presumptuously.' This passage shows the basic meaning of the verb— 'to cook, prepare, seethe,' which developed into 'become heated, animated,' and then 'act presumptuously.' "[5] Try to put yourself in Jacob's position. Imagine being told by your mother that you will rise as the more dominant brother, yet day in and day out you see no sign of it. Instead, you constantly witness your father's blatant partiality to his other son—the outdoorsman.

How do you imagine words like "cooking, preparing, and seething" describe Jacob? Think beyond a pot of stew.

_____

Jacob was stewing all right, and the pot boiled over. Goodness knows, being Esau's brother had to be uncomfortable. After all, from the look of Genesis 25:28-29, Esau brought home the bacon, and Jacob fried it up in a pan.

Esau would have been a kinder, gentler little brother's worst nightmare. A close look at Scripture suggests why. First take a look at Esau's manners. He burst through the door making a demand that more literally could be translated, "Quick! Let me swallow some of that red stuff." The intent of the Hebrew implies gulping it down with hardly a taste.[6] One commentator labeled Esau an "uncouth glutton."[7] (I don't think he washed up before dinner either.) I know for a fact that bad manners and skillful hunters don't always go together. Like Isaac, I happen to be very partial to a skillful hunter, but the difference is that I only have one husband. That kind of partiality is appropriate, and he does happen to have manners.

Scripture rounds out the crass picture of Esau. What does Hebrews 12:16 say?

_____

The Amplified Version lends the verse a broad understanding: "That no one may become guilty of sexual vice, or become a profane (godless and sacrilegious) person as Esau did, who sold his own birthright for a single meal."

We cannot tell from any of the major translations of the Bible whether sexual immorality characterized Esau or if profanity or godlessness was the only intent. I learned in research, however, that nonbiblical Jewish literature certainly attributed sexual vice along with profanity and overall godlessness to Esau.[8] If these images are vaguely accurate, can you imagine what Esau was like? I imagine him talking in grunts and belching at the table—on a good day.

We may infer two characteristics about Esau from our present text in Genesis 25.

- He was driven by instant gratification. (I am starving! I'll do anything you ask only satisfy my appetite *now!*)
- He placed no value on what was truly valuable.

Genesis 25 concludes with profoundly telling words: "So Esau despised his birthright." He was cynical about family and sacrilegious about spirituality (see *Amplified* text quoted earlier). Although he was loved by his father with immense partiality, Esau did not value his place in the family. Based on the picture Scripture paints, he may have been the kind who made merciless fun of his father behind his back. His birthright as his father's firstborn son and principal heir would have allowed him to inherit twice as much as any other son. At that point in his life, Esau so deeply devalued his family that he probably couldn't think of anything his father had that he wanted. Supper was all Esau wanted in that moment.

The message of Esau's life has nothing to do with stew. It has to do with thinking so little about who you are that you'd forfeit a godly heritage for instant gratification.

As we conclude, let's not miss the New Testament application. The Apostle Paul characterized himself as a Hebrew of Hebrews (Phil. 3:5). He knew every Hebrew priority and could not help teaching new covenant concepts through old covenant practices. Paul taught believers in Christ about the value of our inheritance. Scripture teaches that Christ is the Son of God, the uncontested heir of His Father's estate and, astonishingly, that we are joint heirs with Christ (Rom. 8:17).

Record what the following Scriptures tell you about your inheritance:

Ephesians 1:18

_____

Colossians 3:23-24

_____

The carnal world surrounding us stirs up fleshly passions like a pot of boiling, red stew. In a worldly sense, we've been set up for failure. We can be the most skillful hunters of satisfaction this earth could boast and fail to ever find what truly satisfies. We can starve ourselves spiritually and expose ourselves so readily to the lusts of this world that we'd trade in the sense of who we are in Christ—our birthright—for the first pot of stew we're offered. Later we realize we never really tasted the stew, and we'll know that the trade wasn't worth the eternal loss.

You have a birthright, Dear One—a real inheritance awaiting you in a real kingdom (Col. 1:12). Value who you are in Christ. I don't believe Scripture teaches that we can trade in our salvation. But, Beloved, we can certainly trade in a personal sense of who we are in Christ for the lusts of this world. Let no one take your crown (Rev. 3:11). Let it never be said of you or me, "So _____ despised her birthright."

Day Three'
The Generational Impact

Week 5 focuses primarily on Jacob, the heel grabber, and the saga that surrounds him. However, today Scripture chronologically casts its light on Isaac for an entire chapter before returning to Jacob in tomorrow's lesson. We will consider all of Genesis 26 today. Its 35 verses contain multiple scenes and stories about Isaac that could seem almost unconnected, but the Holy Spirit, however, will bring us understanding and application through the common denominator many of the themes share.

Any of us not raised by wolves know we bear similarities to our parents. The least of these may be physical—though the copy of my father's nose perched on my face begs to differ. Parents were meant to impact their children's lives, otherwise their job would be finished in the delivery room. Instead, their impact powerfully reaches past their funerals and grows faster than the grass on their graves. Through parents' influence, we not only take on many of their characteristics, but we also can take on much of their character. *Or lack of it.* I'm sorry, but we all know it's true. Let's put it this way: sometimes our parents leave us more than a china cabinet.

Short of surgery (I've been so tempted!), we have little choice regarding the physical characteristics we inherit. Those of us who want badly enough to be free in Christ and filled by His Spirit *can*—through the mighty power of God—decide which emotional and spiritual characteristics we are willing to maintain as an inheritance. One reason we want to be careful and deliberate about what we agree to inherit is that we too will pass on multiple characteristics and much character. *Or lack of it.* We don't want to judge our parents lest God and the next generation judge us by the scorecard we kept.

In your own words, how does Luke 6:37-38 express this concept?

_____

_____

Today's Treasure
Isaac reopened the wells that had been dug in the time of his father Abraham, which the Philistines had stopped up after Abraham died, and he gave them the same names his father had given them.
Genesis 26:18

Considering my past, I don't want to use a measuring cup as I mete out mercy toward others. I need a water hose hooked up to the bottomless well of God's supply. While being merciful to preceding generations, we need to be careful not to be merciless to those who follow. For them, we need to sort the benefits from the hindrances in our inheritance. The key is to be discerning, loving, and godly in a truthful approach to all we've inherited so we can mark our family lines with blessing.

As you read Genesis 26 in the following three segments, keep in mind that Abraham is already dead and buried. In each segment look for every tie—spiritual, behavioral, or circumstantial—Isaac has to his father, Abraham, and briefly describe them. Every mention of Abraham's name flags an obvious tie, but also look for circumstantial and behavioral similarities he and Isaac shared. You'll be happy to know that most of the elements tying Isaac to Abraham in Genesis 26 are positive.

Keep in mind that Abimelech and Phicol are considered to be dynastic or royal Philistine names repeated through generations much like King George or King Edward in the English monarchy. The "Abimelech" in Genesis 26 is almost certainly different from the one in Abraham's account.

What similarities do you see between Abraham's and Isaac's actions in …

Segment 1: Genesis 26:1-11; glance at Genesis 12:10-20 and Genesis 20:1-11.

Abraham's Actions	Isaac's Actions

Segment 2: Genesis 26:12-22

Abraham's Actions	Isaac's Actions

Segment 3: Genesis 26:23-34 (Read the entire segment so you can finish the chapter and maintain context, but focus on verses 23 and 24.)

Abraham's Actions	Isaac's Actions

Now let's consider the ties suggested in each segment between Isaac and Abraham. How about segment 1? Did you have the same reaction I did? For crying out loud, if Isaac and Abraham had to be deceitful, you'd think they could at least have come up with a new ruse! I am dumbfounded that scholars who don't hold to the veracity of God's Word think the accounts are so suspiciously similar that they must be different renditions of one occasion. How many of us have carried on the tradition of some of our parents' poor decisions? When we are tested by a difficult decision, how we saw our parents respond (whether poorly or well) in a similar situation is ordinarily first among our multiple-choice answers. We may not choose their response, but it is always among the first responses that pop into our heads.

Examples of repeated approaches to life between parents and children are endless, but today's text highlights one too insidious to overlook. Deception, passed down through example from parent to child, can be a frightfully contagious approach to life. If honesty is not held in high esteem and practiced in the home, children learn the destructive art of deception. Unless something dramatic breaks the cycle, it carries into adulthood and can invade any realm of life. If your parents rarely made a disciplinary issue of your childhood "fibs," honesty may not have been a premium in your upbringing. Let's ask ourselves some difficult questions: did either of your parents practice deception? Was either of them entirely different in private than in public? Did your parents openly and easily lie for you? Or for one another? If your answers are largely affirmative, you are wise to ask God to mercifully reveal any similar tendency lurking in you.

If you're willing, please use this space to ask God to free you from any stronghold of deception, no matter where it originated.

_____

_____

_____

_____

Allow me to point out another potential tie to following parental example. Did you know that the statistics for second-generation adultery are overwhelming? If you were raised in a home where a parent committed adultery—even if you despised it and judged it harshly—adultery can tend to be higher on the list of your multiple choice answers in your own time of temptation. Don't misunderstand me to say that second-generation sins are the fault of first-generation sinners. Ezekiel 18 clearly teaches that each person is responsible for his or her own sins. My point is that we must guard against repeating the same mistakes our parents made. Our propensity toward those parental choices is strong even if we hated them. We have to be deliberate about behaviors and life approaches that we don't want to repeat.

My older daughter, Amanda, and I share a standing joke. She has been raised to love women's ministry, particularly the ministry of God's Word. Living Proof Ministries is in her blood since she works with and for me. She has participated in endless Bible studies, but she has avoided *Breaking Free: Making Liberty in Christ a Reality in Life.* I've teased her unmercifully because *Breaking Free* is her mother's life message. Why has she been so resistant? When Amanda was in college, *Breaking Free* broke out like a virus among young Christian women on her campus. Every time Amanda walked past someone she knew who was taking the study, they'd say something like, "*Breaking Free* is about to kill me!"

Several days after Amanda and Curt's temporary relocation to northern England, I got a call from her. "Mom, you are not going to believe what happened. One of the women from the church told me that the ladies here are just about to start *Breaking Free.* She enthusiastically suggested that I arrived just in time to help facilitate it!" My staff and I laughed our heads off. Don't you love God's sense of humor? He'll take us on the other side of the world to perform a work if that's what it takes! Every Tuesday night Amanda helps facilitate the Bible study in a small British home, and she has fallen in love with the house full of women. I know *Breaking Free* practically by heart, so a few days ago I realized she was coming up on the week dealing with generational sin. (I don't teach generational curses, but I certainly believe in the generational effects of sin.) My heart was so full I decided to write her a note about it. I'm about to do something I have never done before. I am going to cut and paste a portion of the e-mail I sent to her because I believe it has a place in today's lesson for you.

Amanda, on a personal note, your father and I want nothing more than for our children to be completely free of any junk we handed down. Don't feel one bit guilty about bringing any of it to the Lord so that He can remove it from you and your descendants. We are so secure in your love for us. We have lived enough of life to know that rejecting something negative that we have passed down is not the same as rejecting us. Feel free, Dear One! Feel free! It's what we want for you! Be merciless in dealing with strongholds. Hold no sympathy or loyalty to them. Your parents' strongholds do not equal your parents. We are confident that you know you have always been loved, so please go forward. Do the work with God! Do not skip a single day, and go right ahead and deal with every issue. You have our blessing, Child. Our complete blessing.

Keith and I have worked hard at parenting, but we still made mistakes. We also have fierce strongholds in our backgrounds. Though we've tried hard to cooperate with God toward healing and wholeness, we aren't foolish enough to think we passed no baggage down to our children. If we managed not to pass down an oversized suitcase, we at least handed them a carry-on. We want them to deal with anything negative they inherited from us so it can be dropped from our family line in the name and power of Jesus!

 What part of the discussion on parenting is speaking most clearly to you at this moment? Please share.

_____

_____

Now let's lighten up with a few brief comments on segment 2. My favorite part of the reading is listed as Today's Treasure. Isaac reopened the "stopped up" wells belonging to Abraham. Few of us have parents who dug literal wells, so let's think in conceptual terms. We've already discussed that we want to be deliberate toward not inheriting any of our parents' destructive habits or approaches. At the same time, we want to unstop any well of blessing from which we were meant to draw and drink. The well of refreshment and blessing that should pass from parent to child can be stopped up by either party or by the enemy. A few examples of well-stoppers are feelings of unworthiness, distance, disrespect, or difference. An adult child stops up a well every time she throws out the positive inheritance with the negative. We can decide that any area of inauthenticity means every area is inauthentic and a fall automatically constitutes a fraud. When we throw out both our positive and negative inheritance, our attitude loudly proclaims, "I want nothing from you, and I want to be nothing like you!" *Nothing* is a big word.

I know a man who sinned against his family for a season, but God prevailed and marked his life with repentance. One of his sons harbored deep bitterness toward his father and didn't want to be anything like him. Every positive characteristic the man possessed was obliterated in his son's eyes by the negative season. In the young man's opinion, to be anything like his father was to be everything like him. Time surfaced a number of the father's wonderful characteristics that are worthy of a son's welcome. One of them was excellent managerial skills. The son is a wonderful businessman but will not consider giving his father any credit for the example. If the younger man is ever going to have peace of mind and fullness of blessing, at some point he may need to reopen some wells.

How about you? Can you share an example of a reopened well or relate in a way you'd be willing to share? Again, be careful not to dishonor anyone. A reopened well is rightly cast in a positive light.

_____

_____

🐫 Segment 3 provides a fitting conclusion to the concepts we've studied today. How did the Lord introduce Himself to Isaac in Genesis 26:24?

_____

Beloved, God is God—holy, wonderful, and merciful—even if someone who held Him up as an example to us didn't reflect His character. Don't confuse God with man! However, when man has something of God to offer, receive it even when the flesh-and-blood channel of blessing is imperfect. Goodness knows, Isaac's father was flawed, but he had a faith Isaac would be wise and blessed to emulate. Spiritual lineage is one of the most precious gifts God offers. He wants nothing more than to reveal Himself to a second generation as the God of the first. Dear One, will we pass down a heritage of faith?

Day Four
Stolen Blessings

Once again we have a lengthy segment of Scripture to consider today. Unlike our previous chapter which contained separate scenes and themes, Genesis 27 tells one story with such description and character development that it stands out like a page in a pop-up book. I'd give almost anything to be part of your small group when you discuss this lesson which is a soap opera if you'll ever see one. Today's Scripture segment is Genesis 27:1-40. We'll read the entire portion before our discussion. This segment naturally falls into four scenes, each involving two interacting characters.

Today's Treasure
Jacob said to his father, "I am Esau your firstborn. I have done as you told me. Please sit up and eat some of my game so that you may give me your blessing."
Genesis 27:19

As you read verses 1-40, please fill in the simple outline below by identifying each pair and the Scriptures depicting their scene. I'll get you started with the first one:

Scene 1: Isaac and Esau, Genesis 27:1-4

Scene 2: _____, Genesis 27:_____

Scene 3: _____, Genesis 27:_____

Scene 4: _____, Genesis 27:_____

Surely you were drawn onto the page through the descriptive character development. Glance back over the text to refresh your memory.

Next write a description of each character. In addition to any obvious information, use some imagination to express what you think each one might have been like based on the text.

Isaac:_____

_____

Rebekah: _____

_____

Esau:_____

_____

Jacob: _____

_____

Now, reduce your description of each character to only one word:

Isaac: _____ Rebekah: _____

Esau: _____ Jacob: _____

OK, let's have a little fun and place ourselves on the hot seat for a moment. Based on your personal history, with which character do you most identify and why? (You have to pick one!)

_____

_____

 What do you consider the most stressful moment in Genesis 27:1-40?

_____

Now let's briefly discuss each scene in the narrative. Scene I takes place in Genesis 27:1-4 between Isaac and Esau. (Verse 5 tells us Rebekah was eavesdropping on the conversation, but she wasn't an intended part of the interaction.) The scene opens on an elderly Isaac, his eyesight failing. One of my least favorite middle age challenges is weakening eyesight. For a rabid reader, it is misery. I wear contacts until bedtime, but I read with glasses until I fall asleep. I invariably have to pull them off Keith Moore's nose. (Yes, he has his own, but he can't remember where he put them.) He's so manly that I wish you could picture him in my pink wire frames.

Isaac was as old as the hills and didn't have the luxury of spectacles. We already know that he loved the taste of Esau's wild game (25:28) but this occasion wasn't just about taste. In ancient cultures a meal was a familiar setting for a blessing.

Even today, many celebrations take place around the dinner table. Name a few examples of dinner celebrations.

_____

_____

Scene 1 concludes with our assumption that Esau is gathering quiver and bow and heading out the door. Perhaps he experienced all sorts of anticipation as his steps quickened toward the open field.

Scene 2 takes place in Genesis 27:5-17 between Rebekah and the mama's boy. Uh, Jacob. Under the one-word description of Rebekah, did anyone happen to use a word like *manipulative*? A fitting two-worder would have been *smooth operator*. *Game* takes on a double meaning in this segment of Scripture. Remember, Rebekah received the prophecy from God concerning the older son serving the younger. Her actions are the continuation of her false belief that she needed to force God's will to come to pass. Somebody needed to rip that junior-God pin off Rebekah's collar and tell her God said not to bother. He faithfully fulfills His Word! I'm sorry, Sisters, but I can't help but relate our gender to Rebekah's actions. Certainly men have their own destructive tendencies. We can trust God to point those out, but let's allow Him to deal with ours.

🐫 Take a look at Rebekah's words in Genesis 27:8 and fill in the blanks: "Now, my

son, _____ _____ and _____ _____ __ _____ _____."

If our loved ones would just listen carefully and do what we tell them, we could whip our families into shape, couldn't we? Hardly! Whoever said, "God couldn't be everywhere so He created mothers," lied!

Can you imagine any more foolish statement than Rebekah's response to Jacob's

fears (v. 13)? "My son, let the _____ _____ _____ _____."

The NIV wording in the second part of the same verse is very telling.

"Just do what I say; go and get them _____ _____."

You know how much I love women. I'm so thankful God made men, but I wouldn't trade being a woman for anything. Please know when I seem to pick on women in Bible study that my deep desire is for us to be all the wonderful things a woman of God can be. The New Testament tells us that God has given us these Old Testament accounts as examples. In the women of God's Word, we see examples of how we want to be and examples of how we don't—often in the same person! Would you agree that not all our family manipulation is selfless? Sometimes what we pressure our loved ones to do is not only for them; something about it is for us as well. Case in point: I love basketball. I desperately did not want Melissa to give up basketball in high school to concentrate on volleyball. The conviction of the Holy Spirit was too strong for me to outwardly blow it, but I was alarmed by the selfishness revealed in my secret feelings.

OK, I've told on myself. What about you? How have you struggled with the compulsion to control family members? Any examples?

_____

_____

So, when we're trying to advise our loved ones, let's ask ourselves three questions:
- *What is our motive?* (Thankfully, God can reveal a pure motive in us as readily as an impure motive. Remember, God doesn't have a critical spirit! He has no problem affirming when we are on target.)
- *Are we giving godly counsel?*
- *How much of our desired outcome has to do with us?*

Let's proceed to scene 3 which takes place between Isaac and Jacob (dressed as Esau), recorded in verses 18-29. Finally! A chance to pick on a male for a moment!

Fill in the following blanks from verse 19 so you can fully experience the weight of deception:

" _____ said to his father, "I am _____,

your _____."

Record every instance in these 12 verses that suggests Isaac's suspicion:

_____

Did you notice that Isaac's suspicions seemed quieted when he caught the smell of Esaus' clothes on Jacob? Any of us who've spent time around outdoor types can grin as we relate. Boys who spend lots of time outdoors smell like it. I always thought the boy I raised for seven years smelled just like a wet puppy. When he was gone, I missed his scent as much as anything. Girls have scents, too, however. Amanda has a four-year old friend at church named Addison. She cannot understand why Amanda and Curt moved overseas for five months. I was with Amanda when she said goodbye to Addy, and I nearly bawled. I held the child in my arms and said, "Let's you and I make a deal. When you really miss Amanda, you come running to me at church and give me a hug. You see, Amanda and I smell just alike." I can hardly count the hugs I've gotten in the last several months. She runs all the way down the corridor, jumps in my arms, inhales deeply and says, "You smell just like Amanda!" (Oh, the power of suggestion!)

The fact that Jacob smelled just like Esau sealed the deal. Isaac ignored a host of suspicions over a single met expectation, and out came the blessing. "Doesn't seem like Esau.

Doesn't sound like Esau. Ah, but it smells like Esau! Must be Esau!" The moral of the story thus far might be this: pay attention to your suspicions … even if everything smells right.

> **Take another look at the blessing Isaac thought he was giving to Esau. What is the key part of the blessing?**

_____

Earlier I asked what you considered to be the moment of highest stress. Though we'd all agree that Isaac and Esau's simultaneous realizations in Genesis 27:33-37 prove climactic, don't miss the opening of scene 4 between Isaac and Esau in verses 30-40. Reread verse 30 and catch how close Jacob and Esau came to bumping into each other. Imagine the look on Esau's face had he beheld how utterly ridiculous Jacob looked in his dress-ups. (Incidentally, all of us who have raised adolescents know how ridiculous a child can look when he or she imitates someone else and the look doesn't fit.)

Do the events recorded in scene 4 frustrate you? Don't you wonder why the blessing couldn't have been annulled under conditions of fraud? Scripture tells us Esau was a crude and profane man, but somehow we can't help feeling sorry for him as he cries out "Bless me—me too, my father!" (v. 34).

The entire theme of Genesis 27:1-40 is blessing. "The root brk occurs no less than 22 times in this chapter, 17 times as a verb and 5 times as a noun."[9] This segment of Scripture confirms one of my own suspicions in my research of Genesis. I don't think we Gentiles have a clue what a true Hebrew blessing entailed. God's ancient people were taught by His Word and example to mean what they said and never to speak or take a blessing lightly. Words are powerful. If the ancients ever erred in assuming fraud wasn't ground for retraction, we moderns tend to err dramatically in the opposite extreme. We speak words hastily and think we can simply take them back at a moment's notice without consequences. Sometimes there are simply no "take backs." Genesis 27 is one of those times.

Our consolation is the sovereignty of God. Though the players in these four scenes proved manipulative, hasty, deceptive, and foolish, a sovereign purpose trumped every play. In a very real sense, Isaac couldn't take back his blessing because it really wasn't his to give in the first place. God foretold the blessing, foreshadowing its higher purpose (Gen. 25:23). In the times of Israel's kings, the prophecy over the nations coming from Jacob and Esau proved true just as God foretold. God would also fulfill the blessings Isaac spoke over his sons in Genesis 27, even the portion about Esau throwing off Jacob's yoke.

> **Read 2 Kings 8:20-22, keeping in mind that the nation coming from Esau was called _Edom_, and the southern kingdom of Jacob's descendants was called _Judah_. What do these verses record?**

_____

These blessings were fulfilled not because Isaac's words were strong enough to bind God but because from the beginning they fit into God's sovereign plan. Isaac was blind long before he got old. Isaac's partiality blinded him to God's prophecy, and his overriding preference for Esau clouded his vision of what God had for Jacob. No, God did not bless the ruse. Rebekah and Jacob were sure to suffer serious consequences. God had His own plan underway, and man's means could not undermine God's purposed result. Only now

Hebrew Root Form

The Hebrew language is built on verbs. The basic form of each verb is called its root. Usually these root words consist of three consonants. From this basic form or root comes not only other forms of the verb, but also related nouns. For example, the root verb _brk_ means "to bless." The noun _brkh_ built off this root means "blessing."

can you and I appropriately grasp the solitary statement regarding Isaac's faith in the Hebrews 10 "Hall of Faith."

Explain Hebrews 11:20 based on all we've studied today. Great job, Sister!

_____

_____

_____

Today's Treasure

"Your brother Esau is consoling himself with the thought of killing you."
Genesis 27:42

Day Five
Destructive Consolations

Dear One, I want to bless you in the Lord Jesus for your spiritual tenacity. As we conclude today's lesson and share video session 5, we have completed half of our journey with the patriarchs. If I can persevere past the halfway point of a demanding journey, I am far more encouraged to press through to the finish. If you feel the same way, be greatly encouraged today. You have done a fabulous job. Once again, I consider being your servant as an unspeakable privilege from God.

This morning I stopped by my cleaners where I regularly deposit something much more important than just clothing. In the loving name of Christ, I make regular deposits into a friendship I've developed with a beautiful Muslim woman who works there. She told me today that she met a woman who attends one of our Bible studies. (I've never had the pleasure of meeting this person face-to-face.) My heart grew tender when I saw how pleased this precious Muslim woman had been to tell her new friend that she and I are personal friends and that she's been to my home. Likewise, I could tell her new friend's reaction had quite an impact. My friend at the cleaners saw that the woman from Bible study and I have a special bond though we've never met, and she found this peculiar and remarkable. I responded, "Dear One, you are going to have to come with me to a study one night and get a taste of our world!" I so hope one day she will.

Once again I was blessed to realize that a loving bond testifies to others that something remarkable takes place between people who love God and His Word. You are truly so dear to me, and as I receive your letters I am astonished to hear many of you reciprocate those feelings. This sisterly side-by-side bond pleases Christ! (What would displease Him is either of us idolizing the other. God forbid it.) Remember, Christ said that the world would know we were His disciples by our love for one another (John 13:35). May this peculiar kinship between us continue to serve as a testimony, whetting appetites for the Savior and increasing hunger for His Word.

You may be relieved to know our Scripture segment today is much shorter than the previous two. At times a few verses are as applicable to our lives as an entire chapter. Today demonstrates one of those times.

Please read Genesis 27:41-46 and complete the following exercise.

On day 3 we witnessed a heart-broken Esau, weeping "aloud" (v. 38) over his forfeited blessing. Draw a diagram depicting the evolution of Esau's emotions from the grief he demonstrated in verse 38 to the unchecked feelings and the resulting plans that followed:

Read verse 42 carefully. How can thinking vengeful thoughts toward people who hurt us be a means of consoling ourselves?

_____

_____

I am so intrigued by what I've learned while researching this lesson that I can't type fast enough to share it with you. Look carefully at the phrase "held a grudge against" in verse 41. The English phrase is a translation of only one Hebrew word: *satam*. *The New International Commentary* footnotes the English translation with the following interesting words: (Keep in mind the Hebrew alphabet doesn't include vowels) "*stm*, apparently a by-form of *stn*, the root from which *Satan* derives." *The Complete Word Study Dictionary of the Old Testament* lists three Hebrew transliterations in a row that I'd like you to consider and compare with a portion of their definitions. Remember these Old Testament words and uses:

#7852 *satam*: (*The word used in today's text.) A verb meaning to hate; to bear a grudge against, to harass. It means to nurse hostility and bitterness toward someone; or even to attack or harass a person physically.

#7853 *satan*: A verb meaning to accuse, to slander, and to harbor animosity toward. The verb is used only six times and presents a negative attitude or bias against something. (*The Old Testament Lexical Aids* prioritize the important English definition "to attack.")

#7854 *satan*: A masculine noun meaning an adversary, Satan, an accuser. This noun is used twenty seven times [in OT]. In Job it is found fourteen times meaning (the) Satan, the accuser.[10]

Please note that the first two Hebrew words are verbs and the third is a masculine noun.

Read Zechariah 3:1 (which uses both words) in the verse below. Circle the word you can assume is the masculine noun, and put a triangle around the word you believe (based on the previous definitions) to be the coinciding verb.

"Then he showed me Joshua the high priest standing before the angel of the LORD, and Satan standing at his right side to accuse him" (Zech. 3:1).

Hopefully, I stated the instructions clearly enough for you to circle the word Satan and put a triangle around the word *accuse*. Now recall the footnote we considered earlier that tells us "*stm* [*satam*] is a by-form of *stn* [*satan*], the root from which *Satan* derives." Please don't miss the very close connections between the Hebrew words for *hate/hold a grudge* (verb: *satam*), "attack/accuse/slander" (verb: *satan*) and *Satan* (noun: *satan*). Malachi 1:2-3 tells us something that can seem disturbing without deeper consideration: " 'Was not Esau Jacob's brother?' " the Lord says, " 'Yet I have loved Jacob, but Esau I have hated.' "

Those are strong words! God's Word tells us He is kind and compassionate, merciful, and just. But did Esau ever have a chance? Did God have it out for Esau from the very beginning? Was Esau simply a victim of God's partiality? I believe some meditation on the connections of these Hebrew words might quiet our concerns enough to rest the remaining mystery in divine sovereignty. Let's discuss the diagram I asked you to draw earlier. Take a glance at yours to refresh your memory. You might have written something expressing these main ideas:

cried ▶ held a grudge ▶ premeditated murder ▶ consoled himself

Beloved, not everyone who suffers loss or feels cheated or betrayed premeditates murder. Modern psychiatry has a name for someone who premeditates murder while finding comfort in the thought of killing. He would be considered a psychopathic personality. Months ago Keith and I watched a news report concerning the arrest of a husband accused of murdering his wife. She was almost full-term with their first child. The report insinuated that another woman provided the husband a possible motive. In horror I said the same thing that occurs to me every time I hear of such a murder: "In this day of quick divorce and instant travel, why in the world would a person go as far as killing someone to get away from her?" You might echo Keith's answer: "Money! It's terrible, but it happens all the time!" How has the distance between greed and murder become so viciously, frighteningly abbreviated?

As the statistics for psychopathic behavior in our culture grow, the need deepens for a flashing red-light reminder: "This behavior is not normal!" Too often we live around aberrant and deviant behavior until we accept it. Only a flagrantly abnormal society accepts the abnormal as normal. Normal people don't murder. Normal people get hurt and angry. They may insult others and even act unkindly, but they don't premeditate a murder. With this in mind, understand that Esau's initial hurt and anger were normal. But notice that his unchecked emotions swelled and multiplied until he consoled himself with the thought of his brother's death. That type of behavior is *psychopathic*.

How do these thoughts connect to our three Hebrew words? Look up John 8:44. This verse eerily casts the devil (Satan) in a paternal role.

According to this verse, what is this evil father's stated desire?

_____

I hope you see that his desire is murder! When a human being premeditates murder, he or she " 'want[s] to carry out [the devil's] desire. He was a murderer from the beginning' " (John 8:44). I am neither saying that all murderers are Demon-possessed nor that murderers cannot repent and be saved. Scripture is, however, telling us that a desire to murder is a desire to carry out the devil's wishes. Don't think for a moment the devil wasn't alive and active during the period of the patriarchs. Furthermore, don't think for a moment he wasn't focused on Jacob's life as a link in the chain of God's people. The holocaust of God's people has been the enemy's plan all along. " 'He was a murderer from the beginning.' " Can you think of a more effective way to kill a people than to kill the individual from whom the promised line would come?

The hate-filled Pharisees whom Christ called "children of the devil" considered themselves to be children of Abraham (John 8). (Keep in mind, not all the Pharisees were hateful and murderous toward Jesus.)

 How did Christ explain the evidence of true parenting from His point of view in John 8:39-41?

The Pharisees natural father may have been Abraham, but from God's point of view a father is more accurately identified by the child's actions. Esau's natural father may have been Isaac, but (based on Christ's teachings) Esau's spiritual father was none other than Satan himself. Esau was profane, perverse, and even murderous. Ultimately (albeit unknowingly), Esau's greatest desire was to fulfill Satan's desire. In his commentary on Genesis, Bruce Waltke writes, "The murder in Esau's heart (fratricide) identifies him as the seed of the Serpent as surely as it marked out Cain and Lamech."[11] I believe this identification is precisely how God could say, "Jacob I have loved. Esau I have hated." Whew!

> **Use this space for any thoughts or insights you'd like to share with your small group. Share your thoughts under the leadership of the Holy Spirit.**

Let's conclude with a look at Hebrews 12:14-17. Read these verses carefully, noting the inclusion of Esau in this text.

 What impact does Hebrews 12:16 have on our understanding of Esau?

Whatever we do, we must not miss the fact that this terrible descent into murderous thoughts began with holding a grudge back in Genesis 27:41. Remember our Hebrew words? *Stn* led to *stn*, eventually sharing the desires of *Stn*. Every time we hold a grudge, Satan holds a foot. The Apostle Paul wrote, " 'In your anger do not sin': Do not let the sun go down while you are still angry, and do not give the devil a foothold" (Eph. 4:26). How can we keep from descending from an understandable sense of offense, betrayal, or loss to the grudges, hatred, and thoughts of revenge that Satan fuels and fans? Context is paramount in the study of God's Word. Esau's name doesn't appear in Hebrews 12 for nothing!

Read Hebrews 12:16-17 again and record the main idea.

_____

Esau missed the grace of God. Yes, grace was available to people in the Old Testament. Grace is kneaded irrevocably into the concept of *hesed*, God's loyal covenant love.[13] In fact, *hesed* is translated "grace" in Jonah 2:8: "Those who cling to worthless idols forfeit the grace that could be theirs."

Esau's own misguided sense of entitlement became his idol, and he forfeited the grace that could have been his. Yes, we could argue that missing the grace of God seemed Esau's destiny in the mystery of divine sovereignty, but murderous people such as Esau and Judas aren't helpless victims. They are humans whose hearts resemble the heart of their spiritual father, Satan.

God offers us the grace to avoid bitterness in every challenge. But if we don't allow God to apply grace like balm to our broken hearts, a "bitter root grows up to cause trouble and defile many" (Heb. 12:15). A single step can be the distance from grief to grudge … unless we take Grace Avenue.

———————

[1] Leon R. Kass, *The Begining of Wisdom: Reading Genesis* (New York: Free Press, 2003), 378-79.

[2] Ibid., 381.

[3] Ibid., 381.

[4] Victor P. Hamilton, *The Book of Genesis: Chapters 18–50* (Grand Rapids: Williams B, Eerdman's Publishing, 1995), 181.

[5] Ibid., 182.

[6] Ibid., 182.

[7] Ibid., 182.

[8] Ibid., 188.

[9] Hamilton, 226.

[10] Spiros Zodhiates et al., eds., *The Complete Word Study Dictionary: Old Testament* (Chattanooga, TN: AMG Publishers, 1994), 113.

[11] Bruce K. Waltke, *Genesis: A Commentary* (Grand Rapids: Zondervan, 2001), 381.

[12] Zodhiates, 41.

SESSION FIVE
The Heel Grabber

The NIV "reached" could be translated more closely with the words _____ _____ or _____ _____. It emphasizes the _____ with which Jacob chose this place to pass at night.

1. A place we think we've _____ happened upon can be a divinely _____ _____ for an _____ _____ with God.

2. God's first stated purpose for the encounter was to tell Jacob that the _____ of _____ and _____ was to be _____ _____ as well.

3. Representations in Jacob's dream:
    • The ladder's obvious purposes of _____ and _____. After the dream Jacob described the place as the _____ of _____ (Gen. 28:17).
    • The dream coming specifically to Jacob who would soon be renamed _____. (See Ps. 105:8-10.)
    • Peter said of Christ, "See, I lay a _____ in Zion, a _____ and precious _____, and the one who trusts in him will never be put to shame" (1 Pet. 2:6). Peter would have well remembered that Christ also promised to _____ His church upon a rock (Matt. 16:18). The emphasis of Genesis 28:14 is clearly upon _____.

4. Jacob's reaction could compel us to ask God to _____ our _____ of His glorious _____.

5. Jacob _____ _____ the stone as a _____.
    • It became unacceptable later when God's people treated memorials as _____ rather than _____.
    • Due to such misuse, the prophet Hosea renamed Bethel (meaning House of God) Beth Aven meaning _____ of _____ (Hos. 4:15).

6. Jacob poured oil on _____ of the standing _____. Both *The New International Commentary* and *The Beginning of Wisdom* treat Jacob's action as an _____ and translate the word "top" as "_____." A more literal interpretation of Genesis 28:18 would be: "He poured _____ upon its _____." A Jewish scholar by the name of Sacks: "Jacob's deed anticipates the need for _____ and _____ who will later be 'the _____ of heaven' for the people." Keep in mind that both words *Messiah* and *Christ* mean "the _____ One."

For the Love of Jacob

I'm not sure any part of our study of the patriarchs displays the complexities of the human psyche better than the week before us. Just when we think we can relate with the feelings of one character, another one looks at us straight from a mirror. We won't always be happy for the glance, but we will always be happy for the grace. Complicated lot that we are, where on earth would we be without Jesus? Without His Spirit to fill us with love, joy, peace, patience, goodness, kindness, gentleness, faithfulness, and self-control? Simply said, Jesus makes us different than we'd be. Get ready for a wild week, Dear One, and watch for the answers to the following questions:

This Week's Principal Questions

Day 1: According to Genesis 29:11, what did Jacob do after removing the stone and watering the sheep?

Day 2: What excuse did Laban offer for deceiving Jacob (Gen. 29:26)?

Day 3: What critical emotional point did Leah reach with the birth of her fourth child (Gen. 29:35)?

Day 4: How was Laban obviously using Jacob (Gen. 29:27)?

Day 5: Why were Rachel and Leah immediately agreeable (Gen. 31:14-16)?

Day One
When Jacob Saw Rachel

I so hope you participate in the weekly video sessions. Without them I fear the written part of our series has meteor-size holes. The sessions are vital to the journey because I often pull out some of the most important segments of Scripture to handle "in person" with you through video. Some things are just better taught orally.

Our fifth week of study concluded with Esau "consoling himself with the thought of killing" Jacob (Gen. 27:42). Pretty heavy stuff. In today's lesson we lighten up significantly. The bridge between the two weeks is the rich segment recording Jacob's dream of a "stairway resting on the earth, with its top reaching to heaven" (Gen. 28:12). If you couldn't join us for the video session, please read Genesis 28:10-22 so you will not have such a drastic shift in gears and your lesson will be in context. Thanks for going the extra mile.

Today's Scripture focus is Genesis 29:1-14. Read this segment and record any elements you find particularly interesting or out of the ordinary.

_____

_____

I'm anxious to discuss those with you in a few moments. Let's set up the scene first. Chapter 29 unfolds with the words, "Then Jacob continued on his journey." I grin as I read this translation of the phrase: "Jacob picked up his feet and went."[1] The terminology echoes the annoying chide of my grade school P. E. teacher, "Pick up your feet, Miss Green!" When I

Day One
When Jacob Saw Rachel
Day Two
An Unexpected Bride
Day Three
Winning Love
Day Four
Speckled Blessings
Day Five
Fleeing from Uncle

Today's Treasure
When Jacob saw Rachel daughter of Laban . . . he went over and rolled the stone away from the mouth of the well and watered his uncle's sheep.
Genesis 29:10

heard those words, I always pictured holding my feet in my hands—shoes and all—while prancing around on stilt-like footless ankles. Don't picture Jacob that way. The Hebrew terminology in Genesis 29:1 suggests a lightness in Jacob's steps, translated in the *Amplified Version* as "briskly and cheerfully."

Glance at Genesis 28:10-22. If you were Jacob—embarking on a pilgrimage of sorts and facing a new life—how would this experience affect your journey?

_____

_____

The stage in today's segment is incomplete without Jacob's encounter at Bethel looming in the background.

What did God tell Jacob in Genesis 28:15? Check all that apply.
❏ I will give this land to your family forever.
❏ I will not leave you until I have done what I have promised you.
❏ I will watch over you wherever you go.
❏ I will protect you from all that try to harm you.
❏ I will bring you back to this land.

Haven't we all at one time or another wished we could encounter a physical, undeniable, and very personal manifestation of God? I've often asked groups how different our prayer lives would be if Christ suddenly showed up while we were having our quiet time. Imagine Him saying, "Don't let me disturb you. Go right ahead," and then we proceed as if He isn't there! Imagine our boldness if all doubt of His nearness, love, and attentiveness were removed. I like to think that if I had a Jacob experience, I'd skip and dance all the way down the road on my subsequent journey as one without fear!

So, why don't I? And why don't you? For those who receive His Son by faith, the promises of God's presence, His call, and His attentive care are among the most repeated concepts we find in the New Testament. The following Scriptures constitute only a smattering of those that speak of God's constant presence and care.

How do the following New Testament promises exceed God's promise to Jacob in Genesis 28:15?

Matthew 1:22-23 _____

_____

Matthew 28:19-20 _____

_____

John 14:16-18 _____

_____

"I am with you and will watch over you wherever you go, and I will bring you back to this land. I will not leave you until I have done what I have promised you."
Genesis 28:15

2 Timothy 4:18 _____

_____

Most of us haven't encountered a physical manifestation of God, but we have His God-breathed promises on paper in permanent marker. Jacob didn't. As Christians we have more than a memory of a dream. We have a written guarantee that we can recheck as often as we need reassurance. We also have the Holy Spirit residing in us as a deposit guaranteeing what is to come (see Eph. 1:14). Let's start walking like it! Let's step out of our shackles of fear and doubt, pick up our feet, and get on with it!

Jacob's feet kicked up miles of dust until they eventually carried him to a well surrounded by flocks of sheep and their shepherds. No doubt you're noting the recurrent theme of wells. Remember, water was life, and those who didn't live close to rivers were entirely dependent on wells. Happening on people at a well in the ancient Middle East was about as coincidental as happening on people at a remote truck stop in a state like Arizona.

> **Read Genesis 29:3 again. What had to happen before the sheep could drink?**
> ❑ The shepherds had to drink. ❑ The sheep had to rest.
> ❑ The stone had to be rolled away. ❑ The sun had to go down.

Jacob's questions to the shepherds seem more like an interrogation than an interview, don't they? He obviously couldn't resist telling them how to do their jobs. (Can anyone relate?) When he told them to "water the sheep and take them back to pasture," the shepherds explained that they couldn't until all the flocks were gathered. The stone at the mouth of the well was obviously more than a few men could budge, and they were forced to wait for more manpower (v. 8).

> That's where the story gets interesting. Even humorous. Review verses 9 and 10 and fill in the blanks:
>
> "While he was still talking with them, Rachel came with her father's sheep, for she
>
> was a shepherdess. When Jacob _____ Rachel daughter of Laban, his
>
> mother's brother, and Laban's sheep, he went over and _____ the
>
> _____ away from the mouth of the well and watered his uncle's sheep."

Might we conclude that one smitten man has the strength of 10 men who aren't? If I could participate in small group, I'd start a discussion on all the funny things we've seen adolescent boys do to win the favor of a girl. I can picture the swagger in their steps. I could nearly get a headache from the scent of Dad's cologne. The term "aftershave" might be a stretch since most of them wouldn't have a patch worthy of a razor for years.

Jacob was a grown man with a full beard, but his emotional growth was squashed under the weight of his overbearing mother. His actions in this scene are delightfully adolescent. Ironically, all Rebekah's pushing on her son Jacob's behalf only pushed the two apart. Jacob had to walk many miles to escape his mother's apron strings. At the well near Laban's house, Mama was nowhere in sight. Esau had been the muscle man in the family, but the sight of

Rachel to Jacob was like an opened can of spinach to Popeye. I like the wording of one of my commentaries: "Jacob acts Samsonesque only on this one occasion."[2] I'm enough of a romantic to believe that every man—no matter his size or type—has some Samson-strength somewhere within him. Of course, Jacob's sudden superhuman strength didn't just come from a sight for sore eyes. Remember, in Genesis 28:15 God promised to be with him … and God specializes in rolling away stones.

 According to Genesis 29:11, what did Jacob do after removing the stone and watering the sheep?

_____

To western readers a greeting of kisses and tears from someone we've never met highlights the "strange" in stranger. Of course, greeting another person with a kiss was—and often still is—a very common custom in the ancient near East and many other parts of the world (see Rom. 16:16). I can relate. In my extended family, we often kiss when we greet. Keep in mind that once Jacob knew Rachel's identity, she was far more like a relative than a stranger to him. You probably noticed that Laban also greeted Jacob with a kiss after "he hurried to meet him" (29:13).

 This might be a fun question to surface our diversities in tastes and practices: What is your customary way of greeting someone you've just met?

_____

Would you greet him or her any differently if you realized you had a tie of some kind? If so, how?

If the tie is business or education, I usually … _____

_____

If the tie is familial, I usually… _____

_____

If the tie is spiritual, I usually … _____

_____

Yesterday my daughter and I were at the mall, and I was approached by a darling young woman who has completed several of the Bible studies. I embraced her enthusiastically and appropriately shook her husband's hand. After we visited for a moment and said our good-byes, I realized that I commonly hug women who tell me we've studied God's Word together; but I extend my hand to shake the hand of virtually everyone else I meet, even if it's a woman. What's the difference? A sense of kinship can invite almost immediate affection.

I was amused by the varied points of view I encountered in my commentaries. I can't resist sharing a portion out of *The Beginning of Wisdom* that might broaden our interpretations of Jacob's actions.

Jacob's boldness with the boulder is matched by his boldness with the woman. The flock he waters, but the woman he kisses. To protect Jacob's reputation, commentators have been at pains to insist that this was a genteel kiss, a sign of respect or familial affection. And Jacob truly has every reason to be overjoyed to have arrived safely and to have met up with his kin; the tears he weeps could be tears of joyous relief, his lifted voice could be an expression of thanksgiving. Indeed, Jacob could well take this fortuitous meeting—a perfect answer in the perfect place at the perfect moment—as a sign that Rachel is his destiny. But his kiss is bold in any case, and, considered as a sequel to his superhuman heroics with the stone, it looks to be love-inspired. He kisses Rachel even before speaking to her. In fact, this is the only instance in biblical narrative in which a man kisses a woman who is neither his wife nor his mother. Jacob acts on strong and immediate passion, and Rachel allows it. Only after the kiss and the weeping does Jacob speak, identifying himself as her father's kin and as Rebekah's son. Rachel, who has apparently remained speechless, runs home to tell her father.[3]

Ah, yes. Jacob was smitten indeed. He will soon discover, however, that the cost of love is sometimes high when tallied on an in-law's ledger.

Day Two
An Unexpected Bride

My childhood family lived right across the street from the high school in Arkansas. Most days I preferred my grandmother's cooking to the school cafeteria, so my saddle oxfords made a beeline home at lunchtime. I invariably walked through the front door to the theme music from the soap opera "As the World Turns."

As we prepare to read today's segment, I feel like that same music should play in the background. I want to warn you that Jacob is going to end up with several wives and eventually four mothers for his children. We'll discover today that Jacob received an unwanted push, but his continuance was his own doing.

Our narrative will not support polygamy but does state it as a fact. In your study of God's Word, be careful not to confuse a statement of fact with divine support. When unclear, God's approval or disapproval of various events is determined by the overriding counsel of His Word. God's plan for marriage *was* and *is* one man and one woman (see Gen. 2:24; Matt. 19:4-6; Eph. 5:31). Jacob's world, however, commonly practiced polygamy and viewed multiple wives as the means to many children.

We live in a culture far removed from Abraham, Isaac, and Jacob's, but I think all of us can relate to family sagas that could rival soap operas. Honestly, I can't think of a societal ill, sin, or challenge we haven't encountered somewhere in my extended family. God help us, one of my great-grandfathers was buried with his wife on one side of him and his mistress on the other! I am adamant that some of those influences not trickle down.

Today's Treasure
When morning came, there was Leah! So Jacob said to Laban, "What is this you have done to me? I served you for Rachel, didn't I? Why have you deceived me?"
Genesis 29:25

Please read Genesis 29:14-30. Identify and describe both the characters that follow on the information given in this text. You might even describe what you think they were like, creating a character sketch of sorts.

Leah: _____

_____

_____

Rachel: _____

_____

_____

 What excuse did Laban offer for deceiving Jacob (v. 26)?

_____

In all, how many years did Jacob work for Laban to win Rachel? _____

I purposely overlapped yesterday's text with today's by including verse 14 in both. I believe this verse is strangely foretelling in the Jacob/Laban saga. What did Laban say when he met and embraced Jacob (v. 14)?

❑ I'm so glad to meet you.   ❑ You are my own flesh and blood.
❑ Why are you persecuting me?   ❑ You will live to regret this day.

The NASB translates the exclamation, "Surely you are my bone and my flesh." Many scholars are convinced Laban's words imply more than a statement of blood kinship. One commentary reads, "While each of these passages includes … the possibility of blood ties, the larger context would suggest that a reciprocal covenant oath is involved as well. Laban is not only celebrating family connections, but is instituting, albeit in an incipient state, a bond between nephew and uncle. Of course, Laban will be the head, while Jacob will be the junior partner."[4] Another reads, "Laban exclaims with gusto, 'Thou are surely my bone and my flesh,' affirming kinship not only in blood but perhaps also of character. This hidden warning is lost on Jacob, who moves in with his uncle."[5]

I was intrigued by the suggestion of yet another commentator that Laban ran with great enthusiasm to Jacob because he was expecting riches like those his family received for Rebekah.[6] Don't forget! Rebekah was Laban's sister, and their family gained much wealth when they agreed to her marriage to Isaac. Jacob, on the other hand, came comparatively empty-handed. But Laban will prove deceptively shrewd as he exacts extravagant payment from Jacob.

We will miss a crucial point, however, if we paint Jacob in this portrait dressed entirely as a victim. We will discover that in Laban, Jacob meets his match. Yes, Jacob had an encounter with God in Genesis 28, but God makes very sure that Jacob also reaps some of what he has sown. Otherwise, what will motivate a permanent change in Jacob's character? Our wise

God will often appoint circumstances and consequences to change what a fresh encounter with Him does not.

> **Suspect an ulterior motive in virtually everything Laban offers. The first example appears in verse 15. How does Laban at first seem thoughtful?**

_____

By hiring Jacob and paying him, Laban is not exalting him nor treating him more like family as it first seems. "As we will see, Laban will treat Jacob not as kin but as servant, and Jacob too will regard himself this way. But in either case, and regardless of Laban's intention, when Jacob names a wage for himself, Jacob agrees defacto to become his uncle's hireling. Blood and business make bad bedfellows."[7]

Not coincidentally, as soon as the business matter is settled, we are introduced to the other daughter. My maternal heart breaks as I see the comparison drawn between Leah and Rachel. My daughters are very different, but each of them possesses strengths and poise that diffuse destructive comparisons. The meanings offered for Leah's name are appalling, ranging from "cow" to "weary" and "disgusted."[8] When you were asked to describe Leah, you probably noted her "weak eyes." The Hebrew word for _weak_ can also be translated "soft," "tender," or "delicate."[9] _Word Biblical Commentary_ suggests, "What makes eyes 'soft' is unclear; most commentators think it means they had no fire or sparkle, a quality much prized in the East. Whether her eyes were the only features that let her down is not said, but the glowing description of Rachel as having 'a beautiful figure and a lovely face' suggests Leah was outshone by her sister in various ways."[10]

> **No matter who we are we have suffered the slings and arrows of painful comparison at some point. How would you describe the feeling of being negatively compared to another person?**

_____

_____

I suppose most of the world's cultures place a high premium on physical attractiveness, but skin-deep beauty has proved remarkably deceptive. "Visible beauty is strikingly obvious; at its extreme, it can be blinding, preventing the viewer from even looking for signs of the soul. For the beautiful look conveys wholeness and self-sufficiency and advertises its bearer as self-evidently good. Indeed, so confident are we in the reliability of the beautiful that we rarely wonder whether it advertises itself truly. In contrast, we somehow know that it is less easy to read the soul, a truth mirrored for us in the biblical text by the difficulty in deciphering the description given of Leah's eyes."[11]

I grieve over our culture's emphasis on physical attractiveness. The media taunts us with doctored images of unattainable perfection. Even at our best, we do not—and often _cannot_—reflect the magazine images that plague us at the grocery checkout. We stare at the covers and then at the foods in our carts. The pressure makes us either want to ditch our groceries or consume them compulsively.

Sorry for the soapbox, but this issue hits close to home. As I shared in the book I wrote on family, _Feathers from My Nest_, our youngest daughter nearly scared us to death with an eating issue during her senior year in high school. Her extreme sadness over a personal loss caused her to lose significant weight from her slender frame. Though she looked almost like death, she got nothing but positive affirmation from her peers. When they crowned her prom queen, I'm not sure how the crown kept from sliding to her ankles. Thankfully, God brought Melissa through the ordeal victoriously, turning our nightmare into a testimony.

Perhaps you have your own soapbox. If so, I'll give you a little space to share it. If you don't have any thoughts on the matter, simply share a time when you learned that beauty can be deceiving. (Remember not to dishonor anyone.)

_____

_____

_____

We'll try to give Jacob a break. Our cultural issues aren't his fault. After all, he obviously fell in love with Rachel at first sight, having never seen Leah. Speaking of seeing Leah, she was the last face he expected to see the morning after.

Let's back up a bit and reread verses 20 and 21. Explain why seven years could seem like only a few days. If you have a personal example when time seemed to pass similarly, share it as your explanation.

_____

_____

At the end of the seven years, Jacob said to Laban, "Give me my wife." The terminology suggests that the couple was betrothed, but their marriage had never been consummated. One commentary translated the Hebrew far more as a demand than a request: "Now then! My wife."[12] Please note Laban's silence. We're simply told that he gathered the people and gave a feast. The breadth of Laban's deception is implied in Rachel's assumed role as bride throughout the actual feast. The bride-swap took place after the feast and presumably in the darkness. The switch itself shows the striking family resemblance between Laban and Jacob.

Laban's mode of deception illustrates his first words to Jacob: "surely you are my bone and my flesh" (Gen. 29:14, NASB). They were cut from the same cloth you might say. Jacob posed as his older brother. Laban posed Leah as her younger sister. We may wonder how Jacob could have fallen for such a ruse. At least Isaac had blindness and old age as an excuse.

Many have reasoned that the customary wedding veil—aided by the darkness—kept Jacob from realizing the swap. The ancient Jewish historian Josephus offered a likely possibility, assessing that Jacob was "deluded by wine and the dark."[13] He could be right since the Hebrew word translated "feast" in today's segment (*misteh*) comes from a word (*sata*) meaning "to drink."[14]

When the confetti was gone and the chalice was dry, the deceiver had been deceived. Jacob reaped what he had sown. *The Beginning of Wisdom* offers profound food for thought: "the story offers a powerfully ironic comment on the love of visible beauty, and shows as well the unreliability of trusting alone to sight. For where is visible beauty in the dark? Jacob, with stars in his eyes, is shown here to be blinded, not necessarily by lust or drink but by the love of the beautiful itself. He does not know one wife from the other except superficially."[15]

We can have stars in our eyes in more ways than romantic love. God calls us to love, but He never calls us to love blindly. In your own words, what was Paul's prayer for believers in Philippians 1:9?

_____

Could Laban have done Leah a greater disservice in his attempt to honor custom? After Jacob promised seven more years of labor, Laban allowed him to have Rachel.

Complete the Shakespearean-like tragedy from Genesis 29:30.

"Jacob lay with Rachel also, and he _____ Rachel _____ than Leah."

You can force a marriage, but you can't force a heart.

Day Three
Winning Love

Take a deep breath because you're going to need it. I can't think of an intellectual way to frame today's lesson. Some things are not intellectual. They are not necessarily even rational. They are red-hot emotional. We're big girls. We can handle this, so let's get to it.

Please read Genesis 29:31–30:24. (Your reading today overlaps two chapters.) Imagine you are a Christian counselor. Leah and Rachel have each come to see you for a one-hour session. Neither knows the other is seeking your counsel. Both talk incessantly the entire hour, leaving you only a minute to advise them. In the space below, offer your succinct advice to each woman.

Leah: _____

_____

Rachel: _____

_____

Today's Treasure

Surely my husband will love me now.
Genesis 29:32

I wish I could hear your advice. When studying an ancient biblical narrative involving such different cultural practices, we might at first be tempted to think we can't relate. After all, hopefully none of us share a husband with another wife and two maidservants, for crying out loud! Women are women, however, regardless of the era; therefore, we can relate to Leah and Rachel. Let's organize our thoughts.

Notice the maidservants are never quoted in this narrative. The wives, Leah and Rachel, took official authority over the maidservants' children who were conceived on the wives' behalf. Though this practice is peculiar and troubling to us, it was not uncommon at the time. Keep in mind that surrogate mothers are not terribly uncommon even in our culture. The striking difference is that labs and test tubes were not used for the process of conception in Leah and Rachel's day.

Search Genesis 29:31–30:24 carefully and record the following.
- **The name of each child born to Jacob in birth order (You will find 12.)**
- **The birth mother's name**
- **Any coinciding statement regarding the mother's feelings or the child's name**
- **Not every birth record has a coinciding statement; when one exists, specify who made it. I've supplied the first entry to get you started.**

Child's Name	Mother	Coinciding Statement	Made By
Reuben	Leah	"It is because the Lord has seen my misery. Surely my husband will love me now."	Leah

Do you wonder why the rapid-fire record of births was interrupted by a business deal over mandrake plants? Are you ready for this? In ancient times, they believed "mandrakes aroused sexual desire and helped barren women to conceive."[16] Leah and Rachel had more than a husband in common. They shared complete desperation (a theme in Genesis) and a certainty that getting something they lacked would complete them and make them happy. That's why we can relate.

What did Leah lack?

_____

What did Rachel lack?

_____

Beloved, with the love and compassion of a woman right next to you, may I ask what you feel you most lack?

_____

Does this lack ever make you feel somewhat desperate? If so, how?

_____

_____

Since Sarah's infertility gave us many chances for application early in our series, we'll focus on Leah today. You can hear Leah's heart as she journeyed through a host of painful emotions in the explanations she gave for her sons' names. You can literally hear her processing through emotional stages.

Look in Genesis 29:31-35. Based on the statements Leah made as she named her first four sons, explain her mindset by describing the process of emotions she experienced. I'll get you started.

Son	Leah's Mindset
Reuben	Surely my husband will love me now.
Simeon	
Levi	
Judah	

The human psyche requires love for wholeness. That's a fact of life. Self-love won't cut it. Unfortunately, we are born into a world with no guarantee we'll be loved. We're all desperate for love, but in some seasons of our lives we become convinced we must have *a certain person's love* to be complete. That person doesn't have to be a spouse or a romantic interest. He or she may be a parent, a relative, a neighbor, a church member, a mentor, or a peer.

I have painful memories of adolescent desperation for my peers to love and accept me. I was (often unfortunately) able to get the guy, but I was desperate for real and trusting female friendships. My desperation finally became the life-gift that led me to a passionate relationship with Jesus. However, if desperation doesn't birth a passion for Him, it will still birth something else.

Paraphrase the following statement as if you were explaining it to a teenager: The troubled child of desperation is obsession.

_____

Dear One, have you ever been obsessed with something? If so, try to pinpoint the desperation at its root. If you feel comfortable writing it, please do.

_____

_____

Leah was *desperate* for Jacob's love, so she became obsessed with having his children. If untreated by the love of God, desperation gives birth to obsession. Invariably we learn what Leah discovered. Obsession neither heals desperation nor fill its lack. The statements Leah made are like mirrors reflecting her heart. They reveal a very private process she experienced emotionally. "It is because the Lord has seen my misery. (Reuben means, 'see, a son.'[17]) Surely my husband will love me now." But he didn't.

Through the birth of her second child, Leah's emotional processing brought her to: "Because the Lord heard that I am not loved, He gave me this one too." (Simeon comes from a word that means "hear.")[18] In other words, Jacob still didn't love her, but at least God "heard" and granted her favor. Leah's comments over the third son break my heart. At this point she decided that if she couldn't have Jacob's love, she'd settle for attachment. The children in her estimation would at least attach Jacob to her. (Levi comes from a word meaning "join.")[19] Beloved, haven't some of us done exactly that? If we can't get a person to love us, have any of us ever tried to manipulate some way they'd at least be tied to us? I've seen this scenario played out countless times to varying degrees. I can think back on my own young life and recall times when I unknowingly did this very thing.

How about you? Can you relate? If so, would you be willing to share how?

_____

_____

_____

What critical emotional point did Leah reach with the birth of her fourth child (29:35)?

_____

The name Judah means praise.[20] Leah finally—if temporarily—progressed to a place where God became the only sense in a senseless spiral, and she gave Him praise. If only Leah could have remained in the mindset of praise for all she had instead of returning to misery for all she lacked, how different her life would have been! Instead, she did what you and I have also done at times. She allowed circumstances (Rachel's children through Bilhah and her own inability to conceive) to eventually catapult her back to the old mindset, and she picked up her familiar obsession again.

Haven't we had similar experiences? Has God ever brought you through a very painful process where you were finally able to think victoriously? Then over time did something happen to catapult you back into the old cycle of defeated thinking? Have we lost ground we worked so hard to gain? Let's regain the freedom we lost! Our Liberator has not changed. Beloved, let's allow God to show us our deepest desperation is for Him. The troubled child of desperation is obsession, but the healthy child of desperation is devotion. Our desperation will birth something. What will it be?

> *The healthy child of desperation is devotion.*

Day Four
Speckled Blessings

What a journey! We've encountered a smoking fire pot, celestial visitors, and a mysterious priest named Melchizedek, who came from who knows where. We've run into sin-infested, half-mad Sodomites who had a run-in with raining sulfur. We've wept in the desert with Hagar and Ishmael and held our breath as Abraham raised the knife to slay his beloved Isaac. We've witnessed the birth of history's first recorded twins and watched a ridiculously-clad Jacob steal his brother's blessing. We attended Jacob and Rachel's wedding supper and wondered how clueless the man had to be not to catch on to the swap. This, my dear, has been a ride. We're a long way from coming into the station where our journey ends, but we can rest assured that we're not likely to get bored.

What has been the wildest part of this journey for you personally and why?

_____

Today's subject matter doesn't break any records on the bizarre barometer, but it's not your run-of-the-mill daily devotional material either. Please read Genesis 30:25-43 and complete the following.

Why do you think Jacob was suddenly ready to go back to his homeland?

_____

> ## *Today's Treasure*
> In this way the man grew exceedingly prosperous and came to own large flocks, and maidservants and menservants, and camels and donkeys.
> **Genesis 30:43**

Reconsider the question Jacob asked in verse 29: "But now, when may I do something for my own household?" Have you ever felt that way? If so, when?

_____

_____

 How was Laban obviously using Jacob (v. 27)?

_____

Briefly explain the deal Jacob offered Laban for payment.

_____

What was the outcome?

_____

Initially Jacob didn't approach Laban to play "Let's Make a Deal." He simply came to him saying he'd served him long enough and wanted to be released to go home with his family. Jacob's beloved Rachel finally had a child destined to become his favorite. Desires met, Jacob was ready to pack up the family and go home. In his plea to be excused, Jacob repeated the obvious to Laban. "Send me on my way ... Give me my wives and children ... You know how much work I've done for you." Laban's response brought Jacob to the realization that, true to form, Laban would never let him go easily.

At first Laban's words may seem innocent: "If I have found favor in your eyes, please stay." Remember, Jacob was desperate to go home. He'd been under his uncle's yoke and working for his uncle's gain long enough. He'd been tricked and manipulated. Had Laban found favor in Jacob's eyes? Hardly! Even if Laban's suggestion been harmless and free of innuendo, Jacob could and would have declined. He'd paid his dues. Doubtless, Jacob knew from his uncle's actions that his smooth talk was a smoke screen for control. Laban had no intention of letting Jacob go. He was too valuable.

I feel for Jacob in this opening scene, don't you? Sometimes we just want a person to be reasonable. At the first familiar sign that they're not going to budge, we lose hope, our hearts sink, and we realize it's no use. The problem is not that unreasonable people don't understand. They won't understand. Their refusal is the epicenter of their control. I suppose I find few things more frustrating than dealing with the unreasonable. Surely you know the feeling.

Is this subject matter hitting a nerve? Without naming or dishonoring anyone, describe how you felt the last time you dealt with an unreasonable person.

_____

_____

_____

Unreasonable people aren't fair people. They only agree to arrangements that grossly favor them. Hence, Jacob's plan against unreasonable Laban. In the Mediterranean world, sheep are ordinarily white, and goats are ordinarily black. Jacob and Laban took their zoology courses on location in the pastures. In classroom terminology, both of them knew the heterozygotes (those with genes for ... how shall I say ... spottedness?) were rare and that genetics would place its bet on the homozygotes. (The ones you wouldn't name Spot.)

The interesting part of Jacob's plan is in the atmosphere he created for producing "streaked or speckled or spotted" animals. You didn't miss the use of the striped branches, did you? Check them out again in Genesis 30:37-38. Jacob didn't learn this technique in zoology. In fact, the chances of the sight of striped branches producing speckled animals were about as good as the mandrakes causing pregnancy.

According to verse 30, Jacob was well aware that the blessing of God was responsible for his shepherding successes. In the scenario with the branches, Jacob had to know God's favor was the cause of the outcome. Jacob's plan was to plainly set God up for success. To make it easier for Him. To increase His chances, we might say.

Have you ever experienced an undeniable act of God then tried to figure out your part in it so you could repeat the formula? In terms of today's lesson, have you ever tried to set God up for success? The plan sounds ridiculous when we put it in these terms, but most of us have tried it nonetheless. I'll share my own case-in-point, but you be thinking of yours.

Only on rare occasions have I attended a conference I was fairly certain God didn't attend. Memories from those occasions still make me shiver. My worst nightmare is that I'll go somewhere God doesn't.

As often as I've experienced God in corporate settings, nothing compares to times His presence seems to fall with holy fire. When His presence seems palpable. When we can practically feel Him on our skin. Times when the Word flows powerfully, effortlessly, and people are so anxious to receive it they nearly jump out of their chairs. Those are the times I return to my hotel room and fall on my face speechless. Times when I know I just happened to be somewhere God visited and no one could have stopped Him. Even now, I shake my head at the wonder of it. Those are moments when all doubts of God as man's greatest present reality evaporate, and all who will are exquisitely scarred for life by holy fire.

Each time it happens—or I should say He happens—I wish He'd do it every time. "Lord, that's what I love to see happen! They knew You were there, Lord! That's what I love to experience most! The Word fell from heaven, Lord! Did You feel it, too? Don't You love it, too?" On and on I boast in Him as if I could talk Him into dropping His presence like that in every gathering.

I've tried my hardest to figure it out. Is the steadfast prayer of the intercessory team the difference? Is fasting the difference? Is the specific city the difference? Did we pray a certain thing? Or were we purer of heart than usual? Did we have more humility? Did God bless the willingness to serve during personal crisis? Did we have more faith?

I could come up with a hundred different scenarios, and the only common denominator would be God. The difference is the sovereign, selective will of God. We don't set Him up for success. He sets us up. We're not worthy enough for Him to bless. He's worthy and has the grace to bless.

God is not about to let us come up with a formula for blessing. If He did, we'd stick to our formula rather than sticking to our God. Yes, God blesses obedience ... and prayer ... and fasting ... and faith ... and certainly a pure heart, but the way He manifests His blessing can differ dramatically from one time to the next.

Nothing compares to God's presence falling with holy fire.

OK, I've given you enough time. How have you tried to "set God up for success" or come up with a formula for blessing?

_____

_____

What did you learn from your experience?

_____

_____

God blessed the flocks of Jacob more than Laban because He was faithful to His promises. At Bethel He told Jacob that He'd spread out his descendants "to the west and to the east, to the north and to the south," and that He'd bless him and be with him wherever he went. God also emphatically promised to bring Jacob back to the land (Gen. 28:14-15). The method God chose and revealed ingeniously to Jacob meant the bleating of spotted, speckled sheep and goats would follow Jacob and his family all the way home. As for the branches? Mere accessories.

Save your trees and bow down to a sovereign God.

Day Five'
Fleeing from Uncle

Today's Treasure

This heap is a witness, and this pillar is a witness, that I will not go past this heap to your side to harm you and that you will not go past this heap and pillar to my side to harm me.

Genesis 31:52

Today's lesson includes all 55 verses of Genesis 31, but it's a great read! Please stop and ask God to give you focus to follow this story line and to help you discern how He desires to apply it to you. Our reading will take place in three parts.

First, read Genesis 31:1-21 and complete the following. As you can see, God once again revealed Himself to Jacob through a dream. In your own words, what did God tell Jacob?

_____

_____

 Why were Rachel and Leah immediately agreeable according to verses 14-16?

_____

_____

What did Rachel steal from Laban? Choose one.
❏ her father's household gods ❏ the inheritance he owed her ❏ her dowry

In our previous lesson we discussed the frustration of dealing with unreasonable people. Note Jacob's words to Leah and Rachel in verses 5-13. Surely nothing places us in a more awkward position than a conflict between our parents and our spouse or—to turn it around the other way—our in-laws and ourselves. If you're married, you can almost feel the acid churn in your stomach as you think about it, can't you? We love our parents and our spouses and feel a certain amount of loyalty to each of them, but we know that our first allegiance is to our spouse. The situation escalates and complicates when the spouse proves to be the primary problem. Times like these demand much prayer, sensitivity, willingness to speak truth in love, and sometimes godly counseling.

Thankfully, Jacob was not the only cause of the conflict between his wives and their father. As you view the verses again, note Jacob's willingness to talk through the situation with Leah and Rachel. Do you hear him using reason? Actually, in the ancient Middle East, cultural practices did not necessarily require reasoning sensitively with a woman. But instead of making demands, Jacob approached his wives with care, essentially saying, "We have been more than fair with your father. Surely you'll agree that enough is enough. God has instructed us to leave." Rachel and Leah had also seen the change in their father and claimed he treated them as foreigners rather than daughters. Jacob's thoughts and plans were not unreasonable, so they followed him willingly. But not without a secret stash of Laban's idols.

Nothing like a little extra baggage in what was already a complicated mess. Thanks, Rachel. In all likelihood she probably stole the idols for the protection these "gods" were believed to bring. In verse 20 the Hebrew phrase "Jacob deceived Laban" literally translates, "Jacob stole Laban's heart."[21] Rachel, on the other hand, stole Laban's gods.

Let's consider a possible application of Rachel's actions. Surely we have been in situations where we were genuinely mistreated; but in the process of gaining our freedom, someone in our camp did something foolish. Have you ever noticed how hard remaining blameless can be in a conflict? I have!

The chances of one side staying spotless while the other side is covered in mud are fairly remote. Do you agree? ❑ yes ❑ no Why or why not?

_____

_____

Read Genesis 31:22-44.

Laban was obviously a polytheist, but when our God desires to issue a rebuke, the recipient doesn't have to be His follower. God can speak to whomever He pleases. In a nutshell, what did God say to Laban (v. 24)?

_____

The NIV rendering sounds like God forbade Laban to talk to Jacob, but He didn't. The following are two closer renderings of the Hebrew: "Refrain from threatening Jacob with any harm."[22] And, "Take care not to contradict Jacob."[23] Laban knew when he approached Jacob which one had the favor of God.

Use your imagination and describe what might have been going through Jacob, Leah, and Rachel's minds "when Laban overtook him, and Laban and his relatives camped there too" (v. 25). You know a little about each of their personalities by now, so try to reflect their possible thoughts accordingly.

Jacob might have thought, _____

_____

Leah might have thought, _____

_____

Rachel might have thought, _____

_____

Genesis 31:27 records Laban's most outlandish excuse for claiming he should have been told of their departure in advance. What did he claim he would have done?

_____

Reread verses 28-29. What do you think Laban meant when he said: "You have done a foolish thing. I have the power to harm you"?

_____

Compare verse 7. To what or to whom does Jacob attribute Laban's inability to harm him?

_____

How did Rachel get away with god-napping (vv. 34-35)?

_____

I didn't bring up the subject. God did. I'm sorry if we're uncomfortable with cycle-talk (and I don't mean the kind with wheels), but as long as God brought it up, perhaps it begs a point. After all, this is women's ministry. Laban differs little from most of the men in our lives. The last thing they want to discuss with us is our periods.

Forgive me, but someone needs to say this. Most moms who have raised teenage daughters have tried to explain to their husbands why the child is insufferable at times. When we attempt to say the "p" word, they invariably throw their hands over their ears and yell, "I don't want to talk about that!" I'm laughing just thinking about it. To men, all PMS need mean is "Pops Move Swiftly." In other words, get out of Dodge till the hormone infestation is properly exterminated. Men aside, here's my point to us girls: since we know our men would rather the whole subject remain mysterious, we can use it for all sorts of excuses we know we probably won't have to explain.

What kinds of behaviors might we excuse this way?

_____

_____

Let's not be like Rachel. Let's walk in truth, *especially* during the worst week—and most convenient excuse—of the month.

After Laban searched for the household gods to no avail, Jacob became furious and "took Laban to task" (v. 36). The words poured forth from his mouth like a dam breaking under the pressure of raging waters.

At the end of his tirade, Jacob called God a very interesting name in connection

with Isaac. What is it (v. 42)? _____

The title "Fear of Isaac," appearing only in Genesis 31, has been the subject of much discussion among scholars. Various proposed alternatives for translating the Hebrew are "kinsman of Isaac," "Thigh of Isaac," "the Dreaded One of Isaac," and, loosely, "fear [is his] shadow/protector."[24] Other scholars have no problem accepting the phrase exactly as it appears in many of our major Bible translations: "the Fear of Isaac." In biblical context, the word "fear" can mean terror or reverence. Succinctly, it is holy fear.

Can't we imagine Isaac intimately knew of the fear of God through both terror and reverence? After all, it was Isaac who encountered God while strapped to an altar and his father's hand raised to slay him. Surely Isaac was terrified of the One who sent him to Mount Moriah, yet he reverenced the One who spared him. I have no trouble picturing that the name of God most closely associated with Isaac is fear. By calling God this name in front of Laban, Jacob was reminding his father-in-law that God isn't to be taken lightly or disobeyed flippantly.

Now, let's consider our third and final segment. Please read Genesis 31:44-55. Why was the heap of stones called "Mizpah" according to verses 49 and 50?

_____

I believe the covenant made between Jacob and Laban suggests an important concept. God desires every wayward individual to be reconciled to Him, but God's desire is not always for two (unmarried) individuals to be reconciled to one another. Certainly the New Testament teaches us to be reconciled to our brothers and sisters in Christ, but sometimes the former bonds of attachment had nothing to do with Christ.

For instance, I am sometimes asked sincere questions about whether or not people who have had wrong or illicit relationships can later have active friendships. Though I'm not a counselor, I've seen too many disasters to ever recommend resuming such relationships. Emotional bonds are far too powerful. And if we have really sorrowed to the point of full repentance, why would we have any affection or sympathy for that relationship? If the repentance was deep, the pain of such a deep offense toward God and man was also probably deep (2 Cor. 7:10). The memory of those relationships ought to give us shivers of terror.

Although God's Word teaches us to forgive and to seek forgiveness, I don't believe Scripture counsels us to reconcile relationships God despised. He loves people, but make no mistake—He can despise relationships. Some relationships are nothing less than an abomination. Sometimes two people who need God to stand between them weren't in an illicit relationship. They simply can't keep from doing one another harm. Too much anger still rages. They need to be sent to opposite ends of the boxing ring with the referee firmly planted between them.

I think Laban and Jacob offer us a prime example of restoration in terms of forgiveness and goodwill—but not togetherness. Sometimes God restores two people to one another on the basis of the cross. Other times He restores them to Himself but stands between them as a witness for their protection and accountability. Consider these two diagrams as a New Testament rendition of two types of reconciliation. Allow the cross to signify Christ.

Conclude today's lesson by studying the two diagrams. Describe the type of reconciliation you see represented in each. After writing your interpretation, circle the one that resembles the covenant of Mizpah between Laban and Jacob. Thanks for your hard work today! I'm nuts about you.

[1] Gordon J. Wenham, *Word Biblical Commentary: Genesis 16–50* (Dallas: Word Books, 1994), 227.

[2] Victor P. Hamilton, *The Book of Genesis: Chapters 18–50* (Grand Rapids: William B. Eerdman's Publishing, 1995), 255.

[3] Leon R. Kass, *The Beginning of Wisdom: Reading Genesis* (New York: Free Press, 2003), 313.

[4] Hamilton, 256.

[5] Kass, 422-23.

[6] Ibid., 422.

[7] Ibid., 423.

[8] Ibid., 423.

[9] Spiros Zodhiates et al., eds., *The Complete Word Study Dictionary: Old Testament* (Chattanooga, TN: AMG Publishers, 1994), 108.

[10] Wenham, 235.

[11] Kass, 233-34.

[12] Hamilton, 261.

[13] Ibid., 262.

[14] Ibid., 263.

[15] Kass, 426.

[16] Wenham, 246.

[17] Hamilton, 267.

[18] Ibid., 267.

[19] Ibid., 268.

[20] Ibid., 268.

[21] Ibid., 295.

[22] Ibid., 299.

[23] Wenham, 282.

[24] Hamilton, 278.

SESSION SIX
For the Love of Jacob

- "I will pacify him with these gifts:" "I may _____ his _____."
   (The word *kapar* translated "cover" is also the word for "make an atonement.)
- "with these gifts I'm sending on ahead:" " ... gifts that go before my _____."
- "later, when I see him:" "when I _____ _____."
- "perhaps he will receive me:" "he will raise _____ _____."
- "So Jacob's gifts went on ahead of him:" "the gifts went on _____ of his _____."

The point? Jacob was _____ to _____ his brother.

Genesis 32:22-31. *Peniel* means " the _____ of _____." When we _____ facing something or _____, what we need most is to _____ _____ God.

Jacob's Face-to-Face Encounter:

1. An _____ _____. Verse 24 tells us Jacob was _____ _____. We are _____ we _____ without our _____ and our _____.

2. An _____ _____.
   - The basic idea behind "could not overpower him" is that he could not _____ him _____. (Compare Hos. 12:3-5.) God taught Jacob how to _____ _____ and _____ _____.
   - Sometimes in the dark of our _____ seasons, we don't know with _____ we're _____ until the _____ begins to dawn.
   - When God allows or even _____ us to wrestle with Him, His constant goal is to make us _____. Even when God appears to be _____ us, He is _____ us.

3. An _____ _____. The name *Jacob* means _____ and _____.
   - In every struggle _____ _____ let go until the _____ _____.

4. An _____ _____ (v. 28). Few things _____ us more than _____ we struggle. When we struggle through the crisis with God all the way to the _____, we are gloriously _____.

God of the House

Our seventh week of study adds broad strokes to the character sketch of our present patriarch, Jacob. However, just when you think you're settling into the flow of the chapter, tragedy will strike with imposing interruption. Be especially prayerful as you engage in each day's study this week. The subject matter at times will be difficult, but the lessons will be deep. Let's stay open to all God wishes to teach us. Keep the following questions in mind as you meet with Him in His Word each day.

This Week's Principal Questions

Day 1: What does Matthew 5:23-24 say about making amends?

Day 2: What was Dinah's intention as she "went out," and what happened instead?

Day 3: How did Jacob alter the name for Bethel on the return visit (Gen. 35:7)?

Day 4: What did Rachel name her second son? What did Jacob name the child?

Day 5: What was the significance of the coat Jacob gave to Joseph?

Day One'
The Embrace of Brothers

My mind whirls at the thought of all the application and discussion that could come from today's lesson. I love God's Word! There's no getting to the bottom of it. It reveals and it conceals. It explains yet purposely awakens questions. Sometimes its truths are too lofty to grasp. Other times it is the foundation beneath our feet ... so relevant that we are strangely shocked by the Most High's ability to lean down and speak our language.

I hope you joined us for video session 6. If you did, perhaps you begin today's lesson by visualizing the sun rising on a limping Jacob as he emerges from an all-night wrestling match with God.

Do you recall how often Jacob repeated the Hebrew word for "face" as he fearfully planned how he'd approach Esau? We surmised that the best way to "face up" to something we deeply want to avoid is to have an honest face-to-face with God.

> **If you missed video session 6, please read Genesis 32 for the rich context from which today's lesson flows. With that in place, please read Genesis 33.**

> **Carefully consider how Jacob arranged his family as they prepared to meet Esau and his 400 men (vv. 1-2). What was he apparently thinking?**

_____

Note verse 3's contrast to a scene in the previous chapter. Recall that in Genesis 32:22-23, Jacob sent his family ahead of him. In Genesis 33:3, he stepped to the front. After Jacob wrestled with God, he had the courage to step ahead and take the lead, meeting his brother first. Though he was still terrified, he knew his place. An intense encounter with God can give us the courage to do the necessary things we wish we didn't have to do. We may still be afraid, but we're more afraid of disobeying God than facing a mess we helped make.

Day One'
The Embrace of Brothers
Day Two'
Nightmare in Shechem
Day Three'
El Bethel
Day Four'
But His Father
Day Five'
Public Dreams

Today's Treasure

Esau ran to meet Jacob and embraced him; he threw his arms around his neck and kissed him. And they wept.
Genesis 33:4

Did you wince as you considered a probable reason for the order of Jacob's family members? Though his children were no doubt all dear to him, Jacob appeared to place them in line according to their mothers' nearness to his heart. The maidservants and their children were in front. Leah and her children were next. His beloved Rachel and Joseph were in the very back—as if to keep them farther from harm. Inevitable partiality: one of many reasons why God meant one man to have one wife.

 Review Genesis 33:12-14. Offer your own thoughts concerning any unspoken reasons why Jacob might not have wanted Esau to accompany him and his family.

_____

_____

I wish I could hear your conjecture. Did you wonder if Jacob thought he and Esau had better stop while they were ahead? Their immediate encounter went well. Why push it? Sometimes a relationship has such a troubled history that short, sweet visits are preferable to longer ones. Volatile relationships are safer in small doses … if you know what I mean.

After no small amount of drama, Jacob and his entourage finally "arrived safely at the city of Shechem in Canaan and camped within sight of the city" (v. 18). Then the 19th verse records a significant action.

What did Jacob buy for a hundred pieces of silver (Gen. 33:19)?
❑ the oaks of Mamre   ❑ the field of Haman the Agagite
❑ the plot of ground where he pitched his tent

What did Jacob call the altar he set up?

_____

Jacob was home … back in the land of promise. The Hebrew name he gave the altar means "God is the God of Israel."[1] But Jacob's reference to Israel was not to Israel as a nation. At this point, Israel was only one renamed man: Jacob himself.

Jacob's reference to God as "the God of Israel" was intensely personal and reminds me of Genesis 28:20-21. Read these verses and explain the connection.

_____

_____

With an overview of the chapter behind us, let's go back and focus on the snapshot capturing the moment of encounter between Jacob and Esau. Perhaps you too noticed the sharp contrast in the physical approach of the brothers. Genesis 32 concludes with Jacob limping. The first thing Genesis 33:1 tells us is that he "looked up and there was Esau, coming."

According to Genesis 33:4, how did Esau approach Jacob?
❑ running   ❑ yelling   ❑ walking   ❑ sobbing

Do you find the contrast peculiar? Ironic? After all, Jacob was God's chosen one, not Esau. God's presence was with Jacob, yet He allowed His own child to limp while the other ran. What is wrong with this picture? At times like these I wish I were sitting right across from you so that I could lean toward you and speak compassionately and tenderly—especially if you are new to the study of God's Word. Beloved, sometimes God will wound His own child to make him walk differently while the profane and ungodly seem to run with endless confidence and vitality.

We are to walk as people who have encountered God, and some of the most transforming encounters are wrestling matches. Dear One, the lost do not wrestle with God nearly as much as we who belong to Him. The profane and ungodly don't care enough to wrestle. We who are His often wrestle with Him most, and at times we also seem to hurt the most.

Please understand that for us wounding and hurt are only temporal, yet they carry great eternal benefits: "For our light and momentary troubles are achieving for us an eternal glory that far outweighs them all" (2 Cor. 4:17). So, let the Esaus of this life run! This is the only chance they'll get! And, yes, let the Jacobs limp. We have been with God! Though our humanity may be wounded, our souls are made whole by the One with whom we wrestle.

Scripture tells us Esau ran to meet Jacob and "embraced" him. In Hebrew the phonetic similarity of the words "wrestle" (Hebrew *abaq*, Gen. 32) and "embrace" (Hebrew *habaq*, Gen. 33) is too obvious to seem coincidental.[2]

Both wrestling and embracing are ordinarily face-to-face actions that involve holding onto one another—albeit with different motivations. In our Jacob-like relationship with God, wrestling and embracing are often separated by the thinnest thread. I've wrestled with God many times until the last thread of my resistance breaks. Then I fall sobbing into His arms in desperate embrace, submitting to His will. When Jacob cried out, "I will not let you go unless you bless me" (Gen. 32:26), I believe he had moved from wrestling to embracing. I'm not at all sure Jacob could have allowed his estranged brother to embrace him had Jacob not first wrestled with God and sustained a wound to his stubborn humanity.

One of the most powerful quotes I've ever read is from the Talmud: "God says to man: 'With thy very wounds I will heal thee.'"[3]

Oh, Beloved, this concept has proved true in my life. Has it in yours? If so, how?

_____

_____

_____

Talmud
the authoritative body of Jewish traditions comprising the Mishnah and Gemara

We should not be surprised that God planned a meeting between the brothers on Jacob's way to his promised land. We too have a God-ordained land of promise where He will fulfill His lofty goals for our lives. God also has promises for us as His children. We too will have the opportunity to face our deepest conflicts and to resolve relational differences on the way. We'll often have to return in our weakest state to those we want to see us at our strongest … our limps in full view.

Think again on the scene depicting Jacob bowing down to the ground seven times as he approached Esau. Imagine the grimace of pain on his weathered face as he took such a humble posture with his wounded hip. Like Jacob, our promised lands are practically under our noses when we're closest to the ground. Bowed down.

Consider the following quote from *The Beginning of Wisdom*: "Jacob's return to Canaan and especially to his father's house means, almost certainly, meeting up with Esau. But confronting Esau is more than a practical inevitability; it is also a moral imperative. Failure to settle accounts with Esau and to make amends for his conniving past would leave a permanent blot on Jacob's supremacy. It would also cast grave doubts on his fitness as the next patriarch under the covenant. For under God's new way—in contrast to the uninstructed human way—a man cannot properly take his father's place by denying or destroying his father's other sons, that is, his brothers ... Thus, when a man fights with his brother, he is indirectly fighting with his father."[4]

At least two concluding points come from this quote. First, our unwillingness to make amends can also "cast grave doubts on [our] fitness" for our promised lands. If we cannot humble ourselves and make amends—whether or not we feel we're chiefly to blame—how are we going to be people who can do "greater works than these" (John 14:12, KJV)?

 What does Matthew 5:23-24 say about making amends?

_____

Finally, when we fight with our believing brothers and sisters, we are also "indirectly fighting with [our heavenly] father." Esau and Jacob were "blood brothers," but no greater kinship exists than the one formed by the blood of Christ. Those of us who are Christians are blood brothers and sisters in the most significant way. We know God has called us to forgive even our enemies and certainly our brothers and sisters.

I think I John 4:20-21 says it best.
Allow these verses to be our benediction today.

Wrestle, yes! But then embrace.

You worked hard today, my blood sister. I joyfully love you.

Day Two
Nightmare in Shechem

Today's Treasure
When Shechem son of Hamor the Hivite, the ruler of that area, saw her, he took her and violated her.
Genesis 34:2

I want to warn you as tenderly as possible that our lesson today is about rape. I am deeply moved by knowing some of you have been victims of this violent crime. Although victimization had a titanic effect on my own life, the resulting isolation made me feel like one of very few. Nevertheless, company I have ... in numbers too staggering to comprehend. I have not been a victim of rape in the sense we will study today, but my background enables me to relate on some level. Yours may enable you to do the same.

I'm going to do something I can't recall ever doing. I'm offering you an exemption from this lesson if you need it. If you have been the victim of rape and have never sought effective godly counsel or experienced significant healing, this lesson could disturb you without providing the ample depth to really help. If you have been sexually victimized, I urge you to please seek godly counsel. Though I pray God will minister healing words today, I lack the experience of a professional counselor. I love you dearly and would be devastated to do you more harm than good.

As for the rest of us, we can't assume for a moment we don't need this lesson. While victims of violent crime need compassion and understanding, all of us could use biblical insight into the life-altering situations His children sometimes face. I am grateful for God's unwillingness to leave us comfortable and ignorant. We'd be hard pressed to think of a single crime or human condition unaddressed in Scripture.

Please read Genesis 34.

What was Dinah's intention as she "went out," and what happened instead (v. 1)?

_____

Search the chapter carefully. Does Scripture record Dinah's response to the trauma and, if so, what was it?

_____

What emotions did Jacob's sons feel in reaction to the news of Dinah's rape (v. 7)?

_____

What did Hamor, Shechem's father, suggest to Jacob and his sons in verses 8-10?

_____

How did Hamor's reaction fail to take seriously the violent crime of rape?

_____

How did Jacob's sons deceive Hamor and Shechem, exacting revenge?

_____

How did Jacob respond to his sons' act of revenge (v. 30)?

_____

Can you imagine anyone saying "this person stole your car or broke into your house, so I think you should marry him"? Yet altogether too often people today, as in ancient times, minimize the crime of rape and even suggest Hamor's solution. Treating rape lightly adds to the horrifying fact that many victims of rape never report the crime.

Several factors add to the under reporting of rape, including embarrassment and fear of retaliation or further injury. Many victims fear the courts, police, and court procedures that too often scrutinize and judge the victim's behavior, history, and credibility.

In case you have questions about the meaning of "violated" in verse 2 of the NIV, the NASB says it clearly: "he took her and lay with her by force." HCSB reads, "raped her."

I purposely asked you to search the narrative for Dinah's reaction to her rape to heighten your awareness of its conspicuous absence. I hope to heaven she was allowed to express her pain and grief and that God simply elected not to have it written down. We don't have to be victims of rape to imagine some of the things we'd need from others in a time of such trauma.

 What do you think Dinah needed from those around her once they brought her home from Shechem's house? Be as specific as possible.

_____

_____

We'd all like to imagine that at least her mother Leah, her Aunt Rachel, Zilpah, and Bilhah poured love and compassion upon her. One thing we can know for certain: God did. And we'll hope she was able to discern it and receive it.

What do the following verses tell you about God's response to the brokenhearted?

Psalm 34:18

_____

Psalm 147:3

_____

A vast number of the rape victims in our world are under 18 years of age. Scholars who have done the math according to the time line offered for Jacob's travels estimate that Dinah was little more than a young adolescent when Schechem violated her. Add to the battery of rape the homicide of innocence. I was abused at such an early age that I don't recall having a sense of innocence. I can't imagine having it shattered so suddenly. The thought of anyone doing such a thing may have never occurred to Dinah. You'll recall I asked you Dinah's intention when she left her home that day. Scripture specifies she was going out to "visit the women of the land." The only daughter in a very large family could have used some female companionship. Unfortunately, that's not what she got.

Consider a very important question: Could some have said Dinah never should have left the family encampment? That she should never have put herself in such a position?

Let's consider the effect similar situations have on women in our culture. In Dinah's culture, her decision to visit the women of the land without male protection was probably considered as risky as a woman in our culture going out alone to a club. The comparison is particularly heightened by the end result. This point needs pressing because many victims of rape are vastly impeded in their healing by the suggestion—however carefully implied—that they were partially to blame. After all, they placed themselves in a vulnerable position. Certainly we can all stand to be wiser about high-risk environments, but to suggest a victim asked to be raped by being in a certain place is not only devastatingly ignorant but also shifts the criminal's blame to the victim.

As we seek to be vessels of Christ's love and compassion, let's separate the victim from the victimizer. Few things are more important to the victim's recovery than the support of those around her.

According to the Rape Crisis Center, sexual assault victims are usually in a state of shock after an assault. They are unsure about what to do and whom to tell. This reaction may last several hours or several days. Fear, shame, anger, loss of trust, detached calm, and depression are common reactions but vary with each sexual assault survivor. The impact of a sexual assault is often felt strongly for a year or more and is never forgotten. In today's case study, Jacob did not learn about the rape from his daughter. Remember, Shechem had not allowed Dinah to return home and was determined to keep her. All we're told is that Jacob "heard" his daughter had been violated (34:5).

I'd like to share with you something God used toward my own healing from victimization and the restoration of personal dignity. Scripture teaches that humans are made up of three components.

According to 1 Thessalonians 5:23, what are they?

_____

Now, what does 1 Corinthians 6:17 say about a believer's spirit?

_____

My body may have been violated and my soul—the seat of emotions—may have been injured, but my spirit—the innermost part of my being, where the Spirit of Christ dwells (1 Cor. 6:17)—cannot be violated. Therefore, what defines me most has never been touched.

In my own healing process, God taught me that the more I allowed the Spirit of truth dwelling in me to take authority over my body and soul, the more the wholeness of Christ would overtake every part of me. In other words, God taught me to live from the inside out. I seek to allow the strongest, most invincible part of me—the spirit—to have dominion over all else, thereby sanctifying them (setting them apart as holy) just as 1 Thessalonians 5:23 suggests. Today I live most consciously out of my healthiest part: the spirit. Through the years, the health of my spirit has been gloriously contagious to my soul and even to my body.

According to Scripture, our bodies are temples of the Holy Spirit (see 1 Cor. 3:16 and 2 Cor. 6:16). In some ways broken temples can be rebuilt. The Spirit of God dwelling within me has so overtaken my whole being that even my body no longer feels violated. I don't know if this perspective speaks to you, but it was a great help to me.

If you have found healing in Christ from victimization, perhaps you could briefly share how He helped you. (Please, don't be graphic. Keep your focus on healing.)

_____

_____

_____

Before we conclude, let's take a brief look at the fathers and sons in Dinah's story. First, I'm sure you noticed Shechem's strange reaction in the wake of the rape. His lust for Dinah only escalated until he demanded of his father, "Get me this girl as my wife" (34:4). Shechem seemed to live by the rule of many predators: take first, ask later.[5]

The Beginning of Wisdom offers these words: "A man who offers a woman reassuring words, his lust now being sated after he has raped her, is no less a rapist. Her abasement means nothing; new love will conquer all."[6] The same commentary also targets the foolishness of Shechem's father, Hamor. He is counted among "fathers serving rather than ruling the passions of their sons; a ruler leading his city into ruin for the sake of satisfying his son's erotic wishes."[7] Perhaps Hamor's actions suggest why Shechem thought he could have anything he wanted. Did he simply want sex? I read over and over in my research for this lesson that rape is an act of violence and power. Its motivation has very little to do with sexual gratification.

Lastly, consider Dinah's brothers and the outcome of the story. We are told "they were filled with grief and fury"—hopefully on Dinah's behalf and not the perceived disgrace upon the family. Grief and anger are understandable reactions to the crime against their sister; however, they did not demand justice. Simeon and Levi concocted a scheme, "attacked the unsuspecting city," and killed every male. Talk about overkill. No wonder God insists that we leave vengeance to Him. Both the victim of a crime and the loved one of a victim will be bound to the same principal outcome: until God is allowed to treat grief and anger, innocent people will pay.

Dear One, God can rebuild shattered lives. Satan will do everything he can to tempt you not to trust God because he knows your willingness to place yourself in God's holy hands will lead to full redemption. What is full redemption? Redemption is when the pain is treated and turned around so thoroughly that it not only loses its power to do you harm but also gains the power to do some good. Of this I'm certain. After treating me with the sound counsel of His Word and putting me back together again, God uses my background of childhood abuse every single day of ministry to someone else's good … even if the subject never arises.

I have known suffering, and it gives me a depth of compassion and understanding that I would never have otherwise possessed. When all was said and done, Satan got caught in the very snare he set for me. Don't stop working with God until Satan's evil plan for your life or your family backfires in his ugly face.

Day Three'
El Bethel

Sometimes we just need to move. Our surroundings can be etched with such painful memories that a change of scenery becomes imperative for our emotional and spiritual health. The dirt under our injured feet can finally become quicksand to us, swallowing us in madness. We still have to deal with our memories and the repercussions of cataclysmic events, but we can do so on our way to a new start.

Your life story is not written in scars. While scars mark us, they don't have to make us. Hopefully today's lesson will lift us out of the depths of yesterday's subject matter, reminding us what makes life in this broken world continually worth it.

Please read Genesis 35:1-15.

God sent Jacob and his family back to a spiritual marker where the patriarch had a life-altering encounter through a dream (Gen. 28:10-22). According to verses 16-17, Jacob awoke and thought, "Surely the LORD is in this place, and I was not aware of it." He was afraid and said, "How awesome is this place! This is none other than the house of God; this is the gate of heaven."

Why do you think God chose Bethel as the place for Jacob to return (Gen. 35)?

_____

What three things did Jacob command his household and entourage to do before they went to Bethel (v. 2)?

❑ change clothes ❑ bow down ❑ cover themselves in sackcloth
❑ get rid of foreign gods ❑ purify themselves ❑ be circumcised

Review Genesis 31:34-35. What was at least one way foreign gods crept into Jacob's home?

_____

What was Jacob's stated purpose for going to Bethel according to Genesis 35:3?

_____

Genesis 35:5 tells us the "terror of God fell upon the towns all around them so that no one pursued them." This verse can only be understood in light of Genesis 34:30.

What repercussions could Simeon and Levi's overkill have invited?

_____

Obviously, the return to Bethel was not only for their morale. Eventually the Canaanite forces in the region would have allied against them.

🐪 **Read Genesis 35:7 carefully. How did Jacob alter his previous name for this place (Bethel) on the return visit?**

_____

The record of Rebekah's nurse's death in Genesis 35:8 initially seems a random addition to this text. Rebekah, Jacob's mother, hasn't appeared in the narrative since Genesis 27:46, more than 20 years earlier. Most scholars assume that Rebekah died at a time left conspicuously unrecorded. But why the mention of her nurse? I found one commentary's explanation especially reasonable: "Deborah, the last remnant of the world of Paddan-aram, the old nurse of his mother who had been sent to watch over her as she left to join the people of God's covenant, now at last departs; with her burial "beneath the oak" are symbolically laid to rest all traces of Mesopotamian influence. It is only at this point that "God appeared unto Jacob again, when he came from Paddan-aram", and blessed him—for the first and only time—with a most abundant patriarchal blessing: a blessing for seed, national profusion, kindly descendants, and the Promised Land.[8]

What poised Jacob for such a fresh encounter with God? I don't know about you, but I never want to believe I've had my last life altering, abundant-blessing encounter with God. I want to be poised in any way I can for another divine encounter at my own Bethel.

Certainly God told Jacob to "go up to Bethel and settle there, and build an altar," but the preparation Jacob demanded from his entire family appears prompted by his own conviction. "Get rid of the foreign gods you have with you, and purify yourselves and change your clothes" (35:2). In other words, "We're going to Bethel all right, but we're not going like this. We're about to clean house." He meant for a moral transformation to be reflected—down to even a change of clothes.

Sometimes we just need to move.

Wisdom hasn't exactly been Jacob's calling card, but at this very moment we see a wise man indeed. Our lesson today began with these words: "Sometimes we just need to move." Broaden the concept now to encompass the move to a new place with God rather than a new physical surrounding. If we are desperate for a move, we too could use a thorough house cleaning—spiritually and perhaps literally.

A volcano can suddenly erupt from within what seems a rock-solid family, a mountain that you thought couldn't be moved. I'm not talking about Dinah's rape. That was external. I'm talking about the homicidal rage that "brought trouble" and made Jacob's family "a stench" to those around them. Today we're talking about eruptions from the inside. They don't have to be nearly as radical as murder to spread noxious lava. All sorts of scenarios can constitute eruptions in a seemingly solid family: the sudden exposure of an extramarital affair, a teen pregnancy, or the DUI of a trusted family member. Even a call from a principal's office informing a parent that a child was a caught cheating on a test can feel like an eruption.

This concept is as applicable to the individual as the family. Let's face it, Beloved. None of us are mountains beyond erupting. But when eruptions come, we are wise to ask ourselves when unnoticed tremors began. Like Jacob, we might start by looking for the cracks of compromise within the rock. As much as we're able, we need to insist on a thorough housecleaning and re-consecration. If we've done something drastically uncharacteristic for a follower of Christ, we need to trace the cracks of compromise.

Our family actively prays together, views Christ as the center of all things, and jealously guards what comes into our home ... but we haven't always been so deliberate. Let me be loud and clear: without exception, every single lasting fortification in the Moore extended family was prompted by a sudden eruption. Something unexpected and unwanted happened that caused us to know we needed to tighten up. Some of the occurrences may have seemed minor to someone else, but to us they were indications of trouble within our walls. Other occurrences were more serious by anyone's standard. All led to housecleaning and an urgent pursuit of purity. They also led to Bethels in our lives: places we encountered our God afresh. Listen, Dear One. Pretty things don't always come pretty ways.

Have you ever examined your household in an urgent pursuit of purity?
Use generalities if you feel the specifics call for too much exposure.

Thankfully, we don't have to wait for an internal eruption before doing some spiritual house cleaning and checking for cracks in our spiritual purity. Let's be spiritually healthy enough not to always need a crisis to increase our holiness.

We need some concentrated time to become more spiritually healthy. Like many of you, I'm very committed to a daily quiet time, but I often long for more time to be alone with God for no other reason but personal consecration. If I find myself confessing the same attitude or action over and over, I begin to realize that while I may be telling on myself … I'm not changing. I want to change! Don't you? We need concentrated times of deep intro-spection when we allow God to shed light on our hearts, minds, attitudes, and motivations. That's the way to tend to the root of our sin problems and not only the symptoms.

Describe the last time you allowed God the time to heal you and grow you spiritually.

_____

_____

Glance back at Genesis 35:4. Before you blame all your problems on your earrings, be advised that the "rings in their ears" were charms associated with idols and pagan superstitions. They weren't accessories to match their scarves. Picture Jacob standing before his family, palms up, saying something like, "Out with it!" One by one, those who had harbored idolatrous relics surrendered them to Jacob until the household was clean. Had they not, the terror of God may not have protected them on their journey. Sometimes I've felt as if God said to me, "I will only cover what you have completely and repentantly uncovered to Me."

How do the vivid words of Psalm 32:1-7 lend biblical support to this?

_____

_____

Genesis 35:6 records the arrival of Jacob's entourage in the place of divine encounter. Earlier I asked you what alteration Jacob made in the name he originally called this place. In Genesis 28:19 Jacob called the place *Bethel*. In Genesis 35:6 Jacob called the place *El Bethel*. What is the difference? *Bethel* means "house of God." *El Bethel* means "God of the house of God."[9]

Renaming Bethel dramatically spotlights Jacob's spiritual metamorphosis. Over a two-decade span of time, the abiding presence of God "who has been with me wherever I have gone" (35:3) gradually shifted Jacob's focus from the things of God—blessings, protection, land—to God Himself. This shift is the single most profound turning point toward spiritual maturity, for Jacob or for us.

Many of us were taught to call our churches "God's house" as children. Using this terminology, think how easily our focus on all the involvements and activities of church can exceed our focus on God Himself. If we're not careful, we can come to love great worship music, small group Bible study, and the whole community of church more than we love God. One of the most obscure traps the Devil sets for the deeply spiritual is to tempt us to love loving God more than we actually love God. Certainly nothing is wrong with enjoying the life surrounding our pursuit of God, but our growth is gravely stunted until our focus shifts decisively from our Bethel to our El Bethel. Without the El, Bethel is just an empty house.

Jacob's fresh encounter with God concluded with three crucial elements: (vv. 9-15)

- The ratification of Jacob's new name, Israel.
- The reintroduction of God as *El Shaddai*. (God Almighty)
- The restatement of the covenant promises.

A new season was coming in which Jacob would need to know above all things that he was a changed man. He needed to be certain that God was his mighty mountain, and His promises were true. Maybe you need to know the same thing today. No matter what trial rocks your house or what crisis erupts within it, ask the God of your house to stand up and show Himself mighty. He alone builds a house that cannot be moved.

At the beginning of today's lesson I promised a reminder of what makes life in this broken world continually worth it: the God of the house of God. That's what.

Day Four
But His Father

Today's Treasure

As she breathed her last—for she was dying—she named her son Ben-Oni. But his father named him Benjamin.

Genesis 35:18

Death is as natural a part of life as birth. In fact, the two life-experiences are strangely similar. Both catapult us—ready or not—from the relative cocoon of our thus-far existence into an inconceivably larger world. Both can be traumatically painful, drawn-out processes. You and I may wish from time to time that God would rapture us out of our present lives, but I seriously doubt any of us long to be back in our mothers' wombs. The thought is absurd. Likewise, we have such a wide "world" waiting for us as citizens of heaven that when we arrive, we won't dare long for the relative dark and smothering cocoon we called earthly life.

Today we'll bury two important players in our narrative. Please read Genesis 35:16-29. Let's comment briefly on the odd scandal within this segment.

What did Israel (the person) "hear of" according to verse 22?

_____

We might wonder what possessed Reuben to sleep with Bilhah. Obviously, he surrendered to evil and disturbing desires, but they may not have been entirely physical. Consider one commentator's notes: "Whatever his actual motives, Reuben's deed represents a powerful challenge to Jacob's authority. He simultaneously exacts revenge for the humiliation of his mother, prevents Rachel's concubine from again usurping his mother's place as Jacob's (primary) wife, lays premature claim to his inheritance, and most important, directly challenges his father for leadership by assertion of greater sexual prowess and preeminence over his own wives. Reuben's incestuous act is, in its inner meaning, an act of patricide, the removal of the father as a father." [10]

Don't automatically discount a motivation of physical attraction, however. Reuben was Jacob's oldest son by Leah, and Bilhah was Rachel's young maidservant when she entered the narrative. The difference in their ages may not have been broad enough to discount mutual desire, however sinful.

Let's proceed to our focus for today. Contrast the deaths—their causes and assumed effects—from Genesis 35:16-19 in as many ways as possible.

Rachel _____

_____

_____

Isaac _____

_____

_____

Among other differences, you probably contrasted the crisis of Rachel's death with the relative peace surrounding the end of an earthly life "full of years." We don't have to read a narrative to draw such a contrast. All we have to do is live a little. Let's try to better understand Jacob's heart by contrasting our own examples of someone who died prematurely with someone who died "old and full of years."

How different is the way we experience grief with …

a sudden or early death _____

_____

death at the end of a long life _____

_____

Though lots of drama and plenty of tears surrounded my mother's lingering death, nothing about it compares to the night we spent in ICU as an aneurysm claimed the life of my husband's young sister. Talk about trauma! Though Jacob surely hated to lose his father, Rachel's death no doubt rocked his world unlike anything he'd ever known.

Last night Melissa and I had a conversation about how modern medicine has been used of God to spare so many mothers' and infants' lives. My grandmother is buried in a small cemetery on the grounds of her country church in the hills of Arkansas. Every year at "homecoming" relatives gather for a service at the old church and then share a fabulous pot-luck meal that country folks alone can cook. The eve of the Sunday celebration is called the "grave cleanin'." (Please don't pronounce it with a "g" on the end of it. It just wouldn't be fittin'.) Schedule and distance have cheated me of the pleasure of participating in the grave cleanin' more than a few times in my adult life, but the same sight hit me profoundly each time. Identical dates of deaths are etched on a chilling number of old, worn gravestones marking paired graves of mothers and babies. I remember the words my own mother said to me after my firstborn's birth turned into an emergency delivery. "A mother walks through the valley of the shadow of death for her baby." Indeed.

In an earthly sense, Rachel never got through that valley. Shadow gave way to reality.

Genesis 35:17 tells us Rachel "began to give birth and had _____ difficulty."

Those words send shivers up the spine of anyone who has ever given birth. Under the healthiest of circumstances and modern care, childbirth can be difficult. Add "great" to the difficulty and our hats go over our hearts in respect. As vocal as I am otherwise, I wasn't one to make a peep during labor and delivery, but Keith claims the bone in his forearm is still bruised. And I thought the "hee-hee" breathing he kept doing was for my sake.

Jacob and Rachel never got the chance to laugh over a retrospective view of labor and delivery. Their son was born gulping the air of tragedy, his first cries were quickly drowned by wails of others.

The midwife's words in verse 17 may at first seem strange. What were they?

_____

In all likelihood, the same woman attended Rachel when Joseph was born. Take a look back at Genesis 30:22-24.

What would the midwife have heard Rachel say right after she named her first baby Joseph?

_____

The midwife was perhaps scrambling to encourage a dying mother, wanting Rachel to know that her prayer had been answered. But the most compelling part of our narrative is the name change of Jacob and Rachel's second son.

 What did Rachel name the child (35:18)?

_____

What did Jacob name the child (v. 18)?

_____

Interestingly, this is the only child Jacob himself named; therefore, let's not take his insistence on a change lightly. Obviously, both names have one syllable in common.

What is it? _____

This Hebrew word *ben* means "son." Ben-Oni means "son of my trouble"[11] or "son of my sorrow."[12] Benjamin, on the other hand, means "son of my right hand." [13]

 Can you think of any reason(s) why Jacob might have insisted on the change?

_____

How I'd love to hear your thoughts! I imagine right about now you and I are thinking something similar. Who in the world knew the power of a name more vividly than Jacob? He was named Jacob because he grabbed his brother's heel, but the name also implied meanings like cheater, supplanter, and deceiver. As he lived up to the broader implications, how often do you think Jacob felt mocked by his name? Surely the self-fulfilling, dark power of his name motivated the following dialogue as Jacob wrestled with the divine by the Jabbok.

But Jacob replied, "I will not let you go unless you bless me."

The man asked him, "What is your name?"

"Jacob," he answered.

Then the man said, "Your name will no longer be Jacob, but Israel, because you have struggled with God and with men and have overcome" (Gen. 32:26-28).

Overcome what, I ask you? His own name, for starters. He'd learned to fight fair, and God in His mercy released him from the noose of his own name.

In the pain and delirium of her dying state, Rachel named her second son after the trouble and sorrow surrounding his birth. Wisely, a man who knew the power of being re-titled trumped a name that could have saddled his son with guilt and sadness. In its place, Jacob gave a name of honor. "You are not to be a son of sorrow, little one. In sorrow you were born but in sorrow you shall not live. You are my youngest. My baby. The one I will have beside me to my oldest days. You, my child, are the son of my right hand."

Opposed to popular opinion, the dead cannot haunt us ... but the living certainly can. Rachel did not know the breadth of repercussions her dying wish to name her baby Ben-oni could have. Jacob did. He would not have his son haunted by them.

Generations later, another mother insisted on naming her child after the negative events surrounding his birth. His name has become very well known in our generation.

Read I Chronicles 4:9-10. What was his name?

What in his prayer reminds you of the situation with Benjamin?

His mother gave away the intent of the name in her coinciding statement in verse 9. "I gave birth to him in pain." She named her son after her pain. Does that shed a little light on why Jabez was so desperate for blessing, for the hand of God, and freedom from "pain"? He was asking to be freed from the power of his own destructive name.

Few of us in our culture have been named after sorrows and hurts, but children can certainly be born into circumstances that deeply and negatively impact their identity.

What kinds of birth circumstances can haunt a child today?

Deliver us, Lord. Deliver us from these negative events or emotions that may have somehow identified us. Deliver us from inheriting someone else's sorrow and taking ownership over something that wasn't our fault. Even if we've not been named after difficult circumstances, we may have felt the heavy burden of association. Jabez needed a dad like Jacob: A dad who

refused to let his son become saddled with his mother's sorrow. A father could as easily saddle a child with guilt as a mother. Maybe checks and balances is another reason God wisely assigned two parents to each child.

You and I have a heavenly Father who refuses to call us by our old identities. God temporarily reversed His own Son's identity that ours might be reversed. The Son of His right hand descended to this broken world to become a Son of Sorrows so that you and I might "be called children of God! And that is what we are!" (I John 3:1). How great is the love the Father has lavished on us.

Day Five'
Public Dreams

My heart overflows with a fresh wave of love toward you today. I've just returned from a conference where I studied God's Word with many women just like you. You are not nameless and faceless to me. Further, you have never been—nor will you ever be—a number to me. Perish the thought. To me, you are so many things: you are smiles and tears, often at the same time (emotional multi-tasking). You are stories. Histories. Testimonies. Intensely unique followers of the Lord Jesus Christ. You are all sorts of wonderful shapes and sizes, personalities, ages, and stages. And you are hair-dos. Every conceivable kind. Thank you for being you.

Except for the briefest glance, today you and I will hopscotch over Genesis 36 and fast-forward to Genesis 37.

Based on a quick look at Genesis 36, what does this chapter record?
❑ Esau's descendants ❑ Jacob's descendants ❑ Joseph's descendants

Read Genesis 36:1-8 and record any noteworthy information you learn about Esau and his family.

_____

_____

The final verse of Genesis 36 offers a bit of Bible "trivia." Fill in the blanks.

"This was Esau the _____ of the _____."

The Old Testament makes a number of references to the Edomites, so henceforth you know to associate them with Esau. Scholars believe the positioning of Esau's descendants in Genesis 36 may be a deliberate divider between the Jacob-Esau saga of recent chapters and the Jacob-Joseph saga to come. The spotlight of the narrative will now shift its gaze from the third generation to the fourth as Joseph takes center stage. With these things in mind, please read our text for today: Genesis 37:1-11.

Today's Treasure
Joseph had a dream, and when he told it to his brothers, they hated him all the more.
Genesis 37:5

Based on the information in these 11 verses alone, describe each person or group and how you would feel about them.

Jacob: _____

Joseph: _____

Joseph's brothers: _____

Now let's try our hand together at some general character sketches. We'll consider Jacob first. One of the many things I appreciate about God is His honest appraisal of our humanity and our embarrassing inconsistency toward living beyond it. He casts our humanness on the pages of Scripture like splattered paint against a canvas of divine white hope. Then, through the broad strokes of fathomless redemption, a brilliant living-color portrait emerges that tells a story of God. Like most of us, Jacob's portrait of faith had taken shape in many ways, but the edges were still undefined and splattered. Partiality had smeared an ugly gray over his parenting, and everybody in the family bore the spots.

When partiality is an issue, everyone in a family pays. The chapters to come will show no one pays more than the one to whom partiality is steered. After our lesson on the birth of Jacob's youngest son, Benjamin, you might be confused by the reference to his (Jacob's/Israel's) partial love for Joseph as the child of "his old age" (37:3). Certainly Benjamin was younger, but two factors probably fed Jacob's partiality toward Joseph.

Compare the physical description of Rachel in Genesis 29:17 to that of Joseph, her firstborn, in Genesis 39:6.

Rachel was ...

_____

Joseph was ...

_____

The first factor that fed Jacob's partiality was the reminder of Rachel's life reflected in Joseph. I believe Jacob saw his beloved Rachel every time he looked into their older son's face.

This is not the first time in our study we've had to face our human tendencies to play favorites. The patriarchal narrative offers repeated opportunities for us to behold partiality's potential destruction. Are you willing to be completely honest with yourself and with God as I commit to do the same? The following question will not be discussed in small group, but I'd like you to answer it privately.

What characteristics bring out your partialities? Appearance? Sophistication? Position? A certain type of personality?

_____

_____

Would you join me in allowing the Holy Spirit to convict and make us aware of the damage partiality does? Write a brief prayer asking God to help you to see with His eyes rather than with biased human eyes.

_____

_____

While the first factor contributing to Jacob's partiality may have been appearance, the second factor may have been the reflection of Rachel's death in Benjamin. Even though Jacob wisely refused to name their younger son after Rachel's sorrow, surely the very sight of him often pricked Jacob's wound of loss.

Happy occasions can as easily cause us to miss a lost loved one as unhappy occasions. Can you relate? If so, how?

_____

 What was the significance of the coat Jacob gave to Joseph (Gen. 37:3-4)?

_____

"The elegant ornamented tunic that Jacob provides is not just a decorative gift to a favorite. The garb of rule, it is the sign of Joseph's elevation. Jacob anoints Joseph as his heir apparent—and he does so relatively early in Joseph's life."[14] I hope you didn't miss the phrase referring to the robe as the "garb of rule." Jacob made a powerful statement when he robed Joseph differently, and the brothers did not misinterpret it.

Granted, Joseph didn't have much competition. Jacob suffered severe disappointments in several of his older sons. You'll recall that Reuben, Jacob's firstborn (by Leah), "slept with his father's concubine Bilhah, and Israel [Jacob] heard of it." Such volatile information was not without consequence. Earlier Simeon and Levi showed an extreme lack of judgment and self-restraint in the wholesale slaughter of Shechem. As Jacob perused his sons for the one who would inherit the blessing usually attributed to the firstborn, his hand landed shamelessly and openly on the head of Joseph.

Joseph had other older brothers who were not blatant poor choices, but as we now consider Joseph, we'll view additional reasons for Jacob's preference.

Look carefully at the terminology in Genesis 37:2 as you fill in the blanks. "Joseph, a young man of _____, was _____ the flocks with his brothers."

Several different commentaries suggest that the original wording in this passage could also be translated "shepherded his brothers."[15] These early descriptions of Joseph may imply what the later narrative will undoubtedly confirm: Joseph was a natural leader.

Unfortunately, at 17, Joseph had the personality of a leader without the maturity. I grin as I recall Melissa's mother's day out teacher pulling me aside to say my three-year-old was a "natural born leader." Before I could thank her and tell her how wholeheartedly I agreed, she said, "And she's leading our whole class astray!" Thankfully, by the time Melissa was Joseph's age, her directional sense had greatly improved.

At 17, Joseph may have been unusually able … but he was also irritatingly arrogant. *New International Commentary* quotes a scholar named Sternberg: "God's future agent and mouthpiece in Egypt could hardly make a worse impression on his first appearance: spoiled brat, tale bearer, braggart."[16] I couldn't agree more! I don't share the impressions of one writer who touted Joseph as the only figure in the patriarchal narrative who was entirely blameless. At this stage, Joseph was a brat.

Not only did he fan the flame of his father's partiality toward him with bad reports and tattle tales (37:2), but I fear he also savored making his family squirm over his dreams. Get a load of the King James rendering of Joseph's show and tell.

Circle every use of the word "behold."
"For, behold, we were binding sheaves in the field, and lo, my sheaf arose, and also stood upright; and, behold, your sheaves stood round about, and made obeisance to my sheaf. And he dreamed yet another dream, and told it his brethren, and said, Behold, I have dreamed a dream more; and, behold, the sun and the moon and the eleven stars made obeisance to me" (Gen. 37:7,9).

The undercurrent of the terminology Joseph used seems to suggest, "Behold my superiority!" Where are the hints of humility that always accompany godly awe? Joseph seemed proud and unable to wait for the others to hear of his honor. Lest you have any doubt, note how unhindered he was to share the second dream even after they "hated him all the more" after the first. Yes, I definitely think Joseph was a brat.

As we lastly consider Joseph's brothers and their hateful reaction to his dreams, let's consider the following applications:

We might be wise to keep some of our dreams to ourselves. In Joseph's case, God allowed the dream to make a prophecy with national ramifications recognizable when it was fulfilled. God alone knows if Joseph told the dream with the right heart to the right people.

Let's think beyond literal dreams to the life dreams God gives to people like us. God has a wonderful, significant plan for each of us to take part in His Kingdom agenda on earth. He will sometimes shed light on a future path by instilling in us this thing we call vision. Beloved, our relationships with Christ are intimate, and some things between us are private. More than a few times the Gospels record Christ telling an individual not to instantly share what He'd done for them.

Why do you think God might not want us to share every ounce of vision He has given us?

_____

_____

Once again, I'd love to hear your answers! I'd add that, 1) we could be perceived (perhaps rightly) as arrogant and, 2) we could prove wrong. Misunderstanding the vision could be embarrassing and confusing at the least!

God's exaltation of a man is never for the man himself but rather to glorify God and to edify others. Dear one, let's allow this truth to abide in our marrow: If God ever exalts one of His own with position, wealth, talents, gifts, or influence, His purpose is never—not ever—human exaltation. In fact, the exalted person would be the last one the exaltation was meant to serve. For him or her, the exaltation would be a test and a profound trust over anything else. Mark this equation on the chalkboard of your brain: Exaltation + Ego = Extravagant Humbling.

Joseph's dreams were for his brothers. Not against them. Joseph, however, had not invited their trust. We'll conclude today with an excerpt I found greatly insightful. "Men resist being ruled by one of their own, and they react angrily when one of their own makes a claim to leadership. Before they can accept him, a leader of equals must first prove himself to them and gain their voluntary assent to his ascendancy."[17]

How might you apply this truth to your own life?

_____

_____

_____

_____

We might be wise to keep some of our dreams to ourselves.

[1]Victor P. Hamilton, *The Book of Genesis: Chapters 18–50* (Grand Rapids: William B. Eerdman's Publishing, 1995), 350.

[2]Ibid., 329.

[3]Carroll E. Simcox ed. *3000 Quotations on Christian Themes* (Grand Rapids: Baker Book House, 1988), 156.

[4]Leon R. Kass, *The Beginning of Wisdom: Reading Genesis* (New York: Free Press, 2003), 446-47.

[5]Kass, 483.

[6]Ibid., 483.

[7]Ibid., 480.

[8]Ibid., 502-03.

[9]*New International Version Disciples' Study Bible* (Nashville: Holman Bible Publishers, 1988), 47 n.

[10]Kass, 505.

[11]*New International Version*, 51 n.

[12]James Strong, *Strong's Exhaustive Concordance of the Bible: Hebrew and Chaldee Dictionary* (Nashville: Holman Bible Publishers, n.d.), 22.

[13]*New International Version*, 51 n.

[14]Kass, 514.

[15]Hamilton, 406.

[16]Ibid., 409.

[17]Kass, 515.

SESSION SEVEN
God of the House

• We might be wise to _____ some of our _____ to _____.

• God's _____ of a man is _____ for the _____ himself. Its purpose is the _____ of God and the _____ of others.

Segment One: Genesis 37:12-14

The patriarch told Joseph to check on the "_____ of your brothers." Jacob _____ the ramifications of his _____.

Segment Two: Genesis 37:14-18

A. Ironically, Joseph turned out to be _____ with the Shechemite than with his own _____.

B. In his lifetime Joseph will look for his brothers' _____, _____, _____, _____, possibly their _____, and finally their _____.

Segment Three: Genesis 37:18-25

A. We must be very careful what we plot at a _____, lest we follow through when _____. Nothing is harmless about a _____. The Greek word for "nursed a grudge against" means, "to be _____ _____ or by anything; to be _____ in something, be enmeshed, to be _____ to."

B. We might find that we are capable of doing some harmful things _____ that we might not have done _____. "Stripped" (Hebrew *pasat*) in "priestly texts is used of the _____ or flaying of a _____."

Segment Four: Genesis 37:25-36

A. The means of _____ was already on its way _____ Joseph was in the _____.

B. Ironically, a _____ was slaughtered both when Jacob _____ and when he was _____. "An _____ beast hath devoured him." Jacob then cried, "_____, _____ is Joseph."

C. Jacob's sons _____ the ramifications of their _____.

Dreams and Disappointments

On day 5 of week 7 we officially began the shift to Joseph as our main character. Before our journey is complete, Scripture will usher Jacob back into the forefront and we'll view father and favored son side by side. After a brief but important look at another of Jacob's sons on day 1 of this week, we will join Joseph on a field trip. The location? Egypt. The name of the course? God's Sovereignty. School supplies needed? Humility and patience. The course load is heavy, but the end result is a lesson that can last a lifetime. Be prepared to answer the following principal questions.

Day One
Tamar's Trap
Day Two
The Lord Was with Him
Day Three
Forgotten
Day Four
A Jog in a Cupbearer's Memory
Day Five
Public Dreams

This Week's Principal Questions

Day 1: What sentence did Judah pass on the woman he thought was a prostitute?

Day 2: What kind of reasons did Joseph give for refusing Potiphar's wife (39:8-9)?

Day 3: What very pointed requests did Joseph make of the cupbearer?

Day 4: What significance did cows have in ancient Egypt?

Day 5: How did Joseph respond to Pharaoh's claim: "I have heard it said that when you hear a dream you can interpret it" (Gen. 41:15)?

Day One
Tamar's Trap

Our study of Genesis has forced us to talk about some subjects that might never have found their way to our Christian women's teas. When God invites us to His table, He's obviously got more in mind than a tea party.

We sit down with our knives and forks for meat that sticks to our spiritual ribs. Some of that meat is tough to cut and even tougher to chew. That's what we may find on our plate today. God uses tough meat at times to make us confront tough places in our own hearts: places "hardened by sin's deceitfulness" (Heb. 3:13). Our meal will take place in two courses. Before the first tough cut of meat, I suggest you sharpen your knife with prayer.

Read Genesis 38:1-11 and complete the following.

Verse 1 unfolds with the words "At that time, Judah left his brothers." The terminology suggests the timing of Judah's departure is important. Check the last six or seven verses of chapter 37. What had happened "at that time"?

_____

I so hope you were present for video session 7 as we studied the murderous rage of Joseph's brothers. The turn of the spotlight to Judah may seem abrupt and out of place, but we will see several important connections today.

Review Genesis 37:23-28 and describe Judah's part in the ruse.

_____

Today's Treasure
"She is more righteous than I."
Genesis 38:26

Now, picture the scene as the brothers lead Jacob to believe the son of his heart has been torn to pieces by a ferocious animal.

Read Genesis 37:35. Judah would have been among those who came to comfort Jacob, but how did Jacob respond?

_____

Day in and day out, the sons of Jacob had to face the gaping wound they had torn in their father's heart. Judah couldn't live with the guilt. "At *that time*, Judah left his brothers and went down" (emphasis mine). We talked about the need that sometimes arises for a move or a change of scenery. A new start without a new heart, however, leads to the same old problems.

Turn your attention back to Genesis 38:1-11. How did Judah try to put his family of origin behind him and begin a life for himself?

_____

Describe briefly what happened to each family member (including in-laws) in these 11 verses.

Judah _____

Daughter of Shua _____

Er _____

Onan _____

Shelah _____

Tamar _____

Er has his unique place in Bible history. He is the first individual about whom we read that God killed him. Although we are not told of Er's offenses, we need not wonder if they were serious. The only other lives God has taken in Scripture thus far are the inhabitants of Noah's world who had hearts that were "evil all the time" (Gen. 6:5) and those of Sodom and Gomorrah whose sins are notorious. Interestingly, in Hebrew the word for "evil is Er spelled backwards."[1] As we'll note in Er's younger brother, whether evil is forward and upfront or backward and hidden, God sees and reacts to it. Before we talk about Onan's offenses, let's discuss the biblical introduction to an ancient custom reaching all the way into the time of Christ (Matt. 22:23-30).

What, according to Judah, was Onan's "duty" (Gen. 38:8)?

_____

This ancient marriage custom is called a "levirate marriage." The word *levir* is Latin for "brother-in-law."[2]

> **Read the description of levirate marriage under the Law of Moses in Deuteronomy 25:5-10. What was its obvious purpose?**

_____

Apparently the *levir* was not forced to marry his brother's widow, but he walked around thereafter with one shoe on and one shoe off, spit upon, and dually scoffed. His entire line was henceforth labeled the "Family of the Unsandaled One." (I love Scripture. Sometimes it makes me grin.) Seriously, the perpetuation of a family name and lineage was critical in ways you and I cannot understand. The survival of a line was everything to many ancient peoples and certainly paramount to the Israelites. In fact, one of the continuous threads weaving the chapters of patriarchal narrative together is the threat against Abraham's line.

In Genesis 38:8, Judah called on his second son, Onan, to act as the *levir* and produce offspring for his brother. "But Onan knew that the offspring would not be his," so he practiced the most ancient and crude form of contraception. I don't feel any more comfortable discussing Onan's sin than you do, but God is adamant that we know He sees the sins in a darkened bedroom as clearly as those in the light of day. You see, Onan took Tamar for sexual pleasure alone and had no intention of giving her offspring. He played Tamar for a harlot "rather than a wife celebrated for fruitfulness."[3] Onan's second motivation for not producing an heir for Er is reflected in Numbers 27:8-9.

> **If a man who died had no son or daughter, who got his inheritance?**

_____

We don't have to wonder what God thought about the way Onan used Tamar. "What he [Onan] did was wicked in the LORD's sight; so he put him to death also" (v. 10).

Reread Genesis 38:11. Judah tried to appease Tamar by telling her that his youngest son, Shelah, would provide an heir when he was old enough to assume the responsibility. Judah, however, had no intention of following through. He was afraid Shelah would die just like his other sons, so he sent Tamar back to her father's house to wait, hoping the whole issue would dwindle with time.

> **Now, let's take a sharp knife and fork to our second course. Please read Genesis 38:12-30. The reading is longer so our comments will be briefer. What descriptive name would you give this passage?**
> ❏ Gotcha!
> ❏ People who live in glass houses shouldn't go to sheep shearings.
> ❏ Be not deceived, for your sins will surely find you out.
> ❏ A lying father-in-law is never a match for a resourceful woman.
> ❏ Two can play at the deception game.
>
> ❏ Other _____

Tamar obviously held Judah personally responsible for her family line. We cannot fathom a woman sleeping with her father-in-law, but hurt and anger can cause people to do amazingly bizarre things. On the other hand, we can certainly understand one person trapping another with sex.

Three elements set Judah up for a fall. First, he deceived Tamar. Just as we learned through the life of Jacob, a deceiver frequently becomes the deceived, and the perpetrator of wrong becomes the victim of wrong. When you and I don't repent from wrongs we've perpetrated, we have to live in fear of their coming back to haunt us. That's what Paul meant in Galatians 6:7 when he told us we'll "reap what we sow." Secondly, Judah had recently lost his wife—vastly increasing his vulnerability. Thirdly, he was probably under the influence of free-flowing wine. A festival with much revelry surrounded the ancient sheep shearing.

Tamar's actions are shockingly premeditated all the way down to the pledge she requested for payment. What did she keep as a pledge? Circle three:

cord belt seal staff turban cloak

"Tamar responds like a hard-headed businesswoman, finally exacting the rather serious pledge of Judah's seal and cord and staff, which as the legal surrogate of the bearer would have been a kind of ancient Near Eastern equivalent of all of a person's credit cards."[4] Somehow we don't expect a female Bible "character" to act like that. Never equate Bible characters with caricatures. They were flesh-and-blood people with the capacity both to sin and to bring glory to God. Also take into account all Tamar had endured. She had lost a spouse, been treated like a harlot, and was deceived and forgotten. Unfortunately, I've noticed fairly closely that the more a person gets treated like a harlot, the more she is liable to act like one. Tamar reminds us how easily the injured turn into the injurious apart from God's healing.

The narrator draws us into the drama as Judah sends his friend to pay the prostitute with a goat—of all things—and take back his pledge. In essence he is told they don't have prostitutes in those parts.

Why did Judah decide to let her get away with keeping the pledge (v. 23)?

_____

The parallels with Judah's famous royal descendant, David, in his sin with Bathsheba are undeniable (2 Sam. 11-12). Neither man expected his tryst to result in a pregnancy. Both men thought the sin's seriousness faded with time; therefore, consequences were past due. Both were caught in self-righteous indignation.

 What sentence did Judah pass on the woman he thought was a prostitute (v. 24)?

_____

Compare 2 Samuel 12:5. What sentence did David pass on the man in Nathan's report who had taken what didn't belong to him?

_____

What do those two reactions tell you about human nature?

_____

Now, look very carefully at the wording in Genesis 38:25 (NIV). Fill in the following blanks from Tamar's message to Judah, her father-in-law:

"I am pregnant by the man who owns these," she said. And she added, "_____

_____ _____ _____ whose seal and cord and staff these are."

Are you ready for this? The wording she used in the blank you filled in is exactly the same wording in the Hebrew that Judah and his brothers used in Genesis 37:32 when they took Joseph's bloodied robe back to Jacob: "We found this. Examine it to see (Hebrew literally 'see please') whether it is your son's robe."[5]

Judah, you've been had.

Don't think for a moment the hair didn't stand straight up on the back of Judah's neck. How wise we are to examine our own lives before we're forced to examine the evidence of our guilt in our own hands! A last parallel can be drawn from the lives of Judah and David. Both recognized their sin when cast against the backdrop of their false piety.

Then David said to Nathan, "I have sinned against the LORD" (2 Sam. 12:13).

" 'She is _____ _____ _____ _____, since I wouldn't give her to my son Shelah.' And he did not sleep with her again" (Gen. 38:26).

We'll conclude with a few remarks on Tamar then Judah. Four women appear in the Gospel of Matthew's genealogy of Christ prior to Mary, the mother of Jesus: Tamar (a Canaanite), Rahab (also a Canaanite and a harlot), Ruth (a Moabite) and Bathsheba (an adulteress who was originally the wife of a Hittite). Some scholars suggest God was already mixing the blood of Gentiles into the lineage of His people through whom He'd promised to bless all nations. Virtually all agree that God made a point of showing that Jesus Christ redeems any lineage, no matter how pagan. No matter how scandalous. "God had worked his will in the midst of whispers of scandal."[6]

And about Judah. The one whose name means "praise the Lord." *Word Biblical Commentary* suggests that "in its biographical sketches, character change is what Genesis is all about: Abram becomes Abraham; Jacob becomes Israel ... cocky Joseph becomes the wise states-man who forgives his brothers."[7] By the time the patriarchal narratives draw to a close in Genesis, we will glimpse a very different Judah. The recognition of his own sin over another's was the beginning of his transformation. Come to think of it, it always is.

If "character change is what Genesis is all about," and if Abram became Abraham and Jacob became Israel, what are you and I becoming? Hebrews 4:12 tells us God's Word is alive and powerful and so sharp that it divides soul and spirit, joints and marrow. The most dramatic "cure" for certain cancers is a bone marrow transplant. God's Word is meant to get all the way into our bones, curing our character sicknesses with the most dramatic of all marrow transplants. Christ is our donor. A perfect match for all infirmed. Is this study getting to us? The real us? Then let's ask ourselves a very pointed question as we close: How are we changing?

🐫 In what specific ways is God changing you as a result of the last eight weeks in His Word? The only thing we want to stay is changeable.

_____

_____

_____

Day Two'

The Lord Was with Him

Today's Treasure

While Joseph was there in prison, the LORD was with him; He showed him kindness and granted him favor in the eyes of the prison warden.

Genesis 39:20-21

OK. Can you handle one more scene involving sexual sin? This will be our final opportunity to discuss this kind of subject matter in *The Patriarchs*.

This subject matter is crucial to us because of the pandemic proportions of sexual sin, disease, and crime in our world. What more pressing cultural crisis do we have in our nation alone? While many of our churches remain silent on sensitive subject matters, God certainly doesn't. People are desperate to hear God's Word—presented in truth, grace, and power—on such pertinent issues. We have real problems that need real answers and real power provided by a real Holy Spirit.

We in the Western world live in a culture surrounded by media intentionally designed to keep our carnal appetites awakened. The distance between temptation and participation closes rapidly when the appetite is already awake. I'll say it as long as anyone listens: none of us will practice purity of living and thinking accidentally. The odds are far too powerfully against us to get away with anything less than a deliberate pursuit of godliness.

The male gender is far from alone in its propensity toward sexual sin. As my husband, Keith, wisely pointed out on behalf of his gender, "Don't you imagine that most of these men are having affairs with women?"

Though today's lesson involves sexual sin once more, you will be delightfully refreshed to discover that it is not on the part of our protagonist. Rather, he'll offer us a powerful lesson in resistance.

As you read our first segment, Genesis 39:1-12, please record every contextual phrase that includes the tetragrammaton: "the LORD." I'll get you started:

Verse 2   <u>The LORD was with Joseph</u> _____

Verse 3a   _____

Verse 3b   _____

Verse 5a   _____

Verse 5b   _____

How impressed are you with Joseph's resistance to Mrs. Potiphar's temptation?

| I'm extremely impressed. | It's no big deal. | I want to be that courageous. |

We have before us today a classic case of sexual harassment on the job … and the man is not to blame. Let's work through the setup together.

How did Joseph become a servant in Potiphar's house (v. 1)?

_____

Why was Joseph elevated to the position of Potiphar's attendant (vv. 3-4)?

_____

How is Joseph described in verse 6?

_____

This is the only time in Scripture that a man is described exactly like this. According to the ancient Hebrew text, Joseph had a well-defined physique, and he was beautiful. As I try to imagine what Joseph must have been like, I think of a godly young man I've had the privilege to watch grow up. He is not just handsome. His face is masculinely beautiful, but he is as wonderful in character as he is beautiful in features. You can imagine how the girls swoon. That the young man has kept his head on straight is a testimony of God's grace alone. Consider the words of one commentary: "Beauty, we have had occasion to see before, is a dangerous gift. It is a grace that enhances and adorns, but it is also a power that overwhelms. It can be Apollonian and inspire admiration; it can be Aphrodisiac and inspire lust. For the bearer, it can be a burden or it can be a weapon."[8]

How could beauty be a burden?

_____

How could beauty be a weapon?

_____

Another commentary adds, "A young unmarried man _handsome in figure and handsome in features_ who is left alone with a wife who has been virtually abandoned by her husband spells potential trouble, and is a 'signal of warning in the midst of blessing that Joseph may suffer from one endowment too many.'"[9] Some scholars believe Potiphar may have been a eunuch because the Hebrew word translated _officials_ in verse 1 is often translated as such.[10] This possibility is used to explain Potiphar's wife's unyielding attraction to Joseph. I lean toward others who quash this theory that eunuchs were rarely if ever married. I believe it more likely Mrs. Potiphar was the bored wife of a busy man and she refused to corral her desires.

What part, if indeed any, did Joseph play in the temptation? One scholar suggested that Joseph may have flaunted his beauty and theorized God's chastising response, "I will let a bear loose against you."[11] He surmises the bear's name was Mrs. Potiphar. I don't agree, but I have a reason for bringing up the theory. You'll recall I did not hesitate to call Joseph a brat in the early scenes where he taunted his brothers with his dreams and his colored coat, but I am convinced his actions were innocent in Potiphar's service.

While I don't believe God loosed Potiphar's wife like a bear against Joseph, I certainly believe God can do something similar. I think we can flirt irresponsibly with a situation, and God can teach us a serious lesson by loosing a bear of sorts against us. Hopefully, we quickly learn the lesson before we are mangled by it, but we are far wiser not to play with the bear at all … lest we get badly mauled.

As far as we can tell from Scripture, Joseph's only contribution to the attraction was his beauty. My research raised two intriguing questions: "What are the responsibilities of the beautiful ones? How should they present and carry themselves?"[12]

How would you briefly answer those questions based on our discussions so far?

_____

_____

Mrs. Potiphar's repeated invitation to Joseph was the sum total of two Hebrew words translated, "Lie with-me." Joseph's response, on the other hand, amounted to 35 Hebrew words.[13] He didn't just give Potiphar's wife a refusal. He gave her reasons.

 What kind of reasons did Joseph give for refusing Potiphar's wife (39:8-9)?

_____

_____

Joseph didn't want to violate the trust of his position, betray a husband, or sin against God.

What about you? What specific motivations do you have for not buckling to worldly temptations?

_____

_____

We are wise to rehearse in advance our reasons for standing firm.

If you and I are going to be victorious under tidal wave temptation, we are wise to rehearse in advance our reasons for standing firm. We have no idea how tempted Joseph may have been to take Mrs. Potiphar up on her offer, but he had learned his lesson from his previous brat-results. He knew that fleeting pleasure could not possibly be worth the violations of trust and subsequent consequences. Let's hear that again: it's not worth it. I asked you earlier if you were mildly or significantly impressed with how Joseph withstood temptation. The tenth verse prompted my question.

How regularly did Mrs. Potiphar approach Joseph?

_____

What happened on her final try (v. 12)?

_____

Now read the conclusion of the chapter: Genesis 39:13-23. What did Joseph seem to "get" in return for his blameless actions?

_____

_____

Please absorb how thoroughly Mrs. Potiphar covered, manipulated, and schemed. First, she made sure her servants knew (v. 14). The servants not only provided witnesses but their knowledge also insured Potiphar's obligation to respond strongly and swiftly. Secondly, notice her deliberate attempt to incite racial prejudice in her reference to Joseph as "this Hebrew" (v. 14) and "that Hebrew" (v. 17). Thirdly, don't miss how effectively she played the blame card by shifting fault to her husband.

Fill in the blank based on verse 17: "That Hebrew slave _____ _____ us came to me to make sport of me."

Lastly, note the repetitive reference to the "cloak beside" her in verses 15, 16, and 18. (Cloaks kept getting Joseph into trouble, didn't they?)

According to verses 12 and 13, where had Joseph actually left the cloak?

_____

Every time Potiphar's wife recounted the story, however, she described the cloak beside her rather than in her hand. Then, in verse 16 she very purposely "kept his cloak beside her until his master came home." Why was the placement of the cloak so important? Because Potiphar's wife wanted the scene to insinuate that Joseph himself had removed his cloak as a preliminary to rape.

The woman was so viciously cunning, one has to wonder how often she'd sharpened her skills. Interestingly, Potiphar could have asked for the death penalty for Joseph, but he didn't. Instead, he threw him in prison.

Genesis 39:19 tells us Potiphar "burned with anger," but he may not have been angry at Joseph alone—particularly if he suspected foul play on the part of his wife but couldn't prove it. Imagine being Joseph. He was thrown into a pit and sold into slavery only to ascend to a lofty position in Potiphar's service.

Surely Joseph thought his nightmares were behind him. How wrong he was.

What do you think might have gone through Joseph's mind as he was in that Egyptian prison?

_____

_____

_____

Surely Genesis 39 and the events that will soon follow represent the lowest point of Joseph's life. We've all been there, haven't we? We've known the glorious concoction of relief and joy over a nightmare safely tucked behind us. We could even wax philosophically about all the good it did ... until we walk into another. Have you discovered like me that "round two" can seem more than you can bear? If so, you and I need to take stock of a stunning inclusion in Genesis 39. Earlier I asked you to record the immediate context of every use of the phrase "the LORD" in the first 12 verses. Follow suit in verses 13-23.

Once again, record every phrase that includes the words "the LORD."

verse 21 _____

verse 23 _____

The Joseph saga continues for the next 11 chapters of Genesis. To the degree that he's been abased, Joseph will abound. Yet we will never again see the constant reminder in Scripture that God was with him. Beloved, we tend to be convinced that God has abandoned us in our abasement and joined us in our abundance. God is never closer to us than when we've been kicked down by life. *The Word Biblical Commentary* translates Genesis 39:21, "The Lord was with Joseph and was loyal to him and gave him favor."[14] Dear One, God is loyal to you ... even when no one else is. He is present with you no matter what your estate. You cannot enter a single place—not even a prison—where God cannot ultimately make you successful. "Because the LORD was with Joseph and gave him success in whatever he did."

Day Three

Forgotten

Today's Treasure

The chief cupbearer, however, did not remember Joseph; he forgot him.
Genesis 40:23

Our previous lesson concluded as Joseph was falsely accused and imprisoned. In the worst of his circumstances, however, we read "the LORD was with him; he showed him kindness and granted him favor in the eyes of the prison warden" (v. 21). Joseph found himself in leadership once again, placed "in charge of all those held in the prison, and he was made responsible for all that was done there" (v. 22). You probably know a "Joseph" in your church, work place, or university—someone who always seems to float to the top in some area of leadership.

Based on personal observation, describe the kinds of traits your "Joseph" possesses that you feel contribute to his frequency of leadership.

_____

_____

Your Joseph and our Genesis Joseph very likely shared those traits—along with another commonality. They held leadership positions in environments where they had little or no experience. I'm by no means a Joseph, but I well remember being elected to positions in school clubs that I knew virtually nothing about. Take Future Homemakers of America, for instance. Yep. I was voted president of my high school FHA when I was just a freshmen. Of course, I wouldn't have been any more qualified as a senior . . . or a senior adult for that matter. My sewing skills amount to the use of a glue gun. My cooking skills amount to managing a car in a drive-thru. And my home decorating skills? Let's put it this way: I haven't moved my furniture around in 20 years. Domestic goddess I'm not. I would have been better suited as president had FHA stood for Fatted Hair of America.

Joseph obviously didn't have to know much about prisons, but he knew a fair amount about people. Our goals are best suited today by reading all of our text first then taking it apart in segments.

Please read Genesis 40 and then complete the following. What two positions did men imprisoned with Joseph hold?

_____

Scripture tells us only that they "offended" the king of Egypt. A bad meal, do you suppose? (Good thing bad meals aren't a punishable offense in our culture, or I fear I'd be writing you from solitary confinement.) The positions of cupbearer and chief baker may seem minor to us, but in reality no one in Pharaoh's service required more trust. Kings in ancient times had a continual fear of being poisoned. Something must have happened surrounding a meal that caused both positions to be suspect. A crucial piece of information is highlighted in verse 3.

Exactly where were Joseph, the cupbearer, and the baker being held in custody? Choose one.
❏ in the dungeon under the city wall
❏ in the kitchen of a future homemaker of America
❏ in the house of the captain of the guard

Please look back at Genesis 39:1. Who was the captain of the guard?

_____

Beloved, Potiphar wasn't called a captain of the guard. He was called *the* captain of the guard. The captain of the guard in both chapters is no doubt the same person. Genesis 39:20 tells us this location was "where the king's prisoners were confined." I'd like to suggest that Potiphar was never truly convinced of Joseph's guilt, or he would never again have placed his trust in him, making him "responsible for all that was done there."

While in the prison together, both the chief cupbearer and the baker had a dream. These dreams had no words or text. They were visual images I want you to picture. Literally.

In the spaces below, please illustrate each dream with a basic drawing. (You can do this! They don't have to be Picassos!)

The cupbearer's dream	The baker's dream

Now, please record a very basic version of Joseph's interpretations in the coinciding spaces:

The interpretation for the cupbearer	The interpretation for the baker

Genesis 40:6 tells us Joseph found the two men looking "dejected." I smiled as I learned the original word for "dejected" could also be translated "pitiful."[15] Any of us can picture a pitiful expression. At one time or another, most of us have probably perfected the pitiful face. I have never personally experienced a dream that I believed was from God, but I have certainly had dreams that upset me. Not long ago I cried so hard in a dream that I woke up trying to catch my breath. I, like the baker and cupbearer, must have looked pitiful because Keith asked me what was wrong. I described the dream to Keith, and he reasoned with me wisely until I knew it was nothing more than a figment of my wild imagination.

 How about you? When was the last time you had a dream that stuck with you and you wondered if it meant something?

_____

_____

I am convinced that if God means a dream to have significance, He'll make sure we learn what it is. Most wild dreams are nothing more than the by-products of tired bodies and spinning minds. The cupbearer's and baker's dreams, however, had great significance—and not only to them. God would use them to bring a gift He'd given Joseph into play. Interestingly, God made the dreamer of dreams the interpreter of dreams. You see, Joseph knew little about prisons, but he'd had slightly more experience with dreams … and what can happen as a result of them.

I'm sure you noted that the dreams in Genesis 29 had opposite interpretations. Through one, Joseph prophesied a position restored. Through the other, Joseph prophesied a death penalty. The order possibly lends insight into the baker's guilt. The cupbearer, presumed innocent, was very quick to share his dream with Joseph as if he had nothing to hide. The baker, on the other hand, didn't share his dream until he "saw that Joseph had given a favorable interpretation" to the cupbearer.

The dreams, their interpretations, and Pharaoh's subsequent actions may invite us to assume that the cupbearer was falsely accused while the baker was rightly accused. Joseph may have made an appeal to the cupbearer based on this common ground as he testified to having "done nothing to deserve being put in a dungeon" (Gen. 40:15).

What very pointed requests did Joseph make of the cupbearer in verse 14?

_____

Just as Joseph's interpretations suggested, three days later Pharaoh brought forth the chief cupbearer and chief baker from prison. In scriptural terms, he "lifted up [their] heads" by presenting them publicly in front of all his officials. The cup was placed in the cupbearer's hand, and the noose was placed around the baker's neck—just as Joseph had said. Only at this point in Scripture are we told the significance of the three days represented in the dreams by the three branches and three baskets. Pharaoh's birthday was on the third day from the dreams. (If you happen to like little pieces of Bible "untrivia" like I do, you'll enjoy knowing that this is the first mention of a birthday party in Scripture. Can you fathom that this custom has been around since the days of Genesis?)

The chapter that awakened hope for deliverance in Joseph concludes with that very hope deferred. Please write verse 23 in this space:

_____

_____

I asked you to write it so that perhaps you'd feel it. The inspired narrator makes sure we feel the impact by telling us of the oversight not once, but twice:
- "The chief cupbearer, however, did not remember Joseph"
- "he forgot him"

The words "did not remember" suggest what the cupbearer didn't do. The word "forgot" suggests what the cupbearer did do. I believe the narrator is intentionally trying to stir a difference in emotion. Joseph didn't just feel unrecalled. He felt forgotten.

Feel the added impact of the second statement as you try to relate on a personal level through a hurt in your own history. Please don't fill in the blank literally. Fill it in mentally.

_____ did not remember me. He or she forgot me.

Feeling forgotten by someone often feels worse than being scorned. At least the scorner knows we're alive! Feeling forgotten can force a bruising blow to one of our most innate human needs: feeling significant. Noticed. Alive. Feeling forgotten makes us feel invisible. Do you feel that you could say to someone, "I feel dead to you. No, I feel something worse. I feel like I may as well never have been alive to you."

According to Genesis 41:1, how long did Joseph remain in his "forgotten" estate?

_____

Imagine: every day from the time of the cupbearer's release Joseph waited for word. The echoes of two more birthday celebrations must have mocked him as he sat inside those prison walls. Like Joseph, some of you have waited many days for some show of remembrance that hasn't come. God knows exactly how you feel. Over and over in His Word He speaks of being forgotten by His people.

Dear One, if that person's remembrance is truly critical to your life's calling and the destiny God planned for you, in time He will make him or her remember.

We'll see this concept in tomorrow's lesson. The cupbearer's remembrance will be critical to Joseph's future, so God in His sovereignty will cause events to provoke it. Furthermore, God won't waste a moment of the meantime to build Joseph into the kind of man his destiny demands.

I do not know whether God will deem your person's remembrance critical to your future, but this I know: God will never forget you. The power of His remembrance shatters the yoke of anyone else's forgetfulness.

Please conclude today's lesson by reading Isaiah 49:14-15. What do you sense God may be saying to you from today's lesson?

_____

_____

_____

Day Four

A Jog in a Cupbearer's Memory

Today's Treasure

Then the chief cupbearer said to Pharaoh, "Today I am reminded of my shortcomings."

Genesis 41:9

I don't want to delay our reading and resulting study for a moment. After all, two years have passed since the conclusion of yesterday's Scripture material and the beginning of today's. Joseph has waited long enough. Make haste and read Genesis 41:1-13!

The first verse unfolds with the words, "When two full years had passed." The semantics of the original language causes us to feel the length far more readily. "The Hebrew translates literally as 'two years of days.'"[16]

Let's go back to basic grade-school multiplication for a moment and complete the following equation based on our own calender: 365 x 2 = _____

Don't just think of Joseph waiting two years. Picture him waiting 730 days! When we're in waiting mode, one month doesn't feel like one anything. It feels every bit of 30 days. The sun rises in the morning, beams with noon heat, and sets again in the evening every single day of our wait. Meanwhile, we can almost hear the echo in the hollow of a clock's relentless tick, "Nothing yet! Nothing yet!" Time can be a liar. Heaven is replete with angelic activity as God faithfully completes in the spiritual realms what He will release in the visible realms when the time is right. In effect we're praying for this very thing every time we recite the words, "Thy will be done on earth as it is in heaven."

Do a little of your own math. Approximately how many weeks, months, or years do you feel like you've been waiting on something—a word of direction from God, an answer, a remembrance—that you feel has great significance for your future? Translate it into days with the appropriate multiplication:

_____

Let's recall what we were told in Genesis 39:21 when Joseph was thrown into prison: "The LORD was with him; he showed him kindness and granted him favor." Sometimes we can be so busy looking for what is missing in our lives that we miss Who is busily present in our lives. We're looking for God to do us future favors when He's trying to open our eyes to present ones. Remember, God purposes to use every second of a divinely-ordained wait to build us into the individuals our future demands we be. One most peculiar and exquisite experience of the faith is realizing that while you haven't seen answers or the way you should take, you've learned how to see the light of God Himself. Right there in the blindness of your circumstances.

Today's text describes two dreams the Pharaoh had "two years of days" after Joseph's interpretation of the cupbearer's and baker's dreams. Mind you, God could have provoked Pharaoh's dreams 23 months earlier.

According to our previous line of reasoning, why in His sovereignty do you think God might have appointed a longer wait?

_____

_____

You will be thrilled that I'm not going to have you illustrate these dreams only because I've never been able to draw a decent cow, and I fear neither have you. I could always get out a gallon of Blue Bell® Ice Cream and trace the brown cow on the front of it, but how unfair would that be to you who live outside of Texas?

 A brief description will therefore suffice. Pharaoh's first dream: Why do you suppose the dream centered around cows? What significance did cows have?

_____

Pharaoh's second dream: Why do you suppose the dream centered around grain? What significance did grain have?

_____

The representation of cows and grain probably isn't a reach even for us. They easily represent productivity to us, but to the Egyptian they represented more. Egypt was the breadbasket of the ancient world[17] and "cows were not simply the typical farm animal of ancient Egypt, but they symbolized Egypt, the primordial ocean, and one of the gods, Isis, among other things."[18] For an Egyptian Pharaoh to dream about cows had great significance.

Whom did the Pharaoh summon when he awakened with a troubled mind (v. 8)? Circle two:

wise men   counselors   dream catchers   physicians   magicians

No one could interpret the Pharaoh's dreams. Why not, I ask you? Think about the two original dreams Joseph had when he was only 17. Unlike the cupbearer's or baker's dreams, the images in Joseph's dreams (sheaves of grain, sun, moon, and stars bowing down) were so plain to his father and brothers that they needed no interpreter. I'd like to suggest that the meanings of the cows and the grain were equally obvious. The question of what they meant wouldn't even win a hundred bucks on Egyptian Jeopardy. The magicians and wise men simply did not want to be the bearers of bleak news. "They are placing a higher premium on diplomacy than on honesty."[19]

Let's boil this down to our level for a moment and think of it in less subjective terms. Do you know someone you can count on for honesty rather than diplomacy when you need help trying to "interpret" confusing events? If so, briefly describe a way this person's honesty has helped you.

_____

_____

A Pharaoh didn't have peers. He was considered "a god incarnate."[20] All who served him were at the mercy of his absolute power. His diplomatic assistants obviously believed that no news was better than bad news. Their inability or unwillingness to interpret the dreams, however, opened the door to the most climactic point of our study today: the sudden jog in the cupbearer's memory.

I'd like you to recall a point from the very end of our previous lesson. Turn back to the conclusion of day 3 and reread the last three paragraphs. Focus especially on the following goal of reassurance: If that person's remembrance is truly critical to your life's calling and the destiny God planned for you, in time He will make him or her remember.

Beloved, if you have a heart to follow God, He is not going to let something critical fulfilling His wonderful "1 Corinthians 2:9" for you slip by. (Look up that glorious promise in Scripture if you don't know it!) At the conclusion of yesterday's lesson, I asked you to consider remembrances of personal significance. These might have included being remembered by a birth parent who placed you for adoption, a spouse who left you, or a busy adult child that doesn't appear to remember you're alive. Remembrances don't have to be so personally significant to seem critical to your future. Think as well of those that could be professionally significant as Joseph's will turn out to be. For instance, you may wonder if a superior at work will "remember" your hard work on that project when an opening at a higher pay scale arises. Or, you may wonder if the personnel director who interviewed you for that company's opening will "remember" you in the midst of many other applicants.

Can you relate to any of these hopes of remembrance? If so, how?

_____

Beloved, what human are we trying to make omnipotent? Who on this earth have you decided is all-powerful in your life? Who do you feel dependent upon for a good, solid future? God means for you and me to cast our utter dependency only on Him. His plan does not depend on any human, and certainly not on human memory! God loves you. He has well-planned a fruitful life for you. Nothing and no one critical to your God-planned future can fail to come through once God says it's time. No human has the power to overlook what God determines to oversee. Oh, Beloved, if we get anything at all out of the Joseph saga, it must be the trustworthiness of God's sovereignty!

How much would you say you trust in God's sovereign ability to work all things through and all things out for the best—not just universally and corporately—but personally for you? Estimate your trust level with a mark on the following scale:

God's sovereignty does not excuse man's culpability.

❧ ▭▭▭▭▭▭▭▭▭▭▭▭▭▭▭▭▭▭▭▭▭▭▭ ❧

Very little trust   **Absolute confidence**

Describe an experience that has contributed to your present level trust, whether you have little or much.

_____

_____

This morning in my quiet time, the author of a Bible study I'm working on asked what lies God was exposing that we believed. One that came to mind was that man's weakness can trump God's strength. I don't consciously believe it, but based on some of my deep-seated fears, I obviously entertain this false belief at times. I'd like to share with you what I felt God spoke into my heart: God doesn't just work through the strengths of man. He also works through the weaknesses of man. While our weaknesses can certainly mess us up, they can't mess up God. Weaknesses can become God's workmen as surely as strengths. Today's lesson provides a perfect example.

The cupbearer's weakness of memory (or character weakness to act on his existing memory) did not delay God. When God was ready for action, He made sure events happened to jog the cupbearer's memory and activity. I believe God very likely used the weakness of the cupbearer to strengthen a weakness in Joseph. God undoubtedly worked on various areas in Joseph through those "two years of days." Perhaps He worked on the weakness of pride in Joseph, a weakness toward manipulation and control, or independence.

Do you have your own theory? If so, offer it.

_____

_____

The cupbearer's words in verse 9 stir me: "Today I am reminded of my shortcomings." The HCSB says, "Today I remember my faults." The NASB: "I would make mention today of my own offenses." The Living Bible: "Today I remember my sin!" We'll talk about this principle at much greater length further in the study, but let's go ahead and lay the groundwork for it now: God's sovereignty does not excuse man's culpability. In other words, though in His sovereignty God undoubtedly used the cupbearer's delay, the cupbearer was wrong to overlook the request of a man who had faithfully served him in his time of need. Likewise, we must be careful not to use the sovereignty of God as an excuse our unfaithfulness to others. Thankfully, God can rightly use a wrong. Nevertheless, the wrong remains and we must take responsibility.

I can think of few things that spiral me into self-condemnation faster than realizing I forgot to come through for someone. If you're like me, we're so focused on our own concerns and so nauseatingly self-centered that we too often forget things of great importance to others. Recently I forgot to write a college recommendation for someone. It was important to her. Embarrassingly, she had to remind me of my oversight. It wasn't too late, but I still felt horrible. I'm also guilty of walking quickly past someone in the hall at church, asking flippantly, "How are you?" Then I accept her "just fine" answer when in wiser retrospect I know better!

How about you? Can you relate to forgetting something until that was important to someone?
❑ Yes, I'm afraid I can relate.
❑ No, I always remember my commitments.

If you are like me, what is something you forgot until someone was already injured by your oversight?

_____

_____

I want a better memory. Don't you? You and I are the cupbearers of Christ offering those around us a taste of God. Would they be able to "taste and see that the LORD is good" (Ps. 34:8)? Or would they get a bitter taste in their mouths? Unfortunately, we are at times the closest people to God that some people know. When we forget them, they sometimes feel that God has forgotten them. According to John 14:26, the Holy Spirit is our Blessed Reminder. Oh, that He'd remind us of the many things Satan would have us forget! If God reminds you of something specific today, have the cupbearer's courage to act upon it!

Day Five

From the Dungeon

Does anything feel like a long-deferred hope finally—and suddenly—fulfilled? Sometimes the resulting joy and adrenaline rush are worth the wait. I have a forty-year old friend rocking a newborn baby she'd begun to think she'd never hold. I have another friend who long dreamed of West Point. He made the grades, met the requirements, and began the torturous wait. When word of his appointment finally came, the feelings were fireworks. I laugh as I think of the musings of my friend, Jeannette Cliff George: "God is never late, but He misses a few good opportunities to be early." I have a feeling Joseph might have given that statement a testimonial, "Amen!"

Immerse yourself in Genesis 41:14-37 until you feel like an eyewitness to the scenes. Then we'll begin our discussions segment by segment.

Let's start at verse 14 and fill in some interesting blanks:

"So Pharaoh sent for Joseph, and he was _____ _____ from the dungeon."

Don't you find the words "quickly brought" ironic? Sometimes our wait can be so extended that our emotions settle in for the long haul. Then it comes in a flash, and we're left in a state of near shock. My friend's newly-adopted son came exactly like that. They had to run to the store to buy a car seat to take him home, and they didn't have a stick of baby furniture when they got there.

Can you relate to a long wait with a quick ending? If so, how?

_____

_____

Today's Treasure

So Pharaoh sent for Joseph, and he was quickly brought from the dungeon. When he had shaved and changed his clothes, he came before Pharaoh.

Genesis 41:14

Beloved, did you know that Christ's coming to clothe our earthly bodies with heavenly bodies will be something like that (1 Cor. 15:53)? In fact, verse 52 tells us it will happen "in a flash, in the twinkling of an eye, at the last trumpet." Over two thousand years have passed since Jesus wrapped up all written revelation with the words, "Surely I come quickly" (Rev. 22:20, KJV). We assume "quickly" can only mean "soon," but it can also mean "speedily."[21] After centuries of waiting, Christ will return, and we will be changed in an instant. Glory!

In Genesis 41:14, Joseph himself needed a quick change. What did he do to prepare to see the Pharaoh?

_____

Joseph undoubtedly shaved at least his beard. "We know that Semites preferred to be bearded, whereas the Egyptians were clean shaven."[22] The future of our story line will suggest that Joseph took on a very Egyptian look. No doubt, he attempted to be as presentable to the Pharaoh as possible.

Joseph may have looked the part on the outside, but imagine how wildly his adrenaline was rushing on the inside. Still, he had the astonishing ability to be calm and articulate before the Pharaoh.

 How did Joseph respond to Pharaoh's claim: "I have heard it said that when you hear a dream you can interpret it" (v. 15)?

_____

_____

Something very interesting takes place in the original language in the dialogue of Genesis 41, but you'll have to look ahead somewhat to make the comparison. "Joseph uses *ha elohim* (lit., 'the God,' i.e., the usual way of referring to God in the OT) in speaking to Pharaoh (vv. 25,28,32 [twice]), but Pharaoh uses *elohim* (i.e., "God" without the definite article) in speaking about Joseph (v. 38) or speaking to Joseph (v. 39). Joseph's use of the article before *elohim* makes his reference to *elohim* a specific one, God. The absence of the article before *elohim* makes Pharaoh's reference to *elohim* a general, all inclusive one."[23] In a land of many gods, including Pharaoh himself in the eyes of the Egyptians, Joseph made the point that his God was *the* God. There is no other. Pretty gutsy for a man fresh out of the dungeon, wouldn't you say?

Let's fast forward and focus on Joseph's interpretations. Read Genesis 41:25-32. Verse 25 is of particular importance. "The dreams of Pharaoh are one in the same." What does Joseph mean?

_____

_____

Fill in the interpretations of each of the following contents of the dreams.

The seven good cows and the seven good heads of grain represented

_____

The seven lean, ugly cows and the seven worthless heads of grain were

_____

In verse 29 Joseph explains that _____.

In verse 30 Joseph explains that _____.

Look carefully at verse 31. Why won't the abundance in the land be remembered?

_____

Can't we relate? Haven't we had wonderful years—whether in a relationship, a church, or a work place—that may have been followed by such a disastrous season that the bad seemed to erase all the good?

I have! Some seasons that seemed "abundant" at the time were in retrospect little more than seasons of sin. God may not desire us to cherish them in any way. Other seasons were wonderful years that have been pillaged and ravaged tragically by difficult years that followed. We would know if something is worthy of cherishing out of those forgotten years only by the harvest that came from them! Some of you have experienced tragic endings to marriages or other close relationships. You may have had some wonderful years and good times in that relationship, but the hardship and resulting rift spoiled every good memory you had. God may want to bring a measure of healing to some memories that you still have the right to cherish. May I gently ask this question: Did any lasting "grain" come out of it? Any harvest? Physically? Tangibly? Spiritually? Did beloved children come of it? Did God introduce Himself to you through it? Did He show you His faithfulness in the midst of it? Did it produce any lasting transformation?

Then, Dear One, something valuable did come of those years. Something worth remembering. Whether or not you ever realized it, God may have fed you with some of the very grain of your abundant season to get you through your famine. Times aren't always good, but God is. Maybe you don't have to forget all of that time. Maybe right now it's too painful to remember, but perhaps one day it won't be. I've pried enough. I just so deeply want us to have healthy souls and healed memories.

Look carefully now at verse 32. What reason does Joseph give for "the dream … given to Pharaoh in two forms"?

_____

I especially like the NIV wording, "the matter has been firmly decided by God." How would you interpret such a statement?

_____

I'd interpret that statement to mean the prophesied future was inevitable. In essence Joseph told Pharaoh that God had spoken and the events were certain. However, the inevitability of events didn't mean the people were helpless in the midst of it. Quite the contrary, God sent Joseph precisely so they could do something to survive and even to thrive. Inevitability doesn't demand passivity.

Dear One, Scripture is full of prophecy. The kingdom calendar contains some future events "firmly decided by God" that nothing on earth can change. The final end will be glorious for Christ and His own, but some of the means will be frightful. The divine forecast for this world system spirals from dismal to awful. That doesn't mean God's people do nothing. God means for us to be Josephs, thinking and planning wisely so that many may be helped and saved in terrible times.

I can't think of a single time in Scripture when God called His people to do nothing in terrible times. In His mercy, God didn't even leave the Egyptians defenseless against a future famine. He incarcerated Joseph among them so that "the God" of all creation, "the" One and only, would be exalted among a foreign people who would in turn provide for His own.

"Oh, the depth of the riches of the wisdom and knowledge of God! How unsearchable his judgments, and his paths beyond tracing out!" (Rom. 11:33).

In our previous lesson, we talked about the probability that the magicians and wise men chose diplomacy over honesty when asked to interpret Pharaoh's dreams. The best part of Joseph's honesty is that it wasn't hopeless. He brought practical answers. Briefly stated, what were they (Gen. 41:33-37)?

_____

_____

Certainly you and I want people to be honest with us but, if you're like me, you'd also prefer they leave you with a little hope. Maybe even a few possible answers for ways to best endure a difficult situation. None of us wants to hear, "There's nothing we can do." A child of God need never sink into hopelessness no matter how dismal an honest appraisal of their circumstances may be. Nothing is impossible with God. In fact, He may have saved back some harvest from those good seasons to faithfully sustain you. We, Dear Ones, of all people on the face of the earth, have a future and a hope. Here, you may ask? Ah, yes, as long as God wills, but an exceeding future awaits us there. Though it tarry, one day we shall be called from this earthly dungeon and brought before the sovereign King of all creation. And every God-given dream will become a startling, glorious reality.

[1]Gordon J. Wenham, *Word Biblical Commentary: Genesis 16–50* (Dallas: Word Books, 1994), 366.

[2]Victor P. Hamilton, *The Book of Genesis: Chapters 18–50* (Grand Rapids: William B. Eerdman's Publishing, 1995), 435.

[3] Leon R. Kass, *The Beginning of Wisdom: Reading Genesis* (New York: Free Press, 2003), 536.

[4]Wenham, 367.

[5]Ibid., 1534.

[6]Hamilton, 456.

[7]Wenham, 364.

[8]Kass, 541-42.

[9]Hamilton, 461.

[10]Kass, 540 n.

[11]Ibid., 543.

[12]Ibid., 542.

[13]Ibid., 542-43.

[14]Wenham, 368.

[15]Spiros Zodhiates et al., eds., *The Hebrew-Greek Key Study Bible: New International Version* (Chattanooga, TN: AMG Publishers, 1996), 1931.

[16]Hamilton, 484 n.

[17]Wenham, 390.

[18]Ibid., 390-91.

[19]Hamilton, 488.

[20]Ibid., 492.

[21]James Strong, *Strong's Exhaustive Concordance of the Bible: Hebrew and Chaldee Dictionary* (Nashville: Holman Bible Publishers, n.d.), 71.

[22]Hamilton, 492.

[23]Ibid., 496.

SESSION EIGHT
Dreams and Disappointments

Genesis 41:33-35 and Genesis 41:37-49.

1. Throughout biblical history God has _____ sought to place His _____ in positions of public _____.

2. God can _____ and _____ people for public _____ and _____ in ways that exceed formal _____.

God can endow people in public positions with . . .

   • The "_____ of _____" (v. 38). "The Spirit of God that _____ over the _____ _____ rests upon . . . Joseph."

   • _____. The Hebrew word for *discernment* means "to discern, _____, observe, _____ _____ to, understand; to be _____; to heed . . . The word implies discernment, distinguishing between _____ and _____." Please don't miss that we have to _____ _____ to discern. Otherwise, we're only giving a dignified name to the undignified practice of _____ to _____.

   • _____. The Hebrew word for *wisdom* shares many concepts with "discernment." A few additions are "experienced, _____, _____."

3. When God _____ the opportunity, _____ the _____.

4. No one is better suited for places of _____ than those who have proved they can _____ to authority. The Matthew 25:21 principle: If we prove _____ in the small and _____ things, God may place us in _____ of _____.

5. Nothing serves us better in places of _____ _____ than our lessons in _____ _____.

6. Never mistake _____ _____ for _____ _____. "A dream together with its interpretation is only a prediction, a _____ but not yet an actual event. Its _____ depends in part . . . on the _____ of the _____."

WEEK NINE
A Fragile Band
of Brothers

When we're young, everything seems black or white. People are either good or they are bad. All things fit into neat little categories, and the answers to questions are obvious. Then we grow up a little and learn that even the best of people are still human. Christ alone dressed in flesh to perfection. As often as we feel dismayed by a fresh discovery of human frailty, we feel strangely relieved by the company. After all, the person staring back at us in the bathroom mirror just can't seem to get it completely together. As Joseph walked down the elegant corridors of the royal residences, do you think he was shocked every now and then by the reflection of himself in the mirror? After all, he dressed the part of an Egyptian on the outside, but deep inside Hebrew blood still coursed through his veins. A secret war waged within him.

Day One'
Can't Quite Forget
Day Two'
Unrecognizable Recognition
Day Three'
And Benjamin Also
Day Four'
Fears to Feasting
Day Five'
A Set Up and a Stand Up

This Week's Principal Questions

Day 1: What did Joseph name each of his two sons and why (Gen. 41:50-57)?

Day 2: How did Jacob react to his sons' insistence on taking Benjamin back to Egypt (Gen. 42:38)?

Day 3: What primary conflict is depicted in Genesis 43:1-15?

Day 4: What did the brothers think the vizier was going to do to them (Gen. 43:18)?

Day 5: What oath did the brothers make in Genesis 44:9?

Day One'

Can't Quite Forget

On day 5 of week 8 we discussed famine-like seasons in our lives that can come on the heels of fruitfulness. In those seasons nothing is more natural than trying to put old personal hurts behind us so we can forget them. But sometimes the harder we try to forget something, the better we remember it. The more we tell the past to get lost, the more determined it seems to be found.

I've borrowed *Encountering the God of Abraham, Isaac, and Jacob,* from a title God gives Himself in Scripture. For instance, in Exodus 3:15 God introduced Himself to the Israelites through Moses as "The LORD, the God of your fathers— *the God of Abraham, the God of Isaac and the God of Jacob*" (emphasis mine). The entire patriarch narrative screams connectedness, but the theme applies to more than the lineage of God's chosen people. It also applies to personal journeys like David's in the Old Testament and Paul's in the New. Our natural tendency is to disconnect ourselves from past seasons we didn't like, desiring to forget them entirely. Interestingly, the Hebrew word often translated *future* in Scriptures like Jeremiah 29:11 comes from the same root as the word translated *behind*.[1] The Hebrews felt that the future was not whole without the past. If we're convinced God is sovereign, good, and purposeful, why would He allow or even ordain a season that has no value or contribution to our futures?

We certainly don't want to march into our futures carrying the baggage of our pasts, but God forbid we'd walk away from our mistakes empty-handed. What we need is a baggage exchange. We need to drop off our destructive, heavy baggage at the foot of the cross then tarry there for healing until God loads us with treasures to carry into our futures.

Today's Treasure

Joseph named his firstborn Manasseh and said, "It is because God has made me forget all my trouble and all my father's household."
Genesis 41:51

Like us, Joseph needed a lesson about connectedness. Today we'll see that Joseph thought the goal of getting on with life was forgetting the past.

 What did Joseph name each of his two sons and why (Gen. 41:50-57)?

_____

_____

According to verse 50, when were these sons born?

_____

Why did people from other countries come to Egypt (v. 57)?

_____

I smell a divine setup. Don't you?

Let's begin with a look at Joseph's young family. What years of joy those "years of abundance" must have been for Joseph after all that he'd been through! He'd no doubt been offered one of the most desirable women of Egypt for his wife. I'd like to believe he loved her and devoted himself to her. After all, we never read of him taking a second spouse. One man. One wife. What a relief! Maybe he'd learned firsthand how dysfunctional a family could be with too many mother figures.

Joseph seems the reflective type. As a father of young sons, Joseph probably thought about what he wanted to do differently from his father … and what he wanted to imitate.

As I write, I, too, am filled with reflective thoughts. Amanda, my firstborn is 25 today. I called her early this morning to do what I do every birthday morning: I recounted the events of that special day from beginning to end. (As my coworker mused, it's rather like the Israelites commemorating the Passover. Everyone knows the story but the blessing is in the retelling.) Amanda savors every detail about it and even asks questions that have answers she already knows. The birth of my first child made me consider like nothing else what I wanted to do differently and what I wanted to do the same as my beloved parents.

Think back over Joseph's life. He was sold to the Ishmaelites at 17. He was 30 when elevated to second in command over Egypt. The boys were born in the first cycle of seven years, the years of abundance. So, Joseph was approximately 35 and had experienced many good things along with the bad.

What differences do you think Joseph wanted to see in his home in contrast to his childhood home?

_____

_____

We humans are mixed bags, aren't we? Maybe even a bag of mixed nuts. As we've discussed before, our biggest consistency is probably our inconsistency. Look back at the meaning of Joseph's firstborn's name. *The New International Commentary* translates the Hebrew as, "God has made me forget entirely all my suffering and my family."[2] Entirely? We might want to ask Joseph, "Is that why you named both boys Hebrew names and your firstborn a name that would always make you remember?"[3] Just think about it. Every time he called his first son by his name, "Making Forget," Joseph ironically reminded himself of what he was trying to forget.[4] Manasseh's whole name might as well have been Making Forget What?

I intended for Amanda to be my Manasseh. Little did I know she'd become the catalyst God would use to make me deal with my past. Not forget it. Ironically, after I recounted my past enough to deal with it God's way, I started forgetting much of it. Have you had a Manasseh of sorts?

Who or what did you believe would cause you to "forget" something painful from your past? _____

Did it work? And if so, did it last?

_____

_____

I can't resist repeating the corny saying: "Denial is not a river in Egypt!" Nor is it the way we get over our pasts. Denial, just like the real Nile, has a way of finally hitting flood stage until we nearly drown in the very past we tried to ignore. Furthermore, saddling a spouse, baby, or friend with the responsibility of being consistently so wonderful that we forget all things terrible is a bit much. Frankly, no one stays that wonderful.

Manasseh, of course, did not have the power to make Joseph "forget entirely all [his] suffering and [his] family." But, don't doubt for a moment that a new addition can be used of God to do all sorts of wonderful things: like giving a dad a new lease on life and reminding him that God is still very good. If Joseph overshot Manasseh's name just a tad, he certainly hit the nail squarely on the head with Ephraim's. You're going to love the meaning of this name: Double fruit.[5]

Look back at verse 52. Where exactly had God made Joseph doubly fruitful? Check one.
❑ **in the Nile**
❑ **in his assistance to Pharaoh**
❑ **in the land of his suffering**

I don't know if God's power and glory is ever more obvious than when He bears a harvest in us in the same land as our suffering. Think more widely than seasons we commonly characterize as suffering. The KJV translates the phrase as "the land of my affliction."

Now take a look at John 15:8 and place it alongside the meaning of Ephraim's name. Share your reflections as you consider the two side by side.

_____

_____

I asked if you'd had a Manasseh in your life. Figuratively speaking, how about an Ephraim? Have you cooperated with God enough to see Him make you doubly fruitful in the very place you've known suffering or affliction? Please explain.

_____

_____

The Bible study *Breaking Free* is one of my Ephraims. I've never lived through a more difficult season than I did while writing it. I was hit by a tidal wave of fear, personal loss, insecurity, self-condemnation, and terrible memories. Honestly, I thought I'd never emerge from that season of affliction intact, yet God used it to bring forth what will likely remain my primary life message: Trust God!

God is so amazing. Not only did He purpose double fruitfulness in Joseph's life, but we'll soon see that He purposed the very people who hurt Joseph most to eat from that fruit. Christ taught us in Luke 6:28: " 'Bless those who curse you,' " Not only for their blessing ... but sometimes for our healing. Dear One, " 'this is to [Christ's] Father's glory, that you bear much fruit.' " God will never lead you anywhere you can't ultimately be productive to the glory of His great name. The very season that seems least likely to bear fruit may be the place of your Ephraim portion.

Day Two
Unrecognizable Recognition

Today's Treasure

Although Joseph recognized his brothers, they did not recognize him.

Genesis 42:8

Studying the patriarchs is like sitting at a window watching life. The costumes and archaic sets may tempt us to sit back from the glass, but the tendencies and crises of the characters make us lean forward, turning the window unexpectedly into a mirror.

In our previous lessons we've seen Joseph making himself comfortable in a life he intends to keep. He has turned his back on his past and embraced the lofty position of his present. As today's lesson opens, unexpected visitors will come and make a royal mess of the tidy set. The good life is about to get complicated.

Please read all of Genesis 42 and complete the following.

Describe the kind of family dynamics you sense in verses 1 and 2.

_____

Why didn't Jacob send Benjamin with his other sons (v. 4)?

_____

How does verse 6 recall Genesis 37:5-7?

_____

What did Joseph accuse his brothers of being?

❏ spies   ❏ conjurers

❏ thieves   ❏ liars

In verse 15 Joseph announced that a test would be given to determine whether they were spies. Compare Joseph's description of the test in verses 14-17 to his actions in 18-20. How did Joseph alter the test?

_____

Why might Joseph have altered how many would stay and how many would go?

_____

Why did the brothers think this misfortune had come upon them (vv. 21-23)?

_____

What kinds of feelings do you think were behind Joseph's hidden tears?

_____

In verse 25 Joseph gave three orders regarding his brothers. What were they?

1. Fill their _____.

2. Put each man's _____.

3. Give them _____.

Two of the three orders are openly thoughtful and generous, but why do you think Joseph returned the silver his brothers had paid?

_____

How did the brothers react to the returned silver (v. 28)?

_____

🐪 How did Jacob react to their insistence on taking Benjamin back to Egypt (v. 38)?

_____

Complicated, isn't it?

Life in Canaan had not ceased for Jacob and his family. They coexisted with all their complexities and conflicts at the very same time Egypt teemed with life for Joseph. Just about the time we grow accustomed to the Egyptian scene, the spotlight in Genesis shifts suddenly to a "meanwhile" moment in Jacob's house.

The sons of Jacob had a skeleton in Egypt's closet.

If you're like me, the opening scene of family conflict made you squirm. Having personally played the role of peacemaker in many family conflicts during my childhood, the mere thought of cutting words and dirty looks can still make my stomach ache. I can almost smell Jacob's disapproval and sense his sons' virtual paralysis in time of need. The more someone belittles us, the less we seem able to do. The negative associations the sons of Jacob had with Egypt surely added to their paralysis. Don't forget, the Ishmaelites who purchased Joseph 20 years earlier were on their way to that land. Let's put it this way: the sons of Jacob had a skeleton in Egypt's closet, and the last thing they wanted to do was open that door.

Of course, the threat of starvation could motivate a houseful of men to do what they'd rather not. After all, haven't we all grinned at the adage that the way to a man's heart is through his stomach? A little math based on verse 3 tells us that somewhere along the way, Judah moved back home. (You'll recall his departure in Genesis 38.) All 12 of Jacob's sons are accounted for in our present chapter with 10 sons traveling to Egypt, one staying home, and one at the right hand of Pharaoh.

By the way, what did you think about Jacob keeping Benjamin at home? The patriarch's youngest son was well into adulthood by this time, yet we see Jacob with Benjamin repeating the same pattern he originally cut with Joseph. Jacob favored the remaining son of his favored wife, Rachel.

Before we judge too harshly, we have the same kind of tendency, don't we? If we don't wise up to it and ask God to help us change, we can transfer an unhealthy pattern in one relationship to another.

 Have you ever wised up to a repeated pattern in your own relationships? If so, how has God helped you break that pattern?

_____

_____

Jacob's (Israel's) family had no idea how dramatically the old patterns were about to be broken, and they will surely wonder if the process will kill them before it heals them. Picture the scene as the brothers bowed down before the viceroy of Egypt who—unbeknownst to them—was their own flesh and blood. The Hebrew adds richness to verses 6 and 7: "And Joseph saw his brethren and *recognized* them [*vayakirem*] but he made himself strange [*vayithnaker*] unto them, and spoke roughly with them, and he said unto them, 'Whence come you?' "[6] Oh, to have been a bug on the royal wall when Joseph recognized his brothers! Don't you know his mind was spinning? Joseph made immediate adjustments in his demeanor in order to be unrecognizable. The translation "made himself strange" is a little amusing as we recall that they thought him strange before.

The scene, however, is deadly serious. The intimidation of Joseph's harsh voice was magnified into sheer terror by the brothers' inability to understand him. Remember, verse 23 says Joseph spoke through an interpreter. The few seconds of delayed comprehension must have been torturous. If so, their troubled hearts must have leapt from their chests when Joseph thundered, "You are spies!" The Hebrew terminology adds interesting insight in verse 9, possibly suggesting a play on words. Joseph accused his brothers of seeing "where our land is unprotected," but a closer rendering of the Hebrew word for *unprotected* is *naked*. "Ye are spies; to see the nakedness *of the land* ye are come."[7] To ancient Hebrew thinkers like Joseph, to be stripped of your robe was to be left virtually naked. The sight of his brothers may have instantly unearthed the humiliating image of being stripped of his robe and thrown into a pit. As the present and the past weaved together in his thoughts, Joseph seemed to say the first thing that came to his mind: You've come to take the robe off of Egypt and leave her defenseless!

Surely you caught the irony of the brothers' response to Joseph's accusation in verse 11. Fill in the blank: "We are all the sons of one man. Your servants are _____ men, not spies."

List several ways they'd proved otherwise.

_____

_____

Imagine you are Joseph. What might you feel upon hearing your brothers say, "The youngest is now with our father, and one is no more." What kinds of things would go through your mind as you were described as "no more"?

_____

_____

What happened over the next few days testifies to the tornadic thoughts and emotions that swayed Joseph from one kind of action to another.

First, he said one brother would go and get Benjamin while the others stayed. Then he placed all 10 of them in custody. Three days later he said one brother would stay while nine fetched Benjamin. Then, of all things, Joseph placed the brothers' silver back in their sacks. Though a pure motive is claimed later (Gen. 43:23), the stress of feeling subject to the suspicion of both their father Jacob and the nation of Egypt vastly exceeded the blessing of having their money returned.

What in heaven's name was Joseph doing? Actually, Dear One, I don't think Joseph had a clue what he was doing. After all, he was in full throttle reaction mode. A number of commentator's feel the need to justify all Joseph's actions and make him above reproach, I suppose so he'll fit neatly into a savior-type role. I see no need. Only one Savior is perfect. I'm fine with giving Joseph some room to wig out.

We've seen Joseph develop character and humility through the course of his challenges, but perfection? Hardly. Sincere tears don't always necessitate sincere actions. Feelings get complicated and reactions mixed. Joseph's actions in today's lesson and those upcoming suggest—at least to me—that Joseph couldn't resist the temptation to exact a tiny bit of revenge, making his brothers squirm.

Take a careful look at Joseph's terminology when he drew up the new plan to retain only one brother instead of nine.

Fill in the blank according to verses 18 and 19: "On the third day, Joseph said to them, 'Do this and you will live, for I _____ _____: If you are honest men, let one of your brothers stay here in prison, while the rest of you go.'"

I'd like to suggest that fearing God had everything to do with Joseph's change of plans. Quite possibly Joseph fell under conviction as he held all 10 men in custody. Perhaps God caused Joseph to ask himself how different he was from his brothers. After all, had Joseph not thrown them as surely "into a pit"?

Let's put ourselves in Joseph's position for a moment. Let's say we each sustained a serious hurt but God was with us in the years that followed, using our pain to build our character and humility. We've come a long way and produced much fruit, but some of the old wounds are still there. We've just chosen to ignore them. Suddenly, we come face-to-face with the person we perceive caused us such pain. We don't give full way to our flesh. Neither do we give full way to the Holy Spirit. In other words, we're not entirely blameless … but who can blame us?

Can you relate with this scenario? If so, how?

_____

What brings us in check when we recognize a measure of our own vindictiveness? I believe it's the fact that we fear God! We know that He tests not only our actions but also our motives. Quite possibly, only the fear of God kept Joseph in check.

I've been there. Bet you have, too. The rich lessons of the story are not dependent upon making Joseph a saint. He's not one. He's a fine man of God, but he's got some wounds that need tending. God is too practical to use the journey Jacob's family has ahead for their sakes and not for Joseph's. Only the most misshapen ego sees conflict resolution as straightening out only the other party. One side may have more work to do, but rarely is the other completely blameless.

The curtain closes on the chapter much like it opened: Jacob, fearful, disapproving and punishing, and 10 guilty sons are scrambling to know what to do. Jacob must have experienced a terrifying sense of *déjà vu*, as once again his sons returned minus one. This time, with a pouch full of silver. Who could believe anything they had to say?

Joseph need not fear he'd been forgotten. After all, the entire family was still completely hamstrung with him.

Day Three
And Benjamin Also

Today's Treasure
So the men took the gifts and double the amount of silver, and Benjamin also. They hurried themselves down to Egypt and presented themselves to Joseph.
Genesis 43:15

Our reading today will be shorter, but our plot will grow thicker. I don't know about you, but I could hardly wait to get back to our story. One of the things I love about Bible studies is getting totally engrossed in the characters' lives. Hebrews 4:12 tells us God's Word is alive. Perhaps that's why ancient figures like Abraham, Isaac, Jacob, and Joseph seem to jump from the page.

 Read Genesis 43:1-15, and describe the primary conflict.

_____

Which son of Jacob took the lead in these scenes?
❏ Joseph ❏ Judah
❏ Israel ❏ Simeon

What did Jacob (Israel) tell his sons to do if the trip was inevitable (v. 11)?

_____

_____

What explanation did Jacob offer for the silver showing up (v. 12)?
❏ It was a plot against his sons.
❏ It was a mistake.
❏ It was theft.

Our chapter begins by implying that time has passed since Jacob's sons returned, minus one (Simeon) and demanding another (Benjamin). Remember, Jacob adamantly refused their request to let Benjamin go to Egypt, and I imagine the issue simmered on the stove of family crises. We did not have the time or space to discuss two very important admissions in yesterday's lesson. Both have tremendous bearings on the current emotional climate in Jacob's home. Glance back at Genesis 42:21-22 and picture the scene.

In our previous lesson I asked you to explain why Joseph's brothers thought misfortune had come upon them, but I wanted to wait until today to stir your thoughts with a compelling quote: "The text profoundly and beautifully displays how guilt lives in the human soul and how it can well up from deeply buried stores to regard as deserved and fitting punishment some distress that is utterly unrelated and, strictly speaking, unmerited. Imprisoned in a 'pit' where there is none who can hear their distress, they recall how they failed to heed Joseph's pleading voice calling to them out of the pit—a fact previously not known to the reader. Perhaps it is the sound of his voice now that triggers a memory of their failure to hear it years ago."[8]

Dear One, the load on the consciences of Joseph's brothers depicts one reason why we've got to go to God, confess our sins, and make whatever restitution He prescribes. If we don't, we will end up attaching every bad thing that happens to us to past sins, chaining ourselves to the perception of endless punishment.

I believe we can all relate. Our pasts may differ dramatically, but surely we've all experienced guilt, whether we earned it or received it as a "gift" from the Evil One.

🐪 Describe how guilt makes you feel.

_____

_____

_____

By Genesis 43, the sons of Jacob are nearly six feet under in guilt. The proverbial elephant in the living room that everyone tried to tiptoe around has finally demanded attention in Genesis 42:36. In the heat of the moment, their father spit words confirming what they'd wondered if he'd suspected all along, "You have deprived me of my children. Joseph is no more and Simeon is no more, and now you want to take Benjamin. Everything is against me!"

"You have deprived me of … Joseph." There. The cat was out of the bag.

Jacob could neither prove it nor explain how it had happened, but he knew his sons were responsible for Joseph's "death." Perhaps they'd disposed of Simeon as well. Can you imagine living in a climate of such guilt and blame? The fact that Jacob had emotionally written off his sons is clear in his reference to Benjamin as the "only one left" (Gen. 42:38). And you thought your family was in a mess! This story should certainly make us feel better about God's ability to redeem messed up families!

By Genesis 43 words have been spoken that cannot be taken back. The elephant is crushing the furniture in the living room, and the cat won't go back in the bag. Jacob's house was an emotional zoo. Don't you know his sons could have wrung his neck when he suggested, "Go back and buy us a little more food" as if it were as uncomplicated as a quick trip to the Stop 'N Go? Had their father forgotten that the holdup was a little family issue called *Benjamin?* Jacob hoped that either time had dropped the Benjamin issue or that obtaining just a "little more food" would not demand such a high price. Jacob is my favorite character in the patriarch story: he offers no end to ways we can relate.

> **Don't we all occasionally hope that time has changed the rules? Can you think of a related example from your life? In what did it result?**

_____

_____

A friend of mine recently left her husband for the umpteenth time. She doesn't even want to live apart from him, but he has a serious addiction that often makes him abusive and frightening. He cries and pleads every time she leaves, they return to counseling, he "re-learns" the ground rules for the privilege of living with his family, she moves back in, and soon he forgets the rules again. You are not meant to take any kind of marriage counsel from that illustration. Rather, view it as a prime example of hoping time has changed the rules.

Earlier I asked you to note the brother who rose to leadership in this segment. We must not miss Judah's rise to the top because we're getting a glimpse of redemption at work. One reason Jacob looked to Joseph as the leader was because the older sons had proved such poor choices. Judah's sins were notorious in the family, but he did not let the appraisal of his past dictate his future. He refused to consider the respect of his family members impossible to earn and reclaim. Judah had a chance to do the right thing and take the strong lead.

> **How about you? Have you ever lamented the loss of someone's respect? I have. Do you tend to think lost respect can never be regained or, on the other hand, do you tend to want to reclaim it without earning it? Briefly explain.**

_____

_____

_____

Toward the conclusion of our study, Jacob's blessing over Judah will show Judah finally earned his father's respect. But the role Judah played in the present scenario and those immediately following are crucial parts of that process. In today's segment we see Judah's willingness to say some strong yet compassionate words to his father.

Fill in the blanks according to Genesis 43:8-9. "Send the _____

along with me and we will go at once, so that _____ and _____ and

_____ _____ may live and not die. I myself will

_____ his safety; you can hold me _____

_____ for him."

Note Judah's endearing reference to Benjamin as "the boy." His age begged to differ with this title, but many of us understand the concept of "relatively speaking." No matter how old my little brother gets, my siblings and I still call him the baby. Benjamin? He remained "the boy." Judah pledged to return Jacob's favored son or "bear the blame" all his life. Judah certainly knew what he was asking for. Guilt and blame were the stakes holding up the family tent. Judah also knew he had to risk the blame in order to save the family. Note also that three generations were implied in the last exercise: we, you, and our children. Without food, all three generations would be lost and the family line obliterated.

In verse 11 we witness the beginnings of Jacob's acceptance. "If it must be, then do this." You noted earlier that Jacob instructed his sons to take "the man" (Joseph) "a gift." If the giver were anyone else, we could consider the action eastern hospitality, but we've already seen Jacob in a tight squeeze where he hoped a gift would appease. Don't forget the lavish gift he sent ahead to Esau so he could "face" him (Gen. 32:13-15).

On the other hand, who could blame Jacob for doing all he could to invite the favor of the harsh viceroy? To the limit of Jacob's understanding, his sons' lives were at stake. The expense of the gift of honey, nuts, and almonds was heavily inflated by the famine. Jacob chanced giving up some of the little food they had in the present to get what they'd need in the future. You can imagine that the old man was stressed nearly to the breaking point.

Reread Genesis 43:14. Do your best to describe Jacob's spiritual state of mind.

_____

_____

Jacob called upon God Almighty: *El Shaddai.* Remember, this is the primary name by which God revealed Himself to the patriarchs (Gen. 17:1, Ex. 6:3). Jacob's father, Isaac, invoked this glorious name over Jacob when he first departed his home: "May God Almighty bless you and make you fruitful and increase your numbers until you become a community of peoples" (Gen. 28:3). With their future bleak and a famine ever-present, Jacob knew that God Almighty alone could keep his family fruitful and increase them into a community.

At this point in his life, Jacob didn't call on God Almighty's blessing. He called on His mercy. I've been there. I remember feeling so undeserving and far gone that I wouldn't

have dared ask for God's blessing. I just hoped for His mercy. How freely He granted it! Sometimes, Dear One, mercy is the blessing.

My heart aches for Jacob as we reach the end of our reading today. Can you imagine his sorrow as his sons, including "the boy," disappeared over the horizon? Read verse 15 slowly and carefully as we conclude. Don't miss the order of things taken on the journey back to Egypt. "So the men took the gifts and double the amount of silver, and Benjamin also."

And Benjamin also. The agonizing phrase almost seems postponed until the last possible second. "The 'and Benjamin' hangs like the resigned sigh of a father trapped between the need to live and the possibility of a life made utterly empty through another loss.' "[9]

I can almost hear the father's prayer: "Have mercy, God Almighty. Have mercy."

Day Four
Fears to Feasting

Today's Treasure

He wants to attack us and overpower us and seize us as slaves and take our donkeys.

Genesis 43:18

Our previous lesson concluded as a heartbroken old man resigned to release his dearest son to meet the demands of Egypt's vizier. The deal was clear: no Benjamin, no food. Interestingly, Benjamin's own thoughts and reactions are not recorded in this segment of Scripture. The bright side of a character's silence is the opportunity for us to use our imaginations to picture his response.

As you visualize the brothers' journey to Egypt, try to imagine the mood of the group. Do you picture them traveling in silence or talking frantically? Do you think the crisis brought them closer, making them kinder to one another; or did it splinter them, shortening their tempers?

What do you think Benjamin thought? Do you think he was glad to finally be considered one of the brothers, or do you think his father and the circumstances surrounding Joseph's disappearance made him fear his brothers? Or did he walk in silent grief, thinking of nothing but his father's sadness?

We'll slightly overlap our reading today with yesterday's so that we can recapture our context. Please read Genesis 43:15-34 and complete the following.

 According to verse 18, what did the brothers think the vizier (Joseph) was going to do to them?

_____

How did Joseph's steward explain the return of the silver to their sacks (v. 23)?

_____

How were the brothers treated differently than they expected (vv. 24-34)?

_____

_____

Why did Joseph have to momentarily leave the room?

_____

_____

What was peculiar about the seating arrangement?

_____

_____

As our scene opens in Genesis 43:16, I can't help but think about the prodigal's father in the Gospel of Luke. Luke 15:20 tells us that " 'while [his son] was still a long way off, his father saw him.' " The image suggests a father's continual search of the horizon for his son's return. Genesis 43:16 indicates Joseph saw his brothers—Benjamin in tow—before they ever saw him. He, too, prepared a feast for those who'd hurt him just as the father in Jesus' story prepared a feast for his wayward son.

A welcome party was the last thing Joseph's brothers expected. In fact, you probably caught the irony of their fears. "He wants to attack us and overpower us and seize us as slaves!" What they feared from this man was ironically identical to what they'd done to him.

Mark the following statements *true (T)* or *false (F)* based on your own perceptions:
_____ I tend to be shocked when someone treats me like I treat others.
_____ I expect a person to treat me as I've treated others.
_____ I see no relationship between the way I treat others and how others treat me.

Though our backgrounds may cause us to mark the three statements differently, Joseph's brothers obviously would have marked the second statement "true." Most of us who have had impure, selfish, or unkind motives in our actions toward others constantly suspect similar motives in others. Highly suspicious people have often been suspect at one time or another. Similarly, if we've done something ugly to someone, we keep waiting and dreading someone acting equally ugly to us. We're not always wrong.

The Bible certainly teaches that we can reap what we sow. And in those times that we don't, we've been the happy victims of something called *grace.*

Do you feel as if you've reaped to the degree you've sown? Be honest. This is a question involving perceptions, not right or wrong answers.

_____

_____

 What reassurance does Psalm 103:10 provide?

_____

Even in His discipline, God is redemptive. We are assured that God disciplines those He loves and that if we're not disciplined, we're not loved (Heb. 12:6). How, then, does God's discipline line up with the mercy described in Psalm 103:10? I believe God disciplines us to the degree we can be taught. Remember, the goal of all true discipline is to disciple. God never chastises His child past the point of teaching. He never punishes just to punish.

No, we don't get what we deserve, but if we continue in the action, we may well get such consequences that the teachable learn not to do it again. The unteachable, on the other hand, can sow the wind and reap the whirlwind (Hos. 8:7). Joseph's brothers did not get away with what they did to him. God allowed them to get a taste of what they deserved all along, yet they ultimately got to feast on grace.

The steward's response to Joseph's brothers in Genesis 43:23 was their first shock. As they frantically claimed innocence over the silver found in their pouches, he spoke peace to them. In Hebrew, "It's all right" is the word *shalom* meaning *peace*.[10] Note that the steward spoke of their God and the God of their father. I believe he knew the story of Joseph and his family well. Focus on the steward's wording: "Your God ... has given you treasure in your sacks." A better translation may be "God ... must have put a treasure" in your sacks.[11] "He avoids using the word *kesep*, 'money.' The word he does use is more dramatic. It refers specifically to buried treasure."[12]

How did God bury treasures amidst the rubble for Jacob's sons in Egypt?

How has he buried treasures amidst rubble for you?

Beloved, I don't know what kind of circumstances this season of your life poses, but could they be worse than those Jacob's sons perceived? They could hardly experience deeper peril or greater risk, yet God's providence was in perfect play. In the midst of His unfolding plan, He'd buried treasures for them to unearth at times they least expected. Do you feel in deep peril? At great risk? Your God ... has given you treasure. Search for it.

Simeon, the brother left behind, was undoubtedly one of those buried treasures unearthed before their eyes. They certainly wouldn't have expected this timing. They expected to present Benjamin to the vizier for his approval before a reunion with Simeon. They had no idea Joseph had already seen them and knew the youngest was in their company.

This is a perfect time to talk about Simeon's incarceration. The last his brothers saw him he was "taken from them and bound before their eyes" (42:24). We have no idea how much time had passed, but we can be certain Simeon was held long enough to wonder if they'd ever return. Imagine how complicated his feelings would be, knowing that Benjamin's life seemed more valuable to his father than his. Scripture records no dialogue between the brothers upon Simeon's return to them.

Next, we see the sons of Jacob treated like royal guests. Suddenly the harshness of "the man" (Joseph) disappeared. He had no apparent reaction to the gifts. Rather, his concerns were for them and their father. Time had passed. Famines were especially fierce for the elderly. Joseph knew his father well enough to wonder if he'd die before allowing Benjamin to leave. Consider the tender moment as Joseph's attention suddenly shifts to Benjamin as if he could no longer resist the pull of a magnet. After all, Benjamin alone among the others was Joseph's mother's son.

The motherless sons of Jacob, no one understood them as they understood one another so many years ago. The memories. The resemblance. The pain. The NIV describes Joseph as "deeply moved," but the Hebrew indicates something more poignant. "And Joseph made haste for *his mercy grew warm (nikhmeru rachamayv)* for his brother, and he sought where to weep" (v. 30, emphasis added).[13]

His mercy grew warm for his brother. I hope I never forget that terminology. Not long ago my own mercy grew warm for a broken young mother. I prayed for her as she sat in a wheelchair caressing her one surviving child from a car crash.

After Joseph returned from gathering his composure, the tone changed dramatically. The peculiarities of the banquet are too rich to miss. First, because he held an Egyptian office, Joseph did not eat with his brothers. An Egyptian and a Hebrew at the same table was a cultic taboo.[14] Joseph, an Egyptianized Hebrew, is simultaneously both and neither.

The second peculiarity was the seating of the brothers in order of age, leaving them utterly baffled. They must have exchanged puzzled glances and unspoken questions. *How did he know? Was it divination?* Then, imagine the whirling thoughts when "Benjamin's portion was five times as much as anyone else's." *Why would the vizier do such a thing?* Do you think they wondered if Benjamin *was obviously* superior and not just the favored son of a shamelessly partial father?

The final scene whispers a telling secret if we're willing to listen. Several commentaries confirmed that the Hebrew doesn't just say they drank freely or merrily. It says they got drunk.[15] Surely we know by now that the patriarchal narrative is not an exemplary thesis on how to live. That was the Law's job in Exodus and Deuteronomy under the old covenant. The point is the faithfulness of God. If Joseph has proved to be anything in his Egyptian tenure, he has shown himself to be a man of restraint. He certainly was not one given to lasciviousness, so why this sudden out-of-character overindulgence?

Why don't you answer first, and then I'll give it a shot.

_____

_____

You and I probably surmised something similar. Joseph felt like he couldn't deal with his emotions—the mercy growing warmer and warmer within him—so he sought to cool them (anesthetize them) with drink. "Joseph, perhaps as much in sorrow as in joy, leads the party-goers to lose themselves in drink, satisfying at once his desire both to forget and to celebrate."[16] Imagine the pitiable scene as he drank alone from his table in the isolation of secrecy while they drank together at theirs. Did he stare forlornly into his cup, remembering long-ago meals they shared?

By the next morning Joseph's temporary fix had worn off. Have you noticed that emotional pain has an uncanny way of hanging over us? Ephesians 5:18 tells us not to "get drunk on wine, which leads to debauchery. Instead, be filled with the Spirit." The fruit of Christ's Spirit introduces His own feelings into the matter: love, joy, peace, patience, kindness, goodness, faithfulness, gentleness, and all in the protective boundary of self-control. Sometimes we have to *feel* the pain for God to *heal* the pain; but when His feelings converge with ours, the process is bearable.

Day Five'
A Set Up and a Stand Up

Now then, please let your servant remain here as my lord's slave in place of the boy, and let the boy return with his brothers.

Genesis 44:33

Free-flowing drink may have cooled Joseph's escalating mercies for a while, but the problem hung over ... probably much like his head. Morning came and so did a bitter reality. He'd promised to return Simeon if the band of brothers brought Benjamin. They complied at no small emotional cost. Was he now to simply let them go? Joseph was not ready to reveal his true identity, yet he could not bring himself to release Benjamin. What was a masquerading man to do? Plot a ruse!

We'll take our reading in two parts today. Please read Genesis 44:1-13 first, focusing on the role of Joseph's steward. Glance back at Genesis 43:23, recalling the steward's explanation for the returned money the brothers found in their sacks. The steward could easily have thought Joseph's initial gesture was simple benevolence, reasoning that his master wanted the brothers to have the grain free of charge.

Now, look back to our present scenes. How could the steward have known that benevolence wasn't Joseph's motive the second time around?

_____

_____

_____

In your own words, what case did the brothers make for their innocence (v. 8)?

_____

 Never dreaming the cup is in their possession, what oath did they make (v. 9)?

_____

In whose possession was the cup found?
❏ Judah's
❏ Benjamin's
❏ Simeon's

According to verse 13, who returned to the city?

_____

At this point in the narrative, can any of us continue to characterize Joseph as completely selfless and pure of motive? When all is said and done, integrity will characterize Joseph, but just like we do, he warred with his own flesh in the process. Joseph was as scarred emotionally as he would have been physically had the wild animal attacked him as his brothers had claimed. With the birth of his first son, Joseph did his best to forget "completely" his troubles and his father's house, but by now these troubles were controlling him. The sight of his brothers picked at every scar but, confusingly, also picked at his heart.

Madness and mercy wrestled. Joseph staggered between feelings like a drunk staggering down Egypt's streets. He loved his brothers. And he hated them. He never wanted to see them again. And he never wanted to let them go. Joseph likely realized that his father had to have Benjamin. But then, so did he.

Some commentators suggest that to give Joseph the benefit of the doubt, we could reason that he was testing his brothers—framing them to see if they would treat Benjamin the same way they treated him.[17] Would they abandon him and make a run for it? Attack him? Return to their father and say he'd been tragically killed? Though the frame-up will prove a test, I'm not sure Joseph was thinking clearly enough to plan it with such noble purpose. I suspect he scrambled to figure out a quick way to retain Benjamin without divulging his identity. That his scheme turned out to be a tremendous test of character was God's redemptive "buy back." Not Joseph's noble purpose.

I cringe as I read that Joseph ordered the steward to frame the Hebrew men and then falsely accuse them of wickedness. Joseph certainly had reason to have known how false accusation felt.

When had Joseph been falsely accused (Gen. 39)?

_____

Surely the steward's eyebrows were pinned to his hairline as Joseph issued his orders. Nevertheless, he obeyed them. The brothers were horrified by the accusation and made a rash oath in verse 9 that could have proved deadly. Thankfully, Joseph's intention was not to kill Benjamin but to keep him. Imagine the terror that shot through their souls when the silver cup was discovered in the beloved son's belongings.

How did the brothers demonstrate their grief (v. 13)?

_____

I hope you noted the significance of their return to the city. They would not forsake Benjamin. They would face his accuser as one. All for one and one for all? Does this sound like Jacob's sons to you? Beloved, we must pause and not miss the change creeping over this fragile band of brothers. The emerging solidarity among these splintered siblings can't be overemphasized. I'd like to suggest that from God's perspective solidarity was the point of their 20-year ordeal. In a very short time, the entire people of Israel will move to Egypt and remain for four hundred years. Though we have difficulty reasoning how their mass transit from Canaan to Egypt fit into the sovereign plan of God, we know that it did because He prophesied it when He first "cut covenant" with Abram.

Succinctly, what was the prophecy in Genesis 15:13?

_____

We know God referred to Egypt because history played out just as He said it would in the land of Pharaohs. Give careful consideration to this point: Centuries passed between the end of the patriarchal narrative and the beginning of the Book of Exodus, yet the people of God retained their solidarity and identity. Look ahead to Exodus 1:9.

What are God's people called in this verse?

_____

How easily they could have been swallowed up by the powerful Egyptian empire, yet they emerged as a people completely distinguishable from the nation surrounding them. I'd like to gently suggest that one reason they held onto their distinct identity and solidarity was oppression. Beloved, a worldly society that fully accepts God's "peculiar people" also invites their integration. You and I tend to think the best thing for believers in Christ is to be surrounded by a friendly society. That is not necessarily true. Had Egypt remained friendly to the sons of Jacob, the tribes would likely have been absorbed into Egypt's pagan culture.

Read John 17: 22-23. What parallels do you see between the road to unity for the sons of Jacob and the road to unity for us?

_____

_____

Up until this point, Jacob's family has been characterized by fragmentation. The only hints we've seen toward solidarity were for wrongful purposes, Joseph's harm for example. Yet suddenly, the brothers unite all for one. The band that would hold them through four hundred years in a strange land first tightened here. If the silver cup was a test, the u-turn back to Egypt was a passing grade that would mark them for centuries. "At last, they clearly show themselves to be their brother's keepers. They will try to stand or fall together ... The ten sons of Israel meet the moral challenge ... and return with Benjamin to face their judge."[18]

The remainder of our reading holds rival significance to the emerging solidarity of Jacob's sons. Please read Genesis 44:14-34. This segment of Scripture contains one of the longest speeches in the Old Testament. Who is the speaker?

_____

Condense the stand he took with Joseph into one statement.

_____

Does anything about Judah's plea move you personally? If so, what and why?

_____

_____

Look ahead to Genesis 45:1. Judah's words were obviously more than Joseph could stand. I just asked what moved you most. What do you think moved Joseph most?

_____

The face-off between Judah and Joseph is critically important. Leader to leader, nose to nose, Judah emerged as the worthy contender. Though we must not dislodge Joseph from his place of God-ordained significance, we will miss the narrative's intent if we fail to see the additional exaltation of Judah. In Genesis 44, he did something far more profound than persuading a change in circumstances. He persuaded a change in heart. True healing comes no other way.

For the remainder of the lesson I'd like to make the case that Judah's speech was every bit the test of Joseph that the silver cup was to his 11 brothers. First, Judah's sincerity tested Joseph's insincerity. Ultimately Joseph's sincerity will trump his moments of insincerity, but in the meantime, circumstances surfaced character flaws in Joseph just like they do in us. We can give Joseph the benefit of the doubt and believe that his ultimate goal was pure, but his means were deceptive.

The questions Job asked in Job 13:7 might have been appropriate for Joseph: "Will you speak wickedly on God's behalf? Will you speak deceitfully for him?" In other words, will you lie and say it was for God?

What power did Joseph tell the 11 sons of Jacob he possessed (Gen. 44:15)?

_____

Egypt was notorious for the practice of divination, so Joseph knew the brothers would believe him. Did Joseph really possess such power? Hardly!

How did he know the brothers had the silver cup?

_____

God had given Joseph the supernatural ability to interpret dreams, but pagan divination was clearly not of God. Nor was it of Joseph. Joseph's insincerity to claim a power he didn't possess was only one line, however, in an entire one-man act. His entire role was insincere. We may understand why Joseph didn't reveal himself in the beginning, but why hadn't he by now? Did some small part of him enjoy the game? Don't miss Joseph's statement in verse 17: "The rest of you, go back to your father in peace."

Why was this suggestion ludicrous?

_____

Judah and his brothers were coming to the quick end of their games. "What can we say? How can we prove our innocence? God has uncovered your servants' guilt" (v. 16). They weren't guilty of stealing the cup, but they were grievously guilty of other sins. Judah saw their crisis as guilt catching up with them. In sincerity, he pled. He also took the risk of pointing out Joseph's role in their impossible position.

Judah concluded his soliloquy with the most astonishing offer of all. He pled to stay in Benjamin's place. In effect, Judah offered to be the substitutionary offering on Benjamin's altar ... the ram for his father's beloved Isaac.

Lastly, Judah's fight *for* his family tested Joseph's fight *with* his family. How often the enemy tries to distract us by tempting us to fight *with* the very people we were meant to fight *for!* Can you imagine Joseph's inner response to the question, "Do you have a father or a brother?" Yes, Joseph had a father and brother—not only one brother. He had 11. His family ties thus far reached only around Benjamin. The partiality of Joseph stood face-to-face with the sudden solidarity of his brothers. The threat to one became the glue that made half-brothers whole. The band around these brothers was no longer fragile. They were not innocent, and they would take their punishment ... but they would take it together. And Joseph? He could stand against them. Or he could stand with them.

Joseph was a man of heart. His heart had simply been wounded. His character endured and his brothers soon learned the most powerful lessons of all at his feet. In the meantime, Joseph had a few things to learn. Through his story we will learn that nothing is more humbling than God teaching a lesson to the more spiritual through the less. And Joseph, too, would pass his test.

---

[1] Spiros Zodhiates et al., eds., *The Complete Word Study Dictionary: Old Testament* (Chattanooga, TN: AMG Publishers, 1994), 11.

[2] Victor P. Hamilton, *The Book of Genesis: Chapters 18–50* (Grand Rapids: William B. Eerdman's Publishing, 1995), 510.

[3] Leon R. Kass, *The Beginning of Wisdom: Reading Genesis* (New York: Free Press, 2003), 571 n.

[4] Gordon J. Wenham, *Word Biblical Commentary: Genesis 16–50* (Dallas: Word Books, 1994), 397.

[5] James Strong, *Strong's Exhaustive Concordance of the Bible: The Hebrew and Chaldee Dictionary* (Nashville, Holman Bible Publishers, n.d.), 15.

[6] Kass, 574.

[7] Ibid., 576.

[8] Ibid., 579.

[9] Hamilton, 548.

[10] Zodhiates, 116.

[11] Hamilton, 547.

[12] Ibid., 550.

[13] Kass, 588.

[14] Hamilton, 555.

[15] Kass, 590.

[16] Ibid., 590-91.

[17] Ibid., 591.

[18] Ibid., 592-93.

SESSION NINE
A Fragile Band of Brothers

Segment One: Genesis 45:1-3

A. Some _____ are _____ moments. No one else can _____.

B. God alone can give us the _____ to be _____ when everyone else is still _____.

Segment Two: Genesis 45:4-11

A. Joseph _____ the entire _____ in the _____ of God. It was their only _____ of _____.

B. Feelings of _____ and _____ toward others sometimes can't _____ those we harbor toward _____. The Hebrew word for *distressed* means "to worry, _____; to _____, cause pain ... denotes _____ and physical _____." The Hebrew word for *angry* means "to burn, be _____, to be angry ... act _____. Points to the fire or heat of the anger just after it has been _____."

C. Our great _____ can mean someone else's _____, even someone who helped _____ us.

D. If we _____ God's means of our _____, we could easily find ourselves _____ (v. 11).

Segment Three: Genesis 45:12-15

In God's process of _____ interpersonal _____, don't expect to reach the same _____ at the same _____. "The _____ of _____ between Joseph and his brothers spells out the _____ of _____."

Segment Four: Genesis 45:16-24

A. Joseph's _____ is not in _____ only. He demonstrates it in _____.

B. Nothing can _____ a family _____ faster than a _____ in the _____ suddenly springing to life.

Segment Five: Genesis 45:25-28

Stunned translates "he was _____, for he did not _____ them." The basic meaning "seems to be that of being _____ or _____, a condition of _____ to _____."

Final point: A fresh _____ of _____ restores _____.

WEEK TEN
Epic Endings to the Beginning

I have had the privilege of journeying with my fellow Bible-students through 10 in-depth Bible studies, yet each of them has been completely unique to me. Our journey through the pages of Genesis has been no exception. In fact, we've been in places with the patriarchs and their families unlike any others I've encountered. The range of themes and subjects has been as deep and wide as the grandest canyon. Surely each of us has had ample opportunity to relate with the great cloud of witnesses that stirred up the dust on Planet Earth so long ago. Aren't you glad God dictated it all to Moses and made sure the patriarchal narratives graced the pages of holy writ? I imagine some of the stories raised his white eyebrows. White or not, they raised a few of ours as well. Our final week awaits us, Dear One. Let's savor every moment of it as we keep an eye out for answers to the following questions.

This Week's Principal Questions

Day 1: What reassurances did God give Jacob about going to Egypt (Gen. 46:1-7)?

Day 2: How did Jacob describe his years in Genesis 47:9?

Day 3: What did Jacob do in Genesis 48:14 that displeased Joseph?

Day 4: What are a few things our future holds for us corporately as believers in Christ?

Day 5: Based on Jacob's words in 49:29-32, what kinds of things do you imagine preoccupied Jacob's thoughts toward the end?

Day One

With All That Was His

As a compulsive reader, few things aggravate me more than a good book with a bad ending. God does all things well. He's seen fit to begin the last leg of our journey in Genesis with the last leg of Jacob's life. Rest assured, we have a good ending coming. I didn't say perfect. Remember, Scripture is not fiction, and real people on this planet don't completely fix. After traveling in Genesis through the twists, turns, and spin cycles of four generations, we have the privilege of seeing the story all come together.

I hope you were able to join us for session 9's video. If you missed the session, familiarize yourself with Genesis 45 before proceeding to our text for today. After all we've endured between Joseph and his unsuspecting brothers, don't cheat yourself of the satisfaction of seeing him reveal his identity. Today's text is Genesis 46. Please begin by reading verses 1-7.

Recently we've discussed the theme of connectedness in the patriarchal narrative. What threads of generational connectedness do you see in this segment?

_____

_____

 What reassurances did God give Jacob about going to Egypt?

_____

_____

Day One
With All That Was His
Day Two
The Years of Pilgrimage
Day Three
Crossing His Arms
Day Four
Prophetic Blessings
Day Five
The Grandest Finale

Today's Treasure
So Israel set out with all that was his.
Genesis 46:1

What was the final tally of Jacob's family members who settled in Egypt (v. 27)?
❑ 30 ❑ 144,000 ❑ 70

Jacob may not have moved since Joseph's disappearance. The last recorded locale for the patriarch was Hebron (Gen. 37:14). I know a mom who is afraid to move away from her home of 20 years in case a young man who lived there for a while tries to find his way back. Perhaps Jacob had similar fears. The news that his beloved Joseph was alive, well, and powerful surely stunned him beyond belief.

His wasn't the only head swimming. Imagine the inner conflict of the sons while they heralded good news sure to raise questions without pretty answers. After all, wouldn't the brothers have to explain how Joseph ended up in Egypt rather than the belly of a wild beast?

So Israel set out with all that was his. We are told Jacob (Israel) "offered sacrifices to the God of his father Isaac" (46:1) when he reached Beersheba. (You probably recorded this among the threads of connectedness.) Why Beersheba?

What happened in Beersheba in Genesis 26:23-25 and to which patriarch?

_____

God appeared at Beersheba to Isaac and identified Himself as the God of his father, connecting the original blessing to Abraham with the family line. Isaac built an altar there, and many years later Jacob offered sacrifices—presumably on that very altar. The old man was surely awash with sentiment over God's faithfulness toward his family line.

Note how Scripture identifies the patriarch in Genesis 46:2 by filling in the blanks: "And God spoke to _____ in a vision at night and said, "_____, _____!"

Perhaps you've wondered why Scripture refers to the third generation patriarch sometimes as "Israel," other times as "Jacob," and often within phrases of one another. God alone knows for certain, but one commentary explains that the name "Jacob" is used most often "when the fretful, apprehensive, suffering patriarch is in view."[1] Certainly, the old man had cause for apprehension—even if it was wrapped in gratitude. With full knowledge of the promised-land perimeters, Jacob was uprooting his entire family and moving to Egypt.

What had happened to Jacob's father, Isaac, in Genesis 26:2?

_____

God reserves the sovereign right to direct one of His children on a path He may have forbidden to another.

God came to Jacob, purposely identified Himself as the God of his father (Isaac), then told him not to be afraid to go to Egypt. Yet decades earlier, as you noted in Genesis 26:2, God forbade Isaac to go to his father. Same God, same line, different plan.

God reserves the sovereign right to direct one of His children on a path He may have forbidden to another. God's overarching laws and principles do not change, but His directions within them can vary drastically. That's one reason we must be careful not to force our personal convictions in gray areas on another believer. God may require something of you He does not require of me and vice versa.

Have you learned this lesson through personal experience? If so, please share.

_____

God not only told Jacob to proceed fearlessly to Egypt but also told him He'd go with him. This prompts me to share a testimony of God's faithfulness. We scheduled the Patriarchs video-shoot trip to Egypt, but political unrest caused us to postpone. Months later, the night before we were to leave, I received a call informing me that we might have to cancel. I stared into my open suitcases and asked the Lord what He'd have us do.

He reminded me of His words to Jacob. "Do not be afraid to go down to Egypt … I will go down to Egypt with you, and I will surely bring you back again." How wonderful can God be? Not surprisingly, I soon received a call assuring me the trip was on. God floors me.

I know you also have occasions when God makes Himself so real you nearly shiver. Share an instance when you felt God's realness.

_____

Take notice of God's promise to Jacob, "I will surely bring you back again" (v. 4). A rich Old Testament feature appears in this promise that I don't want you to miss. Would Jacob actually return to the land of promise alive? No. His body would be buried there, but he'd never lay eyes on it again. The prophecy of Genesis 15 was already set in motion, and the children of Israel would remain in Egypt 400 years. God had not forgotten the prophecy, and He certainly hadn't lied about its fulfillment. God's promise to bring the patriarch back was to Jacob's family line and not just his dry bones.

Notice the three references to "you" or "your" in Genesis 46:4. In "I will go down to Egypt with you," the word *you* applies to Jacob and his family. In "I will surely bring you back again," *you* applies to his descendants or what will ultimately become the nation. Finally, in "Joseph's own hand will close your eyes," the word *your* refers to Jacob himself. Ancient Old Testament thinkers may not have had a problem with the oscillating meanings of "you," but I believe New Testament thinkers do. I'm not sure we've been taught to open our minds to this possibility when we are convinced God has made a promise.

Read Hebrews 11:13 carefully, and explain it in your own words.

_____

Promises "fulfilled from a distance" can mean a number of things. Hebrews 11:39-40 refers to promises God is waiting to fulfill until we're all together. What an incredibly exciting thought! Today's text suggests something else "distance" can mean. God can speak a promise to His faithful child that will actually be fulfilled in the life of his or her descendant.

Modern, drive-thru thinkers like you and me frame events in such immediate terms that we decide we either misunderstood God or He misled us if His promises are not fulfilled in our personal lives. An ancient Hebrew thinker would have considered the possibility of a promise fulfilled in his descendant a great honor because such fulfillment signaled God's continued blessing over the extended line.

Exodus 20:6 tells us God shows His love to a thousand generations of those who love Him and keep His commandments. The last thing I want to do is discourage you from

Consider the possibility of God's promise fulfilled in a descendant an honor.

believing God for the fulfillment of countless promises before your earthly eyes. Let's be open to the possibility, however, that if the years slip away and we find ourselves on our deathbed without seeing a promise fulfilled, it may have been intended for our physical or spiritual descendants.

God's promises to us are bigger than us and reach far beyond us. Their ultimate purpose is glory. His. He is always faithful, and He will never make a promise He won't keep. His promises to "you" could be for you personally, your family, or your line. If precious promises aren't fulfilled in the fruitful years of our lifetimes, let's believe God and welcome His promises from a distance. What kind of faith could be more pleasing to Him?

Now let's look to the end of our present chapter for the climactic reunion of Jacob and his long-lost Joseph. Please read Genesis 46:28-30.

What do we see in Jacob's choosing Judah to go ahead of them to Joseph?
❑ **trust** ❑ **responsibility** ❑ **send one to keep the others safe**

I know I keep drilling the point of Judah's exaltation among the brothers, but it has a place of importance before our series concludes. Keep it in mind.

Once Joseph knew Jacob was near, he went straightaway on his chariot to see him. Let's not hurry past this scene. Surely moments like these are why God gave us imaginations. Picture it: Jacob has not seen his son in over 20 years. To him, Joseph was gone, leaving behind only a bloodied robe. One wonders how long he kept it in his possession. He's been told by the others that Joseph is alive, well, and in the power seat. But could anything have prepared the old man for the sight of Rachel's firstborn arriving in a cloud of dust on a chariot from the Pharaoh's fleet?

Surely Jacob's sons said something like, "That's him, Father! That's Joseph in the distance. Do you see the dust? Can you hear the horses?" I can picture Jacob squinting against the desert sun, welcoming this beloved promise from a distance. Then there he was! Right before his father's aging eyes: Joseph. His Joseph. So different from the Hebrew boy of 17 he'd lost. So different from his bearded brothers. Was it truly him? This Egyptianized man, clean-shaven, maybe bare-chested and bedecked in brass and jewels? No beast-inflicted scars in sight?

Jacob's thoughts swirled. Twirled. In all the sentiments that stampeded through his heart and mind, do you think he was also able to silently wonder, *What have you done to your hair?* Or, *Why didn't I bring that coat?*

As we're told that Joseph "threw his arms around his father and wept for a long time," we can imagine Jacob in shock. We have no record of immediate reciprocation.

Weeping "for a long time" doesn't just come from a sudden explosion of emotion. Those kinds of tears spring quickly and dry quickly. No, weeping "for a long time" comes from a storehouse in the soul. Saving up. Stuffing back. Long-term investments. Though Joseph had wept for his brothers, nothing could have compared to the sight of his daddy. Beautiful sight! Difficult sight. The lines on the old man's leathery face were etched deeply— and not just by years but by the scalpel of grief. Joseph's tears forged a Nile down the desert dry lines of the old patriarch's neck.

What words finally came to the wrestler God renamed *Israel* (v. 30)?

_____

Jacob would not die soon. As God would have it, he'd live 17 more years in Joseph's company: exactly the same number he'd shared with him before. Bookends of seventeen years with painful, precious volumes of estranged life wedged between them. Time that could not be made up. Nor time enough to lament it.

The father-son saga began with telling words in Genesis 37:2, "This is the account of Jacob. Joseph ..."

And it will end with the same.

Day Two
The Years of Pilgrimage

I wrote the previous lesson in route to Egypt; Today I write from an airplane as I fly home. God has been so good I could weep. He was not just faithful to help us in our efforts in Egypt. He was graceful, exceeding what we had asked. With you, His dear ones, in mind, God showed me things to enrich our present path. I took you with me in heart and mind to every single sight. Serving Him through serving you is one of the greatest joys of my life, and in your faces I see the face of Christ. That's why, in the midst of a whole lot of hard work on the other side of the world, God gave you a specific name: Sonya.

Toward the end of the week, we were taping an on-location spot as inconspicuously as possible in front of the Sphinx at Giza. Just as we were growing frustrated over the restrictions placed on us by the authorities, a darling young woman sitting at a nearby table blurted out, "Beth Moore? Is that you?" Yep, she was one of you all the way over in Egypt: a dear sister I'd never met face-to-face but with whom I'd studied many chapters of God's living Word. Sonya and her husband transferred to Egypt three months ago, and God made sure we just happened to be in the same place at the same time. I embraced her over and over, almost as if I could hug every one of you by hugging her. I could cry telling you the story. God used her as such a boost at the end of a busy week of taping, reminding me again that the point of all this is not writing Bible studies. The point is serving Him ... through serving Sonyas. I love you so.

Genesis 47 becomes our focus today. As you recall, Jacob and his entire family arrived in the land of Egypt toward the end of Genesis 46.

Today's Treasure
And Jacob said to Pharaoh, "The years of my pilgrimage are a hundred and thirty. My years have been few and difficult."
Genesis 47:9

Please read Genesis 47 and answer questions that will launch our discussion. Give particular attention to the scenes involving Jacob. Describe how you see Jacob in these verses.

_____

What was the positive outcome of Joseph's solutions during the years of famine?

_____

What, if anything, seems negative about the outcome of Joseph's solutions?

_____

Genesis 47 offers us the chance to explore two important elements in our narrative today: Joseph's agrarian reforms and Jacob's evolving character. The latter will be richest for our purposes, but Joseph's plans are important too.

Commentators are divided as to the value of Joseph's reforms during the severity of famine. He did all he could to serve both Pharaoh and the people, but the bottom-line question plaguing several scholars is this: Did Joseph preserve life at the cost of liberty? Joseph saved the people, but he reduced them to servitude. The people in effect became royal tenants who retained four-fifths of their harvest.

Did the famine reforms ironically help set up a system that would ultimately enslave the Israelites under unfavorable Pharaohs? Fodder for thought perhaps, but remember, the entire point of the Joseph saga is God's sovereignty. If the Israelites were later enslaved by the feudal system set up in Joseph's time, God used it to make the conditions in Egypt so miserable that His people would cry out for deliverance (Ex. 2:23). Furthermore, before we feel too sorry for the Egyptian people enslaved by Joseph's reforms, note the approval rating they gave him in Genesis 47:25.

In the midst of otherwise severe circumstances, how did the Israelites fare in Egypt according to Genesis 47:27?

_____

Verse 27 makes a fluorescent point: God can cause His children to prosper in the midst of terrible circumstances far from their Canaans. How? Obedience is the key. The Israelites were blessed in Egypt because God sent them there for a season to fulfill His good purposes. The land became their temporary shelter, making Egypt to Jacob what the ark was to Noah.[2] Once God's purposes were accomplished, He provoked circumstances to move them.

Joseph's reforms are sandwiched between two moving scenes starring aged Jacob. Glance back at the first scene recorded in Genesis 47:1-10. After presenting five of his brothers before Pharaoh, Joseph brought in his father Jacob.

Jacob's approach to Pharaoh was altogether different than that of his sons. They presented themselves as Pharaoh's "servants" (v. 3). Jacob approached Pharaoh with respect but also as one with the authority to bless. He, in fact, "blessed" Pharaoh twice (47:10).

Genesis 12:2-3 set the tone for the concept of blessing in Genesis. How do these verses seem reflected between the Pharaoh and the family of Jacob (Israel)?

_____

I also think Jacob might have been too old to care much about protocol. We've seen something similar in some of our dear grandparents, haven't we? Speaking of age, you no doubt noticed it became a surprising topic of conversation.

What strange question did Pharaoh ask Jacob (v. 8)?

_____

Seem odd? Not to an ancient Egyptian. "By Egyptian standards [Jacob] outlived the law of averages. Egyptian literature has many references to 110 years as the ideal span of life for an

Egyptian."[3] The Pharaoh was obviously intrigued to know the 130-year old man's secret to longevity. The king may have gotten more than he bargained for in Jacob's answer.

 How did Jacob describe his years (v. 9)?

_____

_____

Let's peer into the heart of Jacob's response. What does it mean to describe life as a pilgrimage?

_____

_____

Compare Psalm 84:5-6. The word *baca* **means "weeping." In what sense is a believer's pilgrimage a journey through the Valley of Weeping?**

_____

_____

We do not know exactly what the patriarchs believed would happen to them after death because Scripture does not record God giving them an explanation. Hebrews 11:14-16 tells us that Abraham and others ancients of faith were "longing for a better country—a heavenly one." Whether or not God told them in so many words, they knew in their hearts something more awaited them. Perhaps this is why Jacob referenced his life as a journey.

 How has your own life seemed like a journey or a pilgrimage?

_____

_____

You also probably noticed that Jacob described his years as unequal to his "fathers." Abraham lived to be 175 (25:7) and Isaac, 180 (35:28). Jacob's tone in this scene makes me wonder if his feeling of not measuring up included more than just age. Perhaps Jacob felt he'd not carried the torch of faith as valiantly as Abraham and Isaac. Perhaps they seemed bigger than life to him. His years were marked by deception. His own. His uncle's. His sons'. The disappointments brought on by his offspring must have added to Jacob's sense of failure. No matter how many comforts he'd known, his eyes saw his life colored by the dark shades of difficulty.

Yes, redemption came and Jacob's family was once again intact. Do you think he felt family unity came too late to lighten the shade of his life? After all, how much would a gallon of white paint change a 30-gallon drum of black? Most of us have experienced Jacob-moments when we felt our lives have been difficult and we haven't measured up.

During a similar Jacob-moment, how would you most likely fill in these blanks?

My years have been _____ **and** _____

and they do not equal _____.

A gallon of white paint may not dramatically alter a 30-gallon drum of black, but a pint of faith can change us. We can place all our years of difficulty on the altar before God as a gift

God can turn our gift of difficult years into benefit and beauty.

for Him to turn into benefit and beauty. We can invite God to fill in the space where we feel we didn't measure up. Beloved, when we do God changes the color.

God didn't give the name Israel to either Abraham or Jacob. He renamed Jacob—the deceiver—Israel. Yes, Jacob had struggled, but he struggled face-to-face with God ... and, therefore, he overcame. "The Light shines in the darkness, for the darkness has never overpowered it" (John 1:5, AMP). The blackness of a thief's entire life was instantly changed by a single drop of faith in the One hanging on the next cross.

Dear One, what do you think it might take to change how you see your life in your Jacob-moments?

_____

_____

_____

Let's conclude with a look at the final scene in Genesis 47. Review verses 28-31. What did Jacob passionately request of Joseph?

_____

After my trip to Egypt, I gained a much clearer picture of Jacob's concern. The fast land of Pharaohs, pyramids, and the flooding Nile would have been unlike anything they'd ever experienced. The roots of the patriarchs were in rural surroundings where they could shepherd their flocks. Egypt surely was a culture shock. The Hebrews stood before the Pharaoh in a spectacular metroplex beyond their wildest imaginations. In our terms, they'd moved from Green Acres to New York City, and one of their own family members was personal assistant to the governor.

Jacob was terrified. What if they liked Egypt? What if they stayed? What if they forgot their true home? What if they lost who they were? So he made his request: "Do not bury me in Egypt, but when I rest with my fathers, carry me out of Egypt and bury me where they are buried." Translation? This is not your father's home. Never forget it. To make sure you don't, I will force you back home with my own bones.

For those of us on true pilgrimage, nothing is riskier than passing through a spectacular Egypt. When the culture shock wears off, so does its protection. This world is not our home. Let's never forget it.

Genesis 47 draws to a close 17 years later with a promise made to an old man on the verge of death. While the NIV describes Jacob "leaning on the top of his staff worshipping," the *Amplified Version* reads, "And Israel bowed himself upon the head of the bed." Since the Hebrew word for "worshipping" means "to prostrate oneself,"[4] the *Amplified Version* probably paints the more accurate picture. So, imagine it. Imagine Jacob lying on his bed, desperate for the assurance that Joseph willingly brings, then in relief and longing, drawing his feeble knees under his aching body, pressing his head downward, and worshipping His God. Perhaps no one worships as honestly as one who has wrestled earnestly.

Day Three
Crossing His Arms

Today's study unfolds "some time later" when Joseph is summoned to the sickbed of his father, Jacob. It seems our patriarch has outlived expectations.

I grin while recalling what my grandmother would say when she heard that someone was still alive long after she expected them to go home to Jesus. "That old man?" she'd say, "Why, I do declare. He's been tryin' to die for 20 years."

I mean no disrespect. Neither did she. I'm fond of Jacob, so I'm just as happy he's still with us.

Please read Genesis 48 and complete the following.

Describe Jacob's physical state.

_____

Does anything about Jacob remind you of his father, Isaac, in old age (27:1)?

_____

What caused Jacob to rally his strength (v. 2)?

_____

What announcement did Jacob make to Joseph in verse 5?

_____

How did Jacob show affection to his grandsons in verse 10?

_____

What did Jacob do in verse 14 that displeased Joseph?

_____

Paraphrase Jacob's blessing over the sons of Joseph (vv. 15-16).

_____

_____

Today's Treasure

Israel reached out his right hand and put it on Ephraim's head, though he was the younger, and crossing his arms, he put his left hand on Manasseh's head, even though Manasseh was the firstborn.

Genesis 48:14

Obviously Joseph resided at his official post near the palace rather than with his family. Word of his father's illness must have been serious enough for him to gather his sons to see their grandfather before he died. "Israel rallied his strength and sat up on his bed" when told of Joseph's coming. I believe no face was dearer to Jacob than Joseph's. His was a face Jacob thought he'd never see again. Although we may not be on our deathbeds, we can imagine those who have a similar effect on us.

Name someone who could motivate you to rally your final strength.

_____

I recall something precious the hospice nurse said to us as my mother tried to hold on to life. All of her children and grandchildren were in the bedroom of my parents' quaint home, gathered closely to her side. One of us asked, "How much longer?"

The nurse replied, "She doesn't want to leave you. She loves all of you so much. Who would want to leave such a family?"

I looked around the room at those familiar faces and nodded my head. If she could have, Mom would have jumped out of that bed and stirred up some biscuits and gravy. Instead, my dad kissed her, whispered something gently in her ear, and she released us to the One calling her home.

Likewise, Jacob still had work to do before resting with his fathers. Blessings to give. Jacob's final tasks were as vital as anything he'd accomplished in his life. The Hebrew blessing was far more than wishful words and lofty benedictions. A blessing was God-spurred revelation with the absolute expectation of fulfillment.

In preparation for the initial blessings, Jacob recounted the story of his encounter with God in Luz (Bethel). Notice the clarity with which Jacob recited the words *El Shaddai* had spoken to him so many years before. While you and I may not hear the audible voice of God, somewhere along the way we've probably felt like He said something so clear and vital to us that we'll take it to our deathbeds.

 Think back on your history with God. What has He told you that you expect to remember with crystal clarity the rest of your life, and why was it so important?

_____

_____

The words of God Almighty at Bethel were critical to Jacob because they confirmed his connectedness to the divine covenant. Imagine how relieved Jacob, a man on the run at the time, was to know that the sins against his brother and father were not strong enough to shatter the bonds of covenant.

God's arm cannot be broken, Sweet One. When God hangs on, nothing—absolutely nothing—can break His grip. Jacob's announcement that Ephraim and Manasseh would be reckoned as his sons came in perfect context with the reminder of God's promise of covenant blessing. We can hardly fathom what Jacob was doing by claiming Joseph's sons as his own, but his actions carried great significance in ancient custom. By naming Ephraim and Manasseh as sons rather than grandsons, they were exalted as co-inheritors with their uncles. Jacob reached to the fullest length to guarantee the utmost benefits of blessing to Joseph's sons. Jacob had 51 other grandsons with him in Goshen, yet none joined Ephraim and Manasseh as sons of Israel. By adopting Joseph's sons as his own, Jacob gave Joseph two tribal allotments rather than one.

>**To which sons did Jacob compare Ephraim and Manasseh in verse 5? (Circle two.)**
>Reuben   Zebulun   Judah   Issachar   Simeon

Nothing is accidental about this comparison. "The first two sons of Leah are singled out because they are being bypassed to give the double portion to Joseph."[5] Thus Joseph, the favored son of the beloved Rachel, received the double portion of the firstborn.

Jacob not only blessed the two grandsons as sons but also blessed the younger as the greater. Take a look in the text at a wonderful clue of what was to come.

>**In what order were the sons of Joseph named in Genesis 48:1?**

>_____

>**In what order did Jacob speak their names in verse 5?**

>_____

>**Glance back at Genesis 41:51-52. Which of Joseph's sons was his firstborn?**
>❏ Manasseh   ❏ Ephraim

>**Refresh your memory concerning their names' meanings in Genesis 41:51-52. Can you think of any reason why Ephraim's name might have had more significance in the long run than Manasseh's? Share your thoughts.**

>_____

>_____

Ephraim didn't receive the greater exaltation over the meaning of his name, but the symbolism in the priority given him could teach us a few things. Manasseh's name represented forgetting one's troubles. Ephraim's, on the other hand, represented fruitfulness in the midst of one's troubles.

Beloved, in God's economy fruitfulness trumps forgetfulness every time. No matter how differently we feel at times, becoming fruitful in our troubles has far greater ramifications of blessing than forgetting our troubles. We're purposely echoing some of the concepts we discussed at the birth of Joseph's sons because they intentionally resurface in today's scene. Jacob's enduring line would not be marked by the troubles they'd forgotten. It would be marked by the faithfulness of a God who remembered His covenant and made them fruitful. Fruitfulness trumps forgetfulness just as surely in your life and mine.

>**Look again at Genesis 48:12. What posture did Joseph take before his father?**
>❏ He stood in his honor, lifting his hands.
>❏ He bowed down with his face to the ground.
>❏ He placed his head in his hands.

The Hebrew words for *bless, kneel,* or *knee* all derive from the same root, *brk.*[6] Though some scholars claim no clear connection between kneeling and blessing, Joseph's posture as he prepares for blessing might make us wonder. *Strong's* definition of the Hebrew word also suggests a possible tie. In addition to the traditional definition of *brk,* "to bless," it also lists "to make to kneel."[7] The possible connection could teach something vital about blessing. God's desire to bless His people is consistent from Genesis to Revelation, but so is His insistence on humility and reverence. I wonder if God's attitude is something like this: "I want nothing more than to bless you, Child, but you will have to humble yourself to receive it."

Why do you think humility would be an important element in receiving blessing?

After Joseph humbly knelt before God, he positioned his sons at his father's hands: Manasseh at his right and Ephraim at his left. What Jacob hinted earlier in his stated order of the boys' names, he demonstrated at this point by crossing his hands: the younger would receive the greater blessing. Once again he ignored the law of primogeniture (priority according to birth order).

When Joseph objected to the placement of his father's hands, Jacob echoed words that are almost haunting. "I know, my son, I know" (v. 19). Of all people, he certainly should know. Jacob was intimately acquainted with the reversal of the law of primogeniture, its blessings, and all its complications.

Glance back at Genesis 25:23-26 and briefly explain why he could so readily say to a confused Joseph, "I know, my son, I know."

Jacob's life was marked from the womb by the prophecy foretelling his own elevation over his older brother (Gen. 25:23-26). Please read Genesis 48:16,19 carefully.

What blessings did both sons of Joseph receive?

What was the only difference (v. 19)?

As you can see, both Joseph's sons were greatly blessed. God's sovereign desire (expressed through Jacob) to exalt the younger is consistent with His Word-wide determination to bring Himself the most glory through the least likely characters. Let's conclude with a last look at Jacob's words in verses 15 and 16.

As the elderly patriarch neared his death, how had his life—tumultuous, often incongruous—finally been reframed entirely by God?

When we lay these bodies down, Dear One, what God has done will be all that matters. Though our physical vision may dim, may our spiritual vision sharpen until we see with stunning clarity how He has led us, shepherded us, delivered us, and blessed us "all my life to this day." And may the God who has blessed us reach across every barrier to bless those who come behind us.

Day Four
Prophetic Blessings

Today we gather around Jacob's deathbed to eavesdrop on his blessings over his 12 sons and their tribes. As you will soon see, Jacob's words draw pictures, and the style of his language comprises what scholars believe to be the first sustained poem in the Bible.[8] We'll begin our study of Genesis 49 by looking at the bookend Scriptures propping up the blessings.

Read only Genesis 49:1 and 49:28 for now. List everything they tell you about the information between the two verses:

_____

_____

Before we consider the important words between these bookends, let's go over what you just learned. Based on Genesis 49:1-28, we know at least the following four things about Jacob's words over his sons:

1. *They are prophetic.* They concern "days to come." God obviously gifted Jacob to foretell something about the future of each son.
2. *They are blessings.* The double reference in Genesis 49:28 left no room for doubt. I'll warn you in advance, however, that some of them won't seem like blessings. In his commentary on Genesis, Bruce Waltke termed several of them "antiblessings" and you'll soon discover why.[9] We'll discuss later how the harsher ones could still be considered blessings.
3. *They are appropriate.* The blessings fit. They are neither unfair nor unwise.
4. *They have long-term effects.* They apply to the descendants of the sons as well as the sons themselves. The name of each son represents the entire tribe that will descend from him.

As we pour over Jacob's deathbed blessings for his sons, keep all four of these elements in mind. As you read the verses, picture the images Jacob mentions, making visual associations for each son. I've provided an exercise to help.

A word of warning: many "commentators agree that this is the most difficult material in Genesis."[10] The Hebrew is treacherous to translate in this chapter, resulting in the wide range of images and expressions offered by the major Bible translations. For this reason, you'll need to stick very close to an NIV for this exercise so the images will be consistent.

Today's Treasure
Then Jacob called for his sons and said: "Gather around so I can tell you what will happen to you in days to come.
Genesis 49:1

Read Genesis 49:1-28 and write the names of each son next to the picture that matches an element of his "blessing." Remember that Simeon and Levi shared the same blessing, so you'll write their names next to the same picture.

Draw a star next to the two sons' names who received the most elaborate blessings. In the margin, describe why you think Jacob [Israel] gave them more prominent blessings than he gave their brothers.

Now, let's explore the four things our bookend Scriptures taught us. First, we learned that Jacob's words were prophetic. The prophecy embraces "both the near and distant future … from the conquest and distribution of the land to the consummate reign of Christ."[11] Ah, the very mention of Christ after such a long tenure in the pages of Genesis is music to my ears! Yours, too? Push the hold button on that last phrase until the end of the lesson.

These verses identify the 12 tribes and "their individual blessings, prophesying their unique destinies within their common destiny as a nation."[12] Absorb the words, "unique destinies within their common destiny." Few of us are biological descendants of Israel, but all of us who have received Christ as Savior are members of His church. We, too, share a common destiny.

What are a few things our future holds for us corporately as believers in Christ?

_____

You have a unique and wonderful destiny that God tailored with you alone in mind.

We each have unique destinies within our common future. Beloved, you have a unique and wonderful destiny that God tailored with you alone in mind.

Jacob didn't miss a single son in the prophecies he gave. How much more can you be assured that God will not miss you? Furthermore, this side of the cross, you don't have to be marked by the actions of your ancestors. We are not obligated to what has come before us in our family lines. You and I can experience freedom in Christ from every yoke (Gal. 5:1). Christ "cancelled the written code, with its regulations, that was against us and that stood opposed to us; he took it away, nailing it to the cross" (Col. 2:9). God has spoken prophetic blessing over your life as surely as Jacob spoke over his sons' lives. When God spoke your blessings, Dear One, He blessed you "in the heavenly realms with every spiritual blessing in Christ" (Eph. 1:3). You are a joint heir with Christ. Because of what He's done on your behalf, you are indelibly marked by His line alone and invited to share His inheritance.

Jacob's words were prophetic. Next, consider that they were blessings.

Which of the blessings seem more like "antiblessings"? Go back and write an "A/B" in the margin beside the appropriate names as a reminder.

Toward the beginning of the lesson I promised we'd consider how "antiblessings" like those given to Reuben, Simeon, and Levi could be labeled "blessings." Since Waltke introduced the term to us, we'll let him explain: "In terms of the nation's destiny these antiblessings are a blessing. By demoting Reuben for his turbulence and uncontrolled sex drive, Jacob saves Israel from reckless leadership. Likewise, by cursing the cruelty of Simeon and Levi, he restricts their cruel rashness from dominating."[13] We might call these blessings of restriction.

We can relate on both a personal and corporate level. Corporately, we are blessed as readily by those who've been restricted and disallowed to have authority or power over us as those who have. Personally, God's decision to disallow us to fill roles we—by temperament or history—are unfitted for is also a blessing. Both what we receive and what we don't receive can constitute blessings for us and those around us. God is all-wise. He blesses us as surely by what He does not grant as what He does.

Describe a blessing of restriction in your own life.

_____

In the Old Testament, God could also sanctify a line and change its course. The tribe of Levi was ultimately set apart as priests or assistants to the priests in the worship system God ordained after the exodus.

What changed the course of Levi's line? After the children of Israel rebelled against God and worshipped the golden calf, the Levites "were the only ones who voluntarily rallied to [God's] side, showing zeal for God's honor."[14] The Levites never received an allotment of land in Canaan, but they were servants of God in His sanctuaries. You see, the blessings of Genesis 49 were not sentences. They were prophecies: intentionally incomplete ones.

The third element from our bookend Scriptures assures us each blessing was appropriate. When Jacob blessed his sons, he gave them "each the blessing appropriate to him." Jacob was led by God who sees into every heart and every future. I'm not at all sure Jacob had rehearsed or written down a single blessing he gave. Quite likely the words fell from his lips under the inspiration of God. Did you notice the interruption in the flow between Dan and Gad's blessings?

Look at Genesis 49:18 where Jacob suddenly addressed God. What did he say?

_____

Jacob seemed almost overwhelmed by the power of the words coming out of his mouth. His own predictions of hostilities against the tribes caused him to stop suddenly and voice his cry of confidence in God's deliverance.

The fourth and final element is the long-term effect of the sons' actions and their subsequent blessings. Each tribe was somehow marked by its ancestor. An undeniable theme in Genesis is the long-term effects of actions, both positive and negative. As New Testament believers, our foolish actions don't "curse" our family lines, but they certainly affect them. However, I'm thoroughly convinced that godly actions affect family lines far more dramatically than ungodly actions.

Look at Exodus 20:5-6. What is the comparison of impact?

_____

Earlier I asked you which of the sons received the most elaborate blessings. The prophecies spoken over Judah and Joseph consume 10 of 25 verses. Though Joseph is named in the tribal blessings in Genesis, those blessings are thereafter fulfilled in the tribes named for his sons Ephraim and Manasseh. Joseph was named "the prince among his brothers" in Genesis 49:26, but an older brother's tribe was exalted even higher. The far reach of blessing upon the tribes of Israel is never more beautifully displayed than in the prophecy Jacob spoke over Judah. The redemption of this once-foolish son is stunning. God tethers his line to eternity with crimson thread, saving earth's crown for His Son's head.

The following Scriptures pertain specifically to our Savior, Jesus Christ. Read each one; then list which portion of Judah's prophecy is reflected or suggested.

Revelation 5:5 _____

Revelation 19:16 _____

The Lion of the Tribe of Judah was the same One who, draped in flesh, rode the donkey's colt down the Mount of Olives to Jerusalem as the crowd cried out, "Blessed is he who comes in the name of the Lord!" (Matt. 21:9). He will be acknowledged as King of all kings, and many crowns will be on His head. Oh, to see Judah's face when he watches every knee bow to King Jesus! The blessed King of the blessed line! No wonder *Judah* means praise! If you hold your peace, the rocks will cry out. Kneel and receive your Blessing, Precious One. Christ is your great reward.

Today's Treasure
When Jacob had finished giving instructions to his sons, he drew his feet up into the bed, breathed his last and was gathered to his people.
Genesis 49:33

Day Five
The Grandest Finale

You'd think after writing 10 Bible studies that I'd get used to endings and that somehow the whole process would lose its freshness and luster. Yet here I sit in tears once again, wrapped in a swirl of emotions. Foremost, I am moved by the love God has given this broken soul for Himself and His Word. He has made Himself at home as the whole of my life, His Word my inexpressible delight. Oh, Sweet One, if He can do it for me, He can do it for anyone.

I also cry because I grieve the end of an in-depth and lengthy time with God. Day in, day out. Month after month. I've been with God in the pages of Genesis for over a year and

a half. I never quite know what to do with myself when a study ends. I also weep because I will never get over the privilege of serving you. That you made it this far, Beloved! That we've walked a thousand miles together over the last 10 weeks! Now, that's something we can celebrate! But, oh, the joy we'll have when we gather around the throne of grace and hear the Word from His own mouth!

Let it be soon, Rabboni! How I hunger for You!

Speaking of hunger, something happened a few days ago that let me know this might be a good time to get out of the pages of Genesis. Amanda and Curt, my daughter and son-in-law, have the most adorable golden retriever puppy you can imagine. Until they give me a grandbaby, I'm nuts about my grandpuppy. Curt has a brand new hand-size Bible with a rich brown cover of exquisite aromatic leather. Aromatic enough, in fact, to incite puppy Beckham's appetite. Day before yesterday Amanda phoned to tell me that Beckham had completely ingested the front cover as well as Genesis chapters 1 through 21. A master at biblical humor, her exact words were, "Thy words were found, and Beckham did eat them" (Jer. 15:16). My mind went into instant overdrive as I tried to figure out which patriarchs Beckham had eaten and how the entire narrative could not be grasped void of chapters 12-21. But thank goodness he did not eat Genesis 22! Where would the Hebrew nation be without Isaac on Mount Moriah?

Yep, time for me to get a life outside of Genesis. The characters are as real as warm flesh, and right about now a few of them have dog bites. OK, at least I've stopped crying.

As sorry as I am for this series to end, I can hardly wait to look at today's verses with you. Though we conclude our written work today in parts of Genesis 49 and 50, the final verses of the Book of Beginnings are treated in video session 10. Please be present, or your ending will seem incomplete. Turn with me one last time to the first book of the Bible and read Genesis 49:29–50:14.

Recall yesterday's lesson. What had Jacob just completed when he gave the last instructions regarding his death (49:1-28)?

_____

What names did he mention in his final wishes (49:29-32)?

_____

 Based on his words, what kinds of things do you imagine preoccupied Jacob's thoughts toward the end?

_____

How is the intensity of Jacob and Joseph's relationship depicted?

_____

How was Jacob's body prepared for burial (v. 2)?

_____

Scripture tells us a "very large company" escorted Jacob's body to its burial place. Circle any of the following that added to the entourage (Gen. 50:7-9).

chariots   horsemen   members of Joseph's household

professional female mourners   the children   the flocks

the herds   dignitaries   Joseph's brothers

What did Joseph and his brothers do after they buried their father (v. 14)?

_____

Refer back to Genesis 47:29-31. How serious was Jacob about being buried back in Canaan as opposed to Egypt?

_____

The old patriarch did not draw his last breath until he reiterated once more the heightened priority of his burial with his "fathers." Jacob's wishes were not for himself. His wishes granted would serve as a life insurance policy of sorts for his descendants. "For it is Israel's memory of these ancestors, preserved through burial in a specific memorialized site purchased for such purpose that will constitute Israel's sole link to the Promised Land through the four hundred years of exile."[15]

 In your own words, why was Jacob's reasoning about his burial important to our understanding of Genesis?

_____

Perhaps many of us can relate on a lesser level. I have lived in Texas since I was 15. From the top of my big hair to the tip of my cowboy boots, I am for all practical purposes a Texan. One thing, however, keeps me from ever completely committing. My roots are six feet under Arkansas soil in the caskets of my grandparents and theirs. I am Texas tall but Arkansas deep.

How about you? Tell me your story.

_____

_____

Jacob's insurance policy tied his sons and their descendants with a hard, fast knot to the bones of their ancestors in Canaan. He intended they never forget. The timing implied in the text suggests that Jacob died almost immediately after blessing his sons. The best thing about the final chapter of Jacob's life is that he was unafraid to face death and unashamed to speak of it.

I can't think of anything that has moved me more than receiving letters from or about someone who did a Bible study all the way through a terminal illness to her death. Recently I exchanged letters with a woman on death row who is in one of the studies with fellow death row inmates. Unless the governor intervenes, she will see the Lord tomorrow night.

Don't picture all of the dying women I've described as elderly. Some of them are disturbingly young. The only common denominator was that all of them made the decision that unless God intervenes with a miracle, they would, like Jacob, meet their ends deliberately. I have no greater respect for anyone. Could you and I make a pact right now to be deliberate about blessing people and about seeking God through His Word all the way to our last conscious breath?

If you agree to it, sign in this space:

_____

My heart surges with the description of Jacob drawing "his feet up into the bed" and breathing his last. The extremities grow cold first, you know. We first "met" Jacob in Rebekah's womb refusing to curl up like other infants. Instead, he stretched, strove, and wrestled with his twin. When all was said and done, wrestling characterized his life. In death, however, he found rest. Finally, Jacob curled up as an infant snuggles down for a long winter's night and closed his tired eyes.

What promise had God given Jacob concerning Joseph in Genesis 46:4?

_____

Joseph washed his father's eyes with his tears and closed them with kisses. The spotlight switches dramatically to a mourning, demonstrative Joseph. We're left to wonder if his grief escalated high above his brothers' and, if so, was it because he felt cheated of time? Let's be honest. He also hadn't dealt with as much family baggage as his brothers had through the years. The death of an elderly parent in families with a turbulent history is dear ... but also complicated. Memories surface. Many wonderful. Others painful.

Surely you noticed that the brothers seem to be mentioned almost in passing throughout the preparations for burial. Have you ever noticed that one person often takes over at a loved one's death? I'm not sure family dynamics are ever more ... uh ... dynamic than during the death and burial of a central family figure. Some of us seem paralyzed, some of us subdued, while others go into automatic overdrive.

What is your tendency during times like this?

_____

Wouldn't you love to know how the brothers felt as they were surrounded by such Egyptian fanfare? And all the way to Canaan! For crying out loud, the Canaanites even named the place after the Egyptians, and who could blame them? Egypt appeared to "claim Jacob in death as one of their exalted own" (v. 11).[16] In fact, *Abel Mizraim* means the "mourning of Egypt."[17] What about the mourning of the Israelites?

Do you think Joseph's brothers were blessed by the Egyptian flare of the funeral proceedings or shocked? Resentful? Or humbled? Were they thinking, "Welcome to the Joseph Show"? Or had they never been so glad he was around?

Perhaps the attentions of the sons of Jacob were stolen so thoroughly by their irreplaceable patriarch that they were oblivious to all things Egypt. I have thoroughly enjoyed—though not always agreed with—the Jewish commentary I've quoted many times throughout this study. Though lengthy, I cannot resist preparing for our conclusion with words once again from *The Beginning of Wisdom*:

> "Whatever the route, the long, hot, arduous journey back to Canaan carrying their father's mummified body to the ancestral grave must surely have produced powerful feelings in the souls of the brothers, as it surely did to their bodies, especially at the end. Lifting and carrying their father, six on each side, each leaning toward his load and all bending toward one another, the brothers would find the walking cumbersome. Now stumbling, now bumping into the one in front or behind, their individual gaits would be hampered as if by a limp, but they would see that progress can be made together, each one now equally dependent on ('curved toward') the others, all equally the sons of Israel."[18]

As if by a limp. How appropriate. After all, the lifeless one they now carried had walked bearing the cadence of divine encounter.

" 'Your name will no longer be Jacob, but Israel, because you have struggled with God and with men and have overcome.' " Jacob said, 'Please tell me your name.' But he replied, 'Why do you ask my name?' Then he blessed him there. So Jacob called the place Peniel, saying, 'it is because I saw God face to face, and yet my life was spared.' The sun rose above him as he passed Peniel, and he was limping" (Gen. 32:28-31).

After burying their father, Joseph and his brothers returned to Egypt. An Israelite would not step foot in Canaan again for four hundred years. The graves of Abraham, Isaac, and Jacob would not cease to call, "Home!"

As for Jacob, he didn't attend his funeral. Missed the whole thing. Long before they laid his body to rest in Canaan's grave, he "saw God face to face. ... The [Son] rose above him as he passed," ... and Jacob was no longer limping.

---

[1] Victor P. Hamilton, *The Book of Genesis: Chapters 18–50* (Grand Rapids: William B. Eerdman's Publishing, 1995), 590.

[2] Ibid., 625.

[3] Ibid., 623.

[4] Spiros Zodhiates et al., eds., *The Complete Word Study Dictionary: Old Testament* (Chattanooga, TN: AMG Publishers, 1994), 114.

[5] Bruce K. Waltke, *Genesis: A Commentary* (Grand Rapids: Zondervan, 2001), 596.

[6] David Noel Freedman ed., *The Anchor Bible Dictionary*, vol. I (New York: Doubleday, 1992), 753.

[7] James Strong, *Strong's Exhaustive Concordance of the Bible: Hebrew and Chaldee Dictionary* (Nashville: Holman Bible Publishers, n.d.), 24.

[8] Waltke, 602.

[9] Ibid., 603.

[10] Leon R. Kass, *The Beginning of Wisdom: Reading Genesis* (New York: Free Press, 2003), 645.

[11] Waltke, 605.

[12] Ibid., 603.

[13] Ibid., 603.

[14] Herbert Lockyer, Sr. ed., *Nelson's Illustrated Bible Dictionary* (Nashville: Thomas Nelson Publishers, 1986), 644.

[15] Waltke, 605.

[16] Kass, 653.

[17] Ibid., 653.

[18] Ibid., 645-55.

SESSION TEN
Epic Endings to the Beginning

Our God is *El Olam,* the _____ _____, who focuses more on _____

than _____. We want God to _____ things _____. God wants us to

grasp how He _____ things _____.

Read Genesis 50:15-26 and consider the following:

1. In His inconceivable sovereignty, God _____ in the _____ of Joseph's brothers to

   the _____ of their _____ (vv. 19-21).

2. In Joseph's final recorded words, God _____ in His original _____

   to _____, then Isaac and Jacob to the _____ (v. 24).

   • A very close literal rendering of Genesis 50:24: "God will surely _____ _____."

   A more literal rendering of Exodus 3:16, "I have _____ _____."

   • The Hebrew word for "_____" in Genesis 50:26 is the same word translated

   "_____" in the Exodus, "_____ of the _____." Though a

   _____ seemed to await Joseph, its ultimate outcome was to allow him to

   indeed see that _____ was _____ with his brothers.

3. In the Gospels Christ _____ in Abraham, Isaac, and Jacob to the _____

   and the _____.

4. The Hebrews "Hall of Faith" _____ in the complete _____

   of the first patriarch's _____ with _____.

5. God _____ in our personal present with our future through an inner _____

   Scripture calls a _____.

CHRISTIAN GROWTH STUDY PLAN

In the Christian Growth Study Plan, *The Patriarchs* is a resource for course credit in the subject area of Bible Studies of the Christian Growth category of diploma plans. To receive credit, read the book, complete the learning activities, show your work to your pastor, a staff member or church leader, then complete the form. Send the completed form to the Christian Growth Study Plan,

One LifeWay Plaza, Nashville, TN 37234-0117. This page may be duplicated. FAX: (615)251-5067. For information about the Christian Growth Study Plan, refer to the current Christian Growth Study Plan Catalog. Your church office may have a copy. If not, request a free copy from the Christian Growth Study Plan office (615/251-2525).

The Patriarchs
COURSE NUMBER : CG-1053

PARTICIPANT INFORMATION

Social Security Number (USA ONLY-optional)	Personal CGSP Number*	Date of Birth (MONTH, DAY, YEAR)

Name (First, Middle, Last)	Home Phone

Address (Street, Route, or P.O. Box)	City, State, or Province	Zip/Postal Code

Please check appropriate box: ☐ Resource purchased by self ☐ Resource purchased by church ☐ Other

CHURCH INFORMATION

Church Name

Address (Street, Route, or P.O. Box)	City, State, or Province	Zip/Postal Code

CHANGE REQUEST ONLY

☐ Former Name		
☐ Former Address	City, State, or Province	Zip/Postal Code
☐ Former Church	City, State, or Province	Zip/Postal Code

Signature of Pastor, Conference Leader, or Other Church Leader	Date

*New participants are requested but not required to give SS# and date of birth. Existing participants, please give CGSP# when using SS# for the first time. Thereafter, only one ID# is required. **Mail to:** Christian Growth Study Plan, One LifeWay Plaza, Nashville, TN 37234-0117. Fax: (615)251-5067.

Rev. 3-03